T0332083

Nature-Inspired Algorithms
Applications

Scrivener Publishing
100 Cummings Center, Suite 541J
Beverly, MA 01915-6106

Artificial Intelligence and Soft Computing for Industrial Transformation

Series Editor: Dr S. Balamurugan (sbnbala@gmail.com)

Scope: Artificial Intelligence and Soft Computing Techniques play an impeccable role in industrial transformation. The topics to be covered in this book series include Artificial Intelligence, Machine Learning, Deep Learning, Neural Networks, Fuzzy Logic, Genetic Algorithms, Particle Swarm Optimization, Evolutionary Algorithms, Nature Inspired Algorithms, Simulated Annealing, Metaheuristics, Cuckoo Search, Firefly Optimization, Bio-inspired Algorithms, Ant Colony Optimization, Heuristic Search Techniques, Reinforcement Learning, Inductive Learning, Statistical Learning, Supervised and Unsupervised Learning, Association Learning and Clustering, Reasoning, Support Vector Machine, Differential Evolution Algorithms, Expert Systems, Neuro Fuzzy Hybrid Systems, Genetic Neuro Hybrid Systems, Genetic Fuzzy Hybrid Systems and other Hybridized Soft Computing Techniques and their applications for Industrial Transformation. The book series is aimed to provide comprehensive handbooks and reference books for the benefit of scientists, research scholars, students and industry professional working towards next generation industrial transformation.

Publishers at Scrivener
Martin Scrivener (martin@scrivenerpublishing.com)
Phillip Carmical (pcarmical@scrivenerpublishing.com)

Nature-Inspired Algorithms Applications

Edited by

S. Balamurugan,
Anupriya Jain,
Sachin Sharma,
Dinesh Goyal,
Sonia Duggal
and
Seema Sharma

Scrivener
Publishing

WILEY

This edition first published 2022 by John Wiley & Sons, Inc., 111 River Street, Hoboken, NJ 07030, USA and Scrivener Publishing LLC, 100 Cummings Center, Suite 541J, Beverly, MA 01915, USA
© 2022 Scrivener Publishing LLC
For more information about Scrivener publications please visit www.scrivenerpublishing.com.

Wiley Global Headquarters

111 River Street, Hoboken, NJ 07030, USA

For details of our global editorial offices, customer services, and more information about Wiley products visit us at www.wiley.com.

Limit of Liability/Disclaimer of Warranty

Library of Congress Cataloging-in-Publication Data

ISBN 978-1-119-68174-8

Cover image: Pixabay.Com
Cover design Russell Richardson

Set in size of 11pt and Minion Pro by Manila Typesetting Company, Makati, Philippines

Contents

Preface

Inspired by the world around them, researchers are gathering information that can be developed for use in areas where certain practical applications of nature-inspired computation and machine learning can be applied. This book was designed to enhance the reader's understanding of this process by portraying certain practical applications of nature-inspired algorithms (NIAs) specifically designed to solve complex real-world problems in data analytics and pattern recognition by means of domain-specific solutions. Since various NIAs and their multidisciplinary applications in the mechanical engineering and electrical engineering sectors; and in machine learning, image processing, data mining, and wireless networks are dealt with in detail in this book, it can act as a handy reference guide. A brief description of the topics covered in each chapter is given below.

- In Chapter 1, "Introduction to Nature-Inspired Computing," Dr. N. M. Saravana Kumar, K. Hariprasath, N. Kaviyavarshini and A. Kavinya introduce a new discipline that strives to develop new computing techniques through observing how naturally occurring phenomena behave to solve complex problems in environmental situations. Characterization of nature-inspired algorithms are also discussed.
- In Chapter 2, "Applications of Hybridized Algorithms and Novel Algorithms in the Field of Machine Learning," Dr. P. Mary Jeyanthi and Dr. A. Mansurali introduce various hybridized algorithms in the field of machine learning (ML) along with their applications. This chapter emphasizes the characteristics of a genetic algorithm (GA) which helps machine learning in GA's consideration of genes (variables).
- In Chapter 3, "Efficiency of Finding Best Solutions Through Ant Colony Optimization (ACO) Technique," Dr. K. Sasi Kala Rani and N. Pooranam address the challenges faced in tourism when a planned vacation to a specific destination is challenged by unforeseen events like adverse climate conditions that threaten to derail the trip. In this case, an optimal solution is generated by using heuristic value and

an ACO algorithm in which the continuous orthogonal ant colony (COAC) method helps to solve real-world problems.

–In Chapter 4, "A Hybrid Bat-Genetic Algorithm-Based Novel Optimal Wavelet Filter for Compression of Image Data," Renjith V. Ravi and Kamalraj Subramaniam explain how three modules, namely optimized transformation module, compression and encryption module and receiver module, are used. Initially, the input image is sub-band coded using hybrid bat-genetic algorithm-based optimized DWT. Subsequently, the encoding using SPIHT and chaos-based encryption is carried out. In receiver module, the received signal from the AWGN channel is demodulated, decrypted and de-compressed to obtain the estimated image. From the results, we can infer that the use of the proposed filter and technique has produced better image quality when compared to existing techniques.

–In Chapter 5, "A Swarm Robot for Harvesting a Paddy Field," N. Pooranam and T. Vignesh discuss how the harvesting process can be improved in a positive way by using the PSO-based swarm intelligent algorithm to help in searching for and optimizing the process. The harvesting process has several steps: Reaping (cutting), threshing (separating process), and cleaning (removing non-grain material from grains). The PSO algorithm will find the positions of all robots to start harvesting and crust-based PSO will help to improve the optimization.

–In Chapter 6, "Firefly Algorithms," Anupriya Jain, Seema Sharma and Sachin Sharma present the working principle of firefly algorithms (FA) in detail with the algorithm explained and its implementation ready for reference. In recent years, variants of FA to accommodate new problems have been introduced. The hybrid or modified models have tremendously improved the performance of a standard FA. These special cases and applications of this metaheuristic problem are discussed in detail.

–In Chapter 7, "The Comprehensive Review for Biobased FPA Algorithm," Meenakshi Rana introduces the concept of flower pollination algorithms characterized by a small number of parameters, which make it promising in solving optimization problems, even multi-objective complex ones. These algorithms are embedded with a mechanism for a local and global exploration feature which is complementary and helps the algorithm work efficiently.

–In Chapter 8, "Nature-Inspired Computation in Data Mining," Aditi Sharma highlights the application of nature-inspired computation in data mining along with its benefits and challenges. For the benefit of the reader, the most used optimization techniques are covered in detail.

–In Chapter 9, "Optimization Techniques for Removing Noise in Digital Medical Images," Dr. D. Devasena, Dr. M. Jagadeeswari, Dr. B. Sharmila and Dr. K. Srinivasan introduce various types of evolutionary computation algorithms inspired by biological, social and natural systems. These methods include the following algorithms: particle swarm optimization (PSO), bat algorithm (BA), firefly algorithm (FA), social spider optimization (SSO), collective animal behavior (CAB), differential evolution (DE), genetic algorithm (GA) and bacterial foraging algorithm (BFA). Thus, the evolutionary algorithms are ones that simulate biological, natural or social level systems to address real-time image processing problems.

–In Chapter 10, "Performance Analysis of Nature-Inspired Algorithms in Breast Cancer Diagnosis," K. Hariprasath, Dr. S. Tamilselvi, Dr. N. M. Saravana Kumar, N. Kaviyavarshini and Dr. S. Balamurugan introduce many successful optimization approaches like swarm intelligence, machine intelligence, data mining and resource management. The swarm intelligence model is one of the popular computation theories that is motivated by common swarm frameworks. The three primary swarm protocols are to move in the same direction as its neighbors, to remain as close as possible to the neighbors, and to avoid collision among neighbors.

–In Chapter 11, "Applications of Cuckoo Search Algorithm for Optimization Problems," Akanksha Deep and Prasant Kumar Dash introduce various optimization algorithms which are classified on the basis of two key elements—diversification and aggregation—generally known as exploitation and exploration. Exploration aims to find a contemporary solution which results in locating global optima, whereas exploitation aims to find local optima of the solution space explored.

–In Chapter 12, "Mapping of Real-World Problems to Nature-Inspired Algorithm Using Goal-Based Classification and TRIZ," Palak Sukharamwala and Manojkumar Parmar present a novel method based on TRIZ to map real-world problems to nature problems. TRIZ is also known as the theory of inventive problem solving. Using the proposed framework, the best NIA can be identified to solve real-world problems. For this framework to work, a novel classification of the NIA based on the end goal that nature is trying to achieve is devised.

To conclude, we would like to extend our appreciation to our many colleagues. We also extend our sincere thanks to all the experts for providing preparatory comments on the book that will surely motivate the reader to read the topic. We also wish to thank the reviewers who took time to review this book, and are also very grateful to our family members for their patience, encouragement and understanding. Special thanks also go to many individuals at Scrivener Publishing, whose talents and efforts made the publication of this book possible. Finally, any suggestions or feedback from readers to improve the text will be highly appreciated.

The Editors
September 2021

Introduction to Nature-Inspired Computing

N.M. Saravana Kumar[1]*, K. Hariprasath[2], N. Kaviyavarshini[2]
and A. Kavinya[2]

*[1]Department of Artificial Intelligence and Data Science, M Kumarasamy
College of Engineering, Karur, India*
*[2]Department of Information Technology, Vivekanandha College of
Engineering for Women, Namakkal, India*

Abstract

Nature-inspired algorithms have significance in solving many problems. This chapter provides an overview of nature-inspired algorithms like bio-inspired algorithm, swarm intelligence algorithm, and physical and chemical system–based algorithm. Many real-world problems are solved using nature-inspired algorithms and the role of optimization plays an important role. This chapter covers the basic working and classification of nature-inspired algorithms along with its area of applications. The purpose and its significance of each and every algorithm have been described. Also, the applications of algorithms comprise most of the real-time problems.

Keywords: Nature-inspired, bio-inspired, evolutionary computing, swarm intelligence, optimization, applications

1.1 Introduction

An algorithm is a finite series of definite procedure for finding significance of the pattern. They are utilized to explain a course of difficulties and then implement calculation. Algorithm are said to unambiguous and utilized for performing computation and dealing with other task.

Corresponding author: saravanakumaar2008@gmail.com

S. Balamurugan, Anupriya Jain, Sachin Sharma, Dinesh Goyal, Sonia Duggal and Seema Sharma (eds.)
Nature-Inspired Algorithms Applications, (1–32) © 2022 Scrivener Publishing LLC

Algorithm has different characteristics; they are unambiguous, well-defined input and output, determinate, realistic, and independent of language. Unambiguous refers to having only one interpretation which leads to only one conclusion. Well-defined input and output refers to defining the input and output clearly. Determinate refers to algorithm that must be finite as the algorithm should not conclude with infinite loop. Realistic refers to the algorithm that is general, simple, and practical which may be implemented with an accessible source. Independent of language refers to the algorithm that must be designed with independent of language that it can be implemented in any language.

The technique of optimization comprises nonlinear problem with huge variables containing design and more composite constraints in the application of real world. The problem of optimization is linked with decrease of cost, waste, and time or increase in performance, benefits, and profits. Optimization can be described as an attempt of generating solutions to a problem beneath bounded circumstances. Optimization techniques have arisen from a desire to utilize current resources inside the excellent possible way.

1.2   Aspiration From Nature

Always nature performs actions in an incredible approach. After the detectable phenomenon, the incalculable conspicuous effects at present are indiscernible. Theorists and experts have been penetrating this type of phenomenon in the centurial essence and making effort to grasp, recognize, accommodate, describe, and simulate the artificial structure. There are countless handler agents and extra energy that is present in both realistic and non-realistic world, nearly which are unfamiliar and hidden risk is beyond manhood apprehension in total. Those agents bear in collateral and usually in opposition to a very few other affording pattern and quality to nature and standardize the kinship, elegance, and agility of survival. This has to be noticed as the dialectical nature which prevails in the theory of the world progression. The expansion of risk in nature pursues a peculiar structure. In addition to this, also, intelligence dealing with the nature is implemented in a shared, self-formed, and optimum response without any fundamental domination.

This type of entire ordination, which is in various types—micro biological, physiologic, chemic, and sociality—is circulated as stated by the risk factor for low level to high level. This series formulate its common dependency and partnership with regard to mutual framework and its personal biography. The behavior retardation owing to the transformed conditions and these entire phenomenon best-known or little-known till now come up with an advanced concepts in science and various technologies, also computation which practice the procedures for resolving problems that is inspired by the nature additionally endeavor to comprehend the fundamental foundations and structures of nature that achieve complicated effort in an advantageous form with narrow assets and capableness. Science intermediates in-between the theorist and the world nature which was emerged before many years by developing advanced hypothesis, techniques, and implementation into well-known system of technological strive.

Manhood has been practicing to comprehend the nature of all time because of evolving advanced mechanisms as well as tools. Nature-inspired computing consists of several branches; one of them is integrative in nature that associates interpolating of knowledge together with information of science among various fields of sciences that permits the emerging of advanced computing processes like algorithms or both software and hardware for understanding the problems, combining of various models and territoriality.

1.3   Working of Nature

Acquiring from nature has become an entrenched practice in processing. The explanations behind this are straightforward. Figuring needs to manage progressively complex issues where customary strategies frequently do not function admirably. Regular frameworks have advanced approaches to take care of such issues. Techniques acquired from nature incorporate the two different ways to speak to and model frameworks, for example, cell automata or neural systems, and methods to tackle complex issues. The inspiration for putting together calculations with respect to nature is that the normal procedures concerned are known to deliver alluring outcomes, for example, finding an ideal estimation of some component. This perception has propelled numerous calculations dependent on nature. In spite of their viability, strategies displayed on nature have frequently been treated with suspiciousness. Customary scientific techniques, for example, straight writing computer programs, depend on notable hypothetical establishments. So, their understanding and their confinements can be tried diagnostically. Interestingly, nature-based techniques are specially appointed heuristics dependent on wonders whose properties are not constantly seen, even by science.

The above issues raise a need to recognize hypothetical establishments to support nature-based calculations. To address this need, we set out to do the accompanying right now. To start with, we recognize highlights that are normal to numerous nature move calculations and show how these are portrayed by a proper model that clarifies why the calculations work. Also, we portray three structures for depicting nature-inspired calculations and their activity. At long last, we examine some more profound issues about the contrasts between normal procedures and techniques dependent on them. This incorporates both the hazardousness of streamlining nature and further exercises that we can get from the manner in which forms really work in nature.

1.4   Nature-Inspired Computing

Nature-inspired computing is an emerging technique which introduces a new discipline by observing the phenomena happening in nature used to give solution to the difficult problem in the surroundings. NIC had has a best presentation for attracting responsiveness in a substantial way. NIC has developed new innovative study with new branch, namely, swarm intelligence (SI), evolutionary computation (EC), quantum computing, neural networks, fractal geometry, artificial life and artificial immune systems (AIS), and DNA computing. It also used in the field of biology, physics, engineering, management, and economics. Some of the examples of nature-inspired algorithms are like evolutionary computing (EC), artificial neural networks (ANN), fuzzy systems (FS), and SI. Nature-inspired computing is also referred as natural-inspired computation which is defined as an expression to include three methods of classes. They are as follows:

i. For the improvement of innovative problem solving, it takes technique which is inspired by nature.
ii. Based on utilization of processer for the manufacture of phenomena by nature.
iii. Based on the molecules of natural material that hire for computation.

To solve optimization problem of real world is challenging and more application need to deal with problem of NP-hard. Even though optimization tool is used to solve this problem, there is no assurance for reaching the optimal solution. There is no efficiency of algorithm for NP problems. As a conclusion for NP problems, technique of optimization is used to solve by experimental method. Some of new algorithm like particle swarm optimization (PSO), cuckoo search (CS), and firefly algorithm (FA) are developed to face this challenging problem of optimization. These new algorithm are developed to gain popularity for the performance with high efficiency. In recent survey, there are about more than 40 new different algorithms. This classification of these different algorithms is risky as it should be based on criteria with no guideline [1].

In growth of new algorithm which is inspiration of nature, some algorithms like SI algorithms and bio-inspired algorithms are developed. Metaheuristic algorithm like nature-inspired algorithm is based on physical, biological, chemical, and SI. These algorithms are called as physical-based, biological-based, chemical-based, and SI-based algorithms depending on the inspiration of nature. As the entire algorithms are not efficient, some algorithms became more common for solving all problem of real world.

1.4.1 Autonomous Entity

Autonomous entities inside the nature-inspired computing concepts comprised of two systems. One is effectors and the other is detectors. There may be various detectors which acquires data considering the adjacent agents and the surrounding. Also, there may be numerous effectors which reveal specified behaviors, purpose of changing to their intrinsic affirm, and propel transformation to the atmosphere. Effectors alleviate the distributing of data between autonomous entities.

NIC software structures are made out of specific conduct regulations that are important to self-governing entity. They are normally used to determine how a self-governing entity has to act on facts or react to nearby stimuli which might be accumulated and shared via the detectors. Autonomous entities are capable of gaining knowledge of because they reply to neighborhood changing situations via modifying their collective rules of behavior over time.

Computational ideal models concentrated by normal processing are preoccupied from characteristic marvels as differing as self-replication, the working of the cerebrum, Darwinian advancement, subgroup conduct, the resistant framework, the characterizing properties of living things, cell films, and morphogenesis. Other than customary electronic equipment, these computational ideal models can be actualized on elective physical media, for example, bimolecular or caught particle quantum figuring gadgets.

Dually, one can see forms happening in nature as data handling. Such procedures incorporate self-get together, formative procedures, quality guideline systems, protein-protein connection systems, natural vehicle (dynamic vehicle and aloof vehicle) systems, and quality gathering in unicellular creatures. Endeavors to comprehend natural frameworks likewise incorporate designing of semi-manufactured living beings and understanding the universe itself from the perspective of data handling. In reality, the thought was even best in class that data is more central than issue or vitality. The Zuse-Fredkin postulation, going back to the 1960s, expresses that the whole universe is an enormous cell robot which persistently refreshes its principles. As of late, it has been proposed that the entire universe is a quantum PC that figures its own conduct. The universe/nature as computational system is tended to investigating nature with assistance the thoughts of process ability and considering normal procedures as calculations.

1.5   General Stochastic Process of Nature-Inspired Computation

In recent days, the evolution of computation has an essential characteristic like model for processing information, which is meant by simulating the character in the basic of intelligent. The character may be biological system or organization in nature. As an example, the algorithm simulating and inspired the evolution of genetic occurrence of organism in nature that has a policy developing from nature like transformation, collection, and boundary that is to find an optimal solution from the group of solutions in nature is called as genetic algorithm (GA). The algorithm inspired by the human brain structure and use the policy of processing modes of information through neural which is human brain interpretation is called as ANN. The inspiration of seeking actions of group of some species like ant or birds from which optimal solution can be found to the problem by algorithms, namely, PSO and ant colony system (ACS).

In nature-inspired computation, to refer essential and possible setup for fundamental and comparative unitive structure that helps to understand the fundamental principle of intellectual modes and to syncretize of intellectual algorithm and to increase the enactment of algorithm is significant. During the procedure of self-motivated computation, a wide range of calculations and computation models of nature-inspired have dispersed enhancement qualities regardless notwithstanding, it is confined by a general system of outer uniform conditions. The general system of nature-inspired computation can be viewed as a hierarchy model, which is partitioned into four layers as indicated by material issues to be get resolved, including the layer of macrostructure plan and strategy improvement, the layer of undertaking flagging and comparing, the layer of computation preparation and data detecting, and the layer of development procedure of controlled elements or items. In the layer of macrostructure structure and technique improvement, client and plan module, information and strategy overhauling module, and significant information and strategy archive are incorporated. In the information and technique redesign module, significant information, smart computation model, and other plan strategies are gathered. Subsequent to being moved up to framework level by information and technique module, the information and strategies are put away to information and strategies storehouse to be moved by the macroscopically plan and dynamic finding of solution module.

In the client and structure module, the reacting specific model outside and general parameters are resolved, and data and related information on the chose smart computation model as indicated by reasonable issues to be comprehended are refined. In the meantime, the refining orders are sent to the information and techniques database. The information and strategies store at that point turn into a strategy archive which is not pointing in any way regular figuring techniques however unique smart calculation models. The information and strategy update module is focusing on a particular module. In the layer of undertaking disintegrating and relating, the fundamental activity is the dynamic appropriation. As per the data of model structure and collectivity parameter introduced by the layer above and as indicated by the macroscopical factor, the depiction of undertaking disintegrating, and circulating and relating procedures of errands, collectivity target request, and dynamic parameters are dissected to the comparing nearby assignment instruction and then transmitted to the lower booking actualize module. This undertaking is an investigation of the macroscopical parameter to neighborhood assignment and guidance. In the layer of computation planning and data detecting, the implementation of schedule module, data trade module, and data detecting and addition module are considered [2].

As by the fractional training from the upper level, relative orders can be completed, conveyed by the implementation of schedule modules of smart operators. Each smart operator can be based on concept of reasoning or a substance idea, contingent upon the problem which is resoled depending on the above. The essential reference control sign of genuine development can be organized by every incomplete crucial continuous programming of assignment, real-time development programming, ongoing development control, and constant guidance momentum. Data of the planning usage module required can be made by the data detecting and gathering module, got through the taking out of original data assortment by fixed-point detecting, distinguishing proof and change, and through optimization of processing signal, data extraction and demonstrating, data collection and redesigning, and data systematization. The manufactured data which is real are dispersed to each planning execution module of operators through the data trade modules, including data arrangement, data order, data test, data transformation, and data distribution.

The layer of development procedure of controlled objective substance incorporates controlled development process and controlled item element, just as comparing sensor framework. In the controlled development process, the controlled article gets continuous control signs of development parameter from the computation planning execution module of upper layer to actualize the items moving. The sensor framework can gather the first data of items and move the data to the above-layer data detecting and collection module.

Decision-making distribution module, information and techniques update module, and computation of schedule module that utilize data trade, detecting, etc., for every specialist are autonomous in the general system of nature-inspired computation. Subsequent to finishing the structure and planning of undertakings, the development of a populace of specialists can be realized in an appropriated and free computational condition which takes on a fundamental attribute of dispersed man-made consciousness remembered for the possibility of nature-inspired computation. It is vibrant that nature-inspired computation is not completely equivalent to an autonomous physical framework or organic populace, yet is a unique structure thought that puts up a sort of relative uniform smart computation mode and is characterized dependent on survey and home investigation of interrelated smart models.

1.5.1 NIC Categorization

Nature-inspired algorithms are characterized into five gatherings:

1. Evolutionary algorithms (EA)
2. Physical algorithms (PA)
3. Swarm intelligence (SI)
4. Bio-inspired algorithms (BIA, however not SI-based)
5. Nature-inspired algorithms.

Figure 1.1 categorize the NIC algorithms in detail.

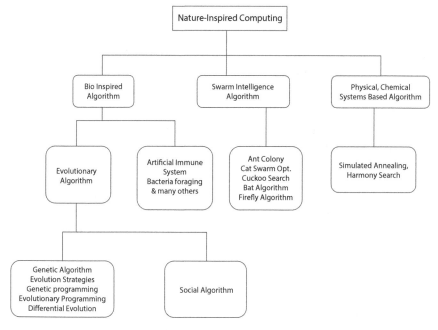

Figure 1.1 Category of NIC.

1.5.1.1 Bioinspired Algorithm

Clearly, SI-based calculations have a place with a more extensive class of calculations, called BIA. Certainly, BIAs are mostly major algorithms of each and every nature-inspired algorithms. From a set of hypothesis perspective, SI-based algorithms are a subgroup of BIAs; while BIAs are a subgroup of nature-inspired algorithms. Numerous BIAs do not utilize straightforwardly the swarming conduct. In this way, this approach is smarter to call them bio-inspired however not as SI based. For instance, GAs are also included in the bio-inspired concept but SI based is not included. Even so, this is difficult to arrange few algorithms, for example, differential evolution (DE). Carefully, DE is not bio-inspired on the grounds that there is no immediate connect to any natural conduct. Nevertheless, it has some similitude to GAs. The BIA comprised of bacterial foraging optimization (BFO), AIS, Krill herd algorithm, and dendritic cell algorithm [3].

Bio-inspired computation serves a gathering of algorithms that focus on gainful processing, for example, for enhancement procedures and coordination acceptance. These algorithms depend upon fields like science, software engineering, and arithmetic. BIAs are major and main set of SI-based and nature-inspired algorithms.

1.5.1.2   *Swarm Intelligence*

In 1989, Gerardo Beni and Jing Wang acquainted SI in connection with cell automated frameworks. Piece of a huge number of animal that have chosen their own will for focus on a typical objective is called swarm. How do swarms (winged animals, fish, and so on) figure out to move so well altogether. How do ants locate the best wellsprings of nourishment in their surrounding? To respond to these inquiries, new incredible streamlining technique, i.e., SI, is planned.

SI is simply the order that manages advanced collection, self-managed, collaborate, flexible, and incredible behavior of class which observes the 35 straightforward principles. The idea of swarm insight depends on artificial intelligence. Individual can be considered as idiotic yet numerous specialists' display self-association conduct and, in this manner, can act like community oriented intelligence. SI-based calculation is famous and broadly utilized. A biologic staging arrangement of nature gives the motivation. Case of SI incorporates ant colony, bird congregation, animal or bird grouping, bacterial development, and fish tutoring. Swarm telerobotics is the methodology of SI, alludes to increasingly regular set-up of algorithms. "Swarm forecasting" is utilized for determining issues [4].

The paradigms of SI are as follows:

1) Ant colony optimization (ACO): Dorigo in his Doctoral exposition presented ACO. It is helpful in discovering better ways through charts.
2) Particle swarm optimization (PSO): This approach promises with issue in that a superlative clarification is constituted as a point in a space of dimension. Advantage of PSO is that it has a huge number of individuals that make the atom swarm, which make the system amazingly intense issue of territorial minima.
3) Artificial bee colony (ABC): In 2005, Karaboga presented this metaheuristic algorithm and animates the chasing conduct of sovereign honey bees. This algorithm is made up of three phases. They are employed honey bees, scout honey bees, and onlooker honey bees.
4) Fish swarm algorithm (FSA): Fish schooling is its starting point. This algorithm works on three conduct of characteristic fish.

   - Searching behavior of fish
   - Swarming behavior of fish
   - Following behavior of fish

SI was firstly introduced by Kennedy and Eberhart in 2001 and is an ongoing and rising prototype in bio-inspired computation for actualizing versatile frameworks. Right now, it is an expansion of EC. While EAs depend on hereditary adjustment of life forms, SI depends on aggregate social conduct of living beings. According to definitions in survey, SI incorporates the usage of aggregate insight of gatherings of basic specialists that depend on the conduct of certifiable organism swarms, as a critical thinking way. The "swarm" word is originated in the periodic developments of particles in the space of issues. SI was created close with the utilization of EA. Few notable scheme are discoursed here. These direction following algorithms being motivated by the aggregate conduct of organisms display decentralized and self-sorted out examples in the scrounging procedure.

Principles of SI: SI is illustrated by thinking about essential standards. They are as follows:

1. **Proximity Principle:** This principle is referred as the community ought to have the option to do basic existence calculations.
2. **Quality Principle:** This principle is referred as the community ought to have the option to react to quality factors in the earth.
3. **Diverse Response Principle:** This principle is referred as the community ought is not submitting to its movement along unreasonably slender channels.
4. **Stability Principle:** This principle is referred as the community ought as not to change its method of conduct each time when the surrounding changes.
5. **Adaptability Principle:** This principle is referred as the community ought to have the option that it can change its conduct method while merits are computational cost.

1.5.1.3 *Physical Algorithms*

Physics-inspired algorithms utilize essential standards of physical science, for instance, laws of movement (motion) and the Newton's laws of attractive energy. They are totally positioned on physical standards of deterministic. The algorithms of physical oriented can be arranged extensively as in following way.

a. Newton's laws of movement (motion) are inspired for Collision Bodies Optimization (CBO).

b. Newton's gravitational power is inspired for Space Gravitation Optimization (SGO), Gravitational Search Algorithm (GSA), Gravitational Interaction Optimization (GIO), and Central Force Optimization (CFO).

c. Heavenly mechanics and stargazing is inspired for enormous detonation of Integrated Radiation Search (IRS), Big Bang Big Crunch (BB BC) search, Artificial Physics-based Optimization (APO), Galaxy-based Search Algorithm (GBSA), and Black Hole Search (BHS),

d. Electromagnetism is inspired for Electromagnetism-like Optimization (EMO), Hysteretic Optimization (HO), and Charged System Search (CSS).

e. Optics is inspired for Ray (Beam) Optimization (RO).

f. Acoustics is inspired for Harmony Search Algorithm (HSA).

g. Thermodynamics is inspired for Simulated Annealing (SA).

h. Hydrology and hydrodynamics is inspired for Water Drop Algorithm (WDA), Water Cycle Algorithm (WCA), and River Formation Dynamics Algorithm (RFDA).

A more prompt for every one of these algorithms is the algorithm of SA dependent on the instruction of thermo dynamics. This algorithm is mimicking the technique of cooling procedure by bit and brings down the temperature of the structure while waiting for its bonds to a state of consistent. This plan is utilized to recreate reinforcing look of possible schedules and associations with arrangement in optimum way that simulatively drove the specialists to investigate different territories of physical science. A concept of sound from the field and auditory range prompted the improvement of HSA motivated by means of a marvel ordinarily determined in harmony. This idea driving the HSA is to locate an ideal condition of harmony controlled by aesthetic estimation.

1.5.1.4   Familiar NIC Algorithms

1.5.1.4.1   Boids

Boids is a one kind of artificial life simulation introduced by Craig Reynolds. The goal of the simulation is to repeat the behavior of group of species especially birds. Rather than controlling the associations of a whole rush, notwithstanding, the boids simulation just indicates the conduct of every individual feathered creature. With just a couple of basic principles, the program figures out how to produce an outcome that is intricate and reasonable enough to be utilized as a structure for computer designs applications, for example, computer created social liveliness in movie films.

The name "boid" relates to an abbreviated adaptation of "bird-oid object", which is known as object like creation of birds. By chance, "boid" is likewise a New York Metropolitan lingo articulation for "feathered creature like bird". In place of with most artificial life simulations, boids is a case of new behavior, that is, the difficulty of Boids emerges from the collaboration of individual specialists which is referred as boids, right now to a lot of straightforward standards. The standards applied in the most straightforward Boids world are as per the separation which is known as direct crowding of local group of local birds; next is alignment which is referred as direct for regular caption of group of local birds; and at last, cohesion which is referred as direct movement of regular location of group of local birds.

Most complicated principles can be included, for example, obstruction shirking, and objective chasing. The development of Boids can be portrayed as either disordered as parting gatherings and wild conduct or methodical. Surprising practices, for example, parting runs and rejoining in the wake of keeping away from deterrents, can be viewed as evolving. The boids structure is frequently utilized in computer designs, giving practical looking demonstrations of groups of feathered creatures and different animals, for example, schools of fish or crowds of creatures.

Another model simulation of group of birds have been developed by Frank Heppner and Ulf Grenander in 1990. The model has three main rules, namely, homing, velocity regulation, and interaction, in which homing is referred as every individual of the group try to be constant in a specific area; velocity regulation is referred as every individual of group tries to make a movement of fly within a definite predefined speed of flight; and interaction is referred to group of birds, where, when they are near to others, they will try to make a movement and, with large distance to others, they will not get impact, else will try to make a movement nearest to each other.

One of the essential highlights of this model (as opposed to Reynolds model) is the consideration of arbitrary unsettling influences. It simulates the unsettling influences with a Poisson stochastic procedure; anyway, one of the shortcomings of this model is that it would not yield satisfiable outcomes without these aggravations. The boid is the demonstration of birds in Reynolds flocking simulation model. Each boid item ought to in any event have the accompanying credits to define the state it is in. Their location is referred as coordinates of the recent location of boid, course is referred as recent course of the boid, and velocity is referred as rate as the boid is migrating.

The course and speed could obviously be spoken to by an equal speed vector. In any case, frequently more credits are expected to make the reproduction all the more persuading. Setting an upper boundary for how quick the boids can move and turn is a typical improvement. Raynolds unique usage essentially characterized the neighbors as the boids inside a specific sweep. Another conceivable meaning of the area is to let each boid take a gander at the N nearest boids. This postulation endeavors to contrast the two definitions with discover qualities and shortcomings in the two definitions and find under what conditions either is unrivaled.

Right now, the rule for the algorithm is that boid has a part around it crossing 300°, fixated on the boid that is ongoing. Some other boids are, right now, considered "neighbors" or (to utilize Reynolds' term) "flockmates".

1. Each boid ought to modify it, making a beeline to stay away from impacts and keep up an agreeable separation of one boid-span with its neighbors. This is the "Division" part of the calculation. The one boid-radius might be avoided; however, it ought to resemble an elastic band, adjusting back properly.
2. Each boid ought to furthermore modify it, making a beeline to be nearer to the normal heading of the different boids in its neighborhood, as long as it does not meddle with the main standard. This is the "arrangement" part of the calculation.
3. Each boid should turn itself toward the normal situation of its group of birds, as long as this does not cause crash or essentially meddle with the subsequent principle.

1.5.1.4.2   Memetic Algorithm

Memetic Algorithm (MA) is an expansion of the conventional hereditary calculation. It utilizes a nearby hunt procedure to diminish the probability of the untimely intermingling. While in streamlining, the work of crossover calculations was at that point being used, a novel and visionary viewpoint that enhances calculations regarding memetic metaphor. MA speaks to one of the ongoing developing territories of research in transformative calculation. The term MA is currently broadly utilized as a cooperative energy of transformative or any populace-based methodology with discrete individual learning or nearby improvement systems for issue search. Regularly, MAs are additionally alluded to the writing as Baldwinian EA, Lamarckian EA, social calculations, or genetic local search.

At the point when a MA approach is structured, it is at the selected time that the conclusive outcome is an algorithm made out of a few sections. These parts can be called images by following the metaphor, administrators if a low level plan is performed, or developmental system and neighborhood search calculations if a traditional MA is considered [5].

Notwithstanding the particular algorithmic execution, a vitally significant issue, if not the most significant issue in MC is to decide how the images associate during the enhancement procedure. The coordination of the images has been acted in one of the following ways:

1. Adaptive hyper-heuristic: This consists of algorithms for which the images are composed by methods for a prefixed plan or calendar. These plans can be randomized or deterministic. In a randomized plan, the images can be randomly initiated individually or in a group by applying an attainment rule. Concerning plans, an ordinary execution is a timetable which subdivides an offered spending plan to every image.

2. Meta-Lamarckian learning: It is an augmentation and an advancement of the hyper-heuristic MA and particularly the decision capacities and establishes a sincere broad and adaptable system for algorithmic structure. All the more explicitly, an essential meta-Lamarckian learning technique was proposed as the standard algorithm for evaluation. This essential technique is a basic irregular coordination of images with no adjustment. At that point, the choice space is disintegrated into sub-regions for the different advancement of each sub-region. This methodology expects that distinctive analyzers are appropriate for various issues, and along these lines, each sub-territory requires an alternate image. So as to pick an appropriate image at every choice point, the procedure accumulates information about the capacity of the images to look on a specific area of the inquiry space from a database of past encounters chronicled during the initial search. The images recognized at that point structure the aspirant images that will get completed, in view of their rewards, to settle on which image will continue with the neighborhood improvement.

3. Self-adaptive and co-evolutionary: The third class depends on the transformative standards for the image improvement and choice. In self-adaptive MA, every arrangement is made out of its hereditary and memetic material. Therefore, the images are directly encoded into the arrangements and their activity is related to the offering solutions. Co-evolutionary MA is adroitly like self-adaptive MA however is actualized in an alternate manner. The memetic material, made out of different images, advances in a populace isolated from the number of inhabitants in arrangements. Populaces of

qualities and images develop independently and all the while and their responses are connected.

4. Fitness diversity adaptive: The fitness diversity adaptive MA naturally executes the image coordination by investigating the populace status. In these adaptive system, wellness that has been mixed with variety is utilized to appraise the populace decent variety.

This decision is finished thinking that, for multivariate issues, the proportion of genotypical separation can be unnecessarily time and memory intense, and accordingly, the adjustment may require an unsuitable computational overhead. Clearly, fitness assorted variety could not give a productive estimation of populace decent variety, since it can happen that altogether different focuses take a similar fitness values.

The applications of MA are multi-dimensional knapsack problem, pattern recognition, feature/gene selection, training of artificial neural networks, clustering of gene expression profiles, traveling salesman problem (TSP), robotic motion planning, etc.

1.5.1.4.3 Evolutionary Algorithms

EC is a prototype that has computerized reasoning domain of targets profiting by aggregate phenomenon in versatile community of issue solvers using the iterative advancement containing development, improvement, propagation, determination, and endurance in a particular community. EA is one of the notable, classic along with recognized algorithms in nature-inspired algorithms as it depends on the organic development in nature that is being answerable to the plan of every living being in the world, and for the techniques, they use to communicate with one another. EAs utilize this incredible structure theory to discover optimal results for difficult issues. EAs are not deterministic and also cost-based enhancement algorithms. EA is motivated from Darwinian development. It is intended to discover optimal result of a given issue. It follows the general ethics of speciation found in nature to resolve the issue.

Algorithms are recited as follows:

- EAs are network based (process an entire choice of chosen one arrangements together).
- A new result is framed by recombination of the preceding data of more members.
- EAs can be stochastic (structure can be examined mathematically but it cannot be used for the prediction process).

In the field of artificial intelligence, EC is a prototype that incorporate interactive iterations of issue decoder which use the iterative procedure comprise of development, advancement, reproduction, selection, and endurance as in populace. Parts of EA are representation, evaluation capacity (or wellness work), population, parent choice component, variation administrators recombination, and change and survivor choice component (substitution).

1.5.1.4.4   Genetic Algorithm

GA is a BIA which is based on search which is constructed based on selection of natural concepts and heredity-based concepts which are introduced by John Holland and his colleagues and students, particularly David E. Goldberg. They have tried a variety of problem based on optimization for huge evaluation of achievement. GA is referred as EC that is subset of huge outlet of computation. GA are randomized in nature, and they can perform more better than random local search, in which an algorithm will try more solution randomly by monitoring the best as they did in historical data. In GAs, for the given set of problem, there will be a possible solution.

These classifications by then experience combination and change which is like ordinary genetic characteristics, conveying new adolescents, and the methodology is repeated over various ages. Each individual is named an estimation of capacity for review the objective of work esteems and the individuals of fitter are provided a maximum chance of comrade that produce immense the people with "fitter". The way is continue growing best individual or gathering about clarification until we arrive at the completion guideline [6].

The pros of GA are that it does not require any derivative data like they are not accessible for most recent world problem, as associated with traditional methods; GA performs more rapidly and efficient way; parallel skills are best in GA; functions like discrete and continuous are enhanced; problems are multi-objective, and they do not provide a single solution rather they provide more solutions; and GA is useful when a searching universe is high and when huge factors are considered.

The cons of GA are that it is not appropriate for all kind of difficulties which are unassuming and derivative data is accessible; GA are more expensive for difficulties as a significance of fitness; when not implemented correctly, it will not give optimal solution; and there are no confirmations on the optimality or the idea of the plan for existing stochastic.

The applications incorporate allocation of document for a distributed system, PC robotized plan, server farm/server center, code breaking, criminological science, robot behavior, PC design, Bayesian inference, AI, game hypothesis, and so forth.

1.5.1.4.5 Ant Colony Optimization

ACO is a populace-oriented approach of metaheuristic which is utilized for discovering inexact results for troublesome enhancement issues. This method is probabilistic in resolving the problems of issues computational that is diminished with the help of discerning new ways through plans. In ACO, a lot of software transmitter called artificial ants will probe for respectable answers for optimal for a given issue of appreciation. For the use ACO, the issue of optimization can be transformed into the issue for identifying the best way on a pattern with weight. The artificial ants gradually built by proceeding onward the pattern.

Artificial ants represent multi-agent techniques roused by the behavior of ordinary ants. The pheromone-based correspondence of natural ants is regularly the overwhelming prototype used. Combinations of artificial ants and neighborhood search algorithms have become a technique for decision for various development jobs including a type of graph, e.g., vehicle steering and web directing. The expanding movement right now prompted conferences devoted exclusively to artificial ants and to various business applications by particular organizations, for example, AntOptima.

This algorithm is hidden for an individual from the ant algorithms, but in SI techniques, it comprises some approach of metaheuristic developments. It was introduced by Marco Dorigo in 1992; the primary algorithm was in the family way to look for an ideal result in an illustration, supported by the ant's behavior of observing for path between the portion as well as the feed root. The major assumption is that it has improved to explain a maximum class of extensive for issues if numeric, and as a result, little issues have been developed and illustration on various types of the ant's behavior. ACO plays out a model-based searching and offer a few reproductions technique with over assessment of circulation algorithms [7].

Its application includes the problem with generalized assignment and the set covering, classification problems, Ant Net for organized directing, and Multiple Knapsack Problem.

1.5.1.4.6 Particle Swarm Optimization

PSO is introduced Kennedy and Eberhart in 1995 aspired by the behavior of social creatures in gatherings, for example, flying creature and fish schooling or subterranean ant colonies. This algorithm imitates the communication between individuals to share data. PSO has been applied to various fields for development and in coordination with other existent calculations.

Swarm optimization (PSO) is a strategy of computational which reduces an issue by regularly and attempting to expand an individual answer based on a specified value of proportion. This understands an issue by the way of having a populace of individual response which is named particles here, and particles move around the space of searching as per the normal statistical principle from the particle's location and promptness. The development of each particle is attacked by its near most popular location but, at the similar period, is guided toward the most popular situations by the seeking environment that is restored with correct location that is sorted by particles of different types.

PSO will make not maximum or no presumptions about the advanced issue and that can stare over massive spaces of individual solutions. Nonetheless, metaheuristic algorithm like PSO will not ensure an ideal solution at all times. Additionally, PSO will not utilize the changing of the issue that is improved and implies that PSO will not impose that the issue of optimization can be differentiated as it is required by strategies of classical development.

Its applications include combination with a back engendering calculation, to prepare a neural system framework structure, multi-target optimization, classification, image clustering and image clustering, image processing, automated applications, dynamic, pattern recognition, image segmentation, robotic applications, time frequency analysis, decision-making, simulation, and identification.

1.5.1.4.7   Harmony Search

Harmony Search (HS) is an approach inspired through the standards of the performer act of harmony. The HS has the distinctive parameters of algorithm that has efficiency in simplicity and search. During the current years, it has been effectively utilized in field such as mechanical structure design, optimization of data classification systems, function optimization, and pipe network optimization. The utilized memory of harmony is significant as it is similar to the result of the best-fit people in GA. This results in the assurance of the best harmonies that will be continued by the new memory of harmony. When performers form the harmony normally attempt different potential mixtures of the music contributes put away their memory. This search for the ideal harmony is without an uncertainty of similar to the technique of finding the ideal answers for building issues. The HS strategy is really motivated by the working standards of the harmony inventiveness. In the HS algorithm, enhancement of constrain by the pitch through modification and randomization as there are two subcomponents for modification which may be a significant feature for the maximum productivity of the HS technique.

The initial subcomponent of forming "new music" or creating new measures through the technique of randomization it would be in any event at a similar degree through productivity as various types of algorithm by randomization. An extra subcomponent by use of HS augmentation is the change of pitch. Pitch changing is completed by modifying the contribution of given data transfer capacity by a little arbitrary sum comparative with the present pitch along with the arrangement from the memory of harmony. Mainly, altering of pitch is a technique based on fine tuning practice of neighborhood activities. Consideration of memory and changing of pitch will assure as the neighborhood activities are detained with the technique of randomization and contract consideration of memory that will consider the worldwide space of inquiry in an effective manner.

The establishment is characterized in the HS algorithm through the technique of memory tolerating rate of harmony. A high amicability response rate implies the great explanation from the past, and recollection is bound to be chosen or acquired. This is identical in a specific way of exclusiveness. When the rate of acknowledgment is excessively low, the activities will meet all the activities with maximum progress. The HS algorithm is simpler to execution. The proof to recommendation of HS will decrease the impatient to the parameters that are selected, in which it implies that it will not need adjustment of the parameters to reach the high quality activities. Besides, the HS algorithm is an approach of populace based metaheuristic that implies various sounds of gatherings and that can be utilized in equal. Appropriate parallelism generally prompts better implantation with higher proficiency. The mixture of parallelism along the elitism just as an equalization of heightening as well as enhancement is the path into the achievement of the HS algorithm and to accomplishment of few approach of metaheuristic. The stochastic subordinates give the choice probabilities of certain discrete factors during the advancement technique of the HS. It is effective at controlling discrete advancement issues and has been utilized in the ideal plan of systems of fluid transport.

In the global best HS (GHS), the alteration of new arrangements is spontaneous as it just founded on the best selected harmony from the HM without the inclusion of the distance bandwidth (BW). This fascinating methodology includes the one of a kind social learning ability to the GHS. The examination of the experiment to 10 benchmark capacities demonstrates that the GHS can perform maximum than HS. The application of the HSA is power systems, power systems, transportation, medical science and robotics, industry and signal, and image processing.

1.5.1.4.8   Social Cognitive Optimization

Social cognitive optimization (SCO) is one of metaheuristic populace-based algorithms for optimization. The algorithm of SCO is the most current perceptive algorithm. The SCO algorithm depends on the theory of social cognitive. The key purpose of the ergodicity which means the ensemble average and time average are equal that is utilized in the procedure of individual learning of a lot of specialists with their own memory and their social learning with the information focuses in the collection of social sharing. It has been utilized for solving problems of optimization which is continuous and combinatorial.

The SCO algorithm is simple with minimum number of parameters and without the changed activity as in genetic-based EA. By contrasting SCO and GA experimentally on the function of benchmark, we are able to get solution with high quality and less time for evaluation. Besides, as in human culture, one learning specialist makes performance with appropriate library size that illustration adaptability is more than in SI. The SCO algorithm can assist the solvers with avoiding stumbling in local optimization while solving the problems of nonlinear restraints. Adjusted and upgraded situations of locality that looks through and acquires the Chaos and Kent functions of mapping to contract increasingly with reasonable information are uniformly distributed [8].

In the method optimization, the algorithm is an approach of high-speed calculation and is applied to the big scale problems that are having multimodal work in optimization worldwide. The speed and the nature of outcome which are the best goals are enhanced than the methods in traditional. The algorithm will contribute to the PC by solving few problems of nonlinear with complex constraints, but regularly trips in the nearby ideal setting, and with cycle of long processing and limits the moderate union rate that extends some of these techniques. The disadvantages are it gets that the social cognitive theory that is applied in the field of the constraint that presents a SCO to take care of the nonlinear constraints. In the SCO algorithm, the procedures that are impersonation and erudition are the most significant idea to characterize the algorithm, and utilization of the procedure of the community is looking to restore the information in which the point is one of the most significant parts. In the SCO algorithm, the area looking through utilizes the irregular capacity to create area of the new information point; however, the subjective capacity depends on the straight congruently strategy. This technique is anything but difficult is that appreciates and has a long processing cycle, and the ergodicity is frail on the off chance that we utilize this strategy and the information point might be a long way from the essential problem and has the likelihood to pass the best goals. In this way, it is important to adjust and improve the social cognitive theory and the SCO algorithm. The area looking of standard SCO algorithm depends on the basic irregular capacity and the ergodicity of basic arbitrary is feeble that can affect the looking through scale of uneven and the recent information point that can have a long way from the essential idea.

1.5.1.4.9   Artificial Bee Colony Algorithm

ABC algorithm is one of the algorithms based on optimization of the hunting behavior of swarm and honey bee introduced by Dervis Karaboga. This was inspired by hunting behavior of honey bees. The algorithm is explicitly constructed on the model introduced by Tereshko and Loengarov in 2005 for the hunting behavior in colonies of honey bee. These approaches consist of three basic segments: food sources, employed, and unemployed. The employed and unemployed segments do the process of searching food resources and the other segment will be close to the hive. The classical model also referred as two dynamic methods of conducting is indispensable for self-organizing and aggregates knowledge that conscription of hunters to food resources is bringing about positive criticism and neglecting poor resources by hunters, causing negative input.

In ABC, settlements of agent like artificial forager bees scan for rich food a resource that is the great answers for a given problem. ABC is applied for the consideration problem of optimization that is initially changed over to the problem of identifying the finest constraint vector that limits a goal work. Artificial bees iteratively identify a populace of beginning planned vectors, and afterward, the process of iteration is improved by them and utilizes the systems as moving toward better arrangements by methods for a neighbor search instrument while neglecting deprived solution [9].

ABC algorithm is based on populace, and the situation of a food resource characterize to a potential solution for the problem of optimization and the measure of nectar in the food resource compared with the eminence of wellness of the solution are related. The utilization amount of honey bees is corresponding with the amount of activities in the general population. Initially, an arbitrarily conveyed beginning populace as food resource positions is produced. After initialization, the general population is unprotected to rehash the patterns in searching actions of the scout bees, unemployed bees, and employed bees separately. The employed honey bee delivers with an alteration on the location of source in the memory of bee and identifies other nourishment location of source. The nectar measure is the upgraded one with maximum of the source, and the honey bee has the ability to recollect the new position of the location and superintend the anterior one, or the situation is kept the memory. Totally employed honey bees complete the quest technique, and then, they share the position of the data sources along with the spectators that move in the region. The onlooker honey bee considers the nectar taken from employed honey bee and afterward preferences a nourishment source contingent upon the nectar measures of sources. As on account of the employed honey bee, they deliver an adjustment on the source of the location in memory of bee and form its nectar quantity. The nectar which has the maximum than that of the past one is collected and the honey bee retains the new location and supervises the anterior one. The sources of location that is relinquished are determined, and new location of sources is arbitrarily transported to be changed along with the unrestricted ones by artificial bee of scouts.

The applications of the ABC algorithm are used in the problem of medical pattern classification, network reconfiguration, minimum spanning tree, train neural networks, radial distribution system of network reconfiguration, and train neural networks.

1.5.1.4.10 River Formation Dynamics

River Formation Dynamic (RFD) is an optimization approach based on heuristic method on the behavior of manner in which the water is dropped from river bed. This mimicks how river water, by decomposition of the ground, saves the silt. The group of droplets that are placed at the beginning stage is exposed to force by gravitation that pulls in the drops to the focal point of the earth. The results of these drops are circulated all through their condition and looking for the absolute bottom in the ocean. Numerous new riverbeds are framed in the process right now. The RFD uses the idea behind the problems of graph theory. The group of drops by agents is made and proceeds onward edges between hubs that investigating a domain for the best arrangement. This is cultivated by components of disintegration and top soil sedimentation that identify with changes in the height that is consigned to every other hub. Drops while transferring to all through a situation of alter hub heights along their way. The change starting with one hub then onto the next is completed by diminishing height of the hubs, which in certainty gives numerous advantages like local cycles that are avoided. When drops change the site by minimum or maximum of the height of spots, the explanations are given by the path of height which is diminishing. Minimizing angles are constructed and the inclines are lag behind the consequent droplets as to create the fresh directions and strengthen the finest direction. This optimization of heuristic approach is introduced by Rabanalin 2007. RFD is utilized to solve TSP.

The working of RFD algorithm is as follows. A measure of soil is allotted to every hub. Drops, as they move, disintegrate their ways like taking some dirt from hubs or storing the conveyed dregs, which is referred, in this way, as expanding the elevations of hubs. Probability of selecting the following hub relies upon the slope which is corresponding to the contrast between tallness of the hub at which the drop lives and stature of its neighbor. Initially, the earth is level, for example, heights of all centers are corresponding, and aside from the objective center which is equivalent to zero during the whole procedure. Drops are put in the underlying center to empower further investigation of the earth. At each stage, a gathering of drops consecutively navigates the space and afterward performs disintegration on visited hubs [11].

The RFD algorithm has some disadvantages which avoid the algorithm for great execution, termed as problem of path generation. On account of an enormous number of coefficients, tuning of the algorithm to a specific case which is unintuitive in high case and regardless of its rate of convergence is little for increasingly confused situations.

1.5.1.4.11 Firefly Algorithm

FA is the swarm-based metaheuristic approach which is introduced by Xin. The behavior such as flashing lights of the fireflies is inspired and utilized in the algorithm. The algorithm utilizes the concept that fireflies are always both sex and implies that any firefly can be engrossed by some firefly and the ability of the desirability of the firefly is directly relational to the ability of its brightness which depends upon the goal work. A firefly will be pulled in to the firefly with more brightness.

The working function FA has the following steps.

1. Objective function is initialized by absorbing the light intensity.
2. Initial population of the firefly is generated.
3. For every firefly, the light intensity is determined.
4. Attractiveness of the firefly is calculated.
5. The firefly which has brightness level of minimum is moved toward the firefly which has brightness level of maximum.

6. Light intensity of the firefly is updated.
7. Fireflies are ranked based on the intensities and best solution is found.

The advantages of the FA are that it has an ability to die with nonlinear more effectively, optimization of multimodal problem can be solved naturally, there is no need of velocity as it is needed in PSO, solution to the global optimization problem can be found as soon as possible, it is flexible to integrate with other technique of optimization, and initial solution is not required. The disadvantage of FA is it consumes more time to reach the optimal solution. FA is used in the field of semantic web composition, classification and clustering problems, neural network, fault detection, digital image compression, feature selection, digital image processing, scheduling problems, and TSP.

1.5.1.4.12   Group Search Optimizer Algorithm

Group search optimizer (GSO) is an optimization algorithm based on approach of heuristic with respect to populace. It implements the model of Producer Scrounger (PS) for modeling the technique of searching through optimization which is inspired by hunting behavior of animal. In GSO, a class may consist of three parameters, namely, producers, rangers, and scroungers. The behavior of producer and scrounger consists of scanning and replication of a particular area, and ranger will perform the task of random walk. The producer is selected by the individual situated in an area that has preeminent ability value in each iteration and scans to search for the resources in the environment. The scroungers are selected in the way who will continue scanning for chances to intersect with the resource setup by the manufacturer. The remaining member in the cluster is referred as rangers which has the ability to scatter from their present locations [10].

The algorithm of GSO is easy, simple, and clear executes, which gives a structure that is open to use the study in actions of animal to handle the hard situation. This algorithm illustrates the robustness and not sensitive for the factors excluding the ranger's percentage. In any case, the complex of computational is expanded significantly on the grounds that it embraces an idea of interest edge that a polar can have Cartesian coordinate that will change according to required needs. PSO is a classification of SI is best algorithm for candidate for problems of NP-hard. It is computational basic and simple to execute structured in Cartesian facilitate. In addition to the benefits of PSO and GSO, to improve GSO for ideal setting of distributed generator (DG) is a stimulating work.

1.5.1.4.13   Bat Algorithm

Bat algorithm was introduced by Xin-She Yang by inspiring the behavior of locating the path by echo which is referred as echolocation of the micro-bats that vary in rating of pulse for the parameter of loudness and emission for the optimization. Echolocation mechanism is as a sort of sonar that bats for the most part micro-bats produce a noisy and short sound of pulse. At the point when they hit an item, after a small amount of time, the reverberation will return back to their ears. The bat gets and identifies the area of the target right now. This location identifying mechanism through echo makes bats ready to recognize the contrast between a problem and a prey and permits them to chase even in full darkness. So as to mimic the hunting behavior of the bats, a technique of the bat algorithm is implemented with the following assumptions:

1. Bats utilize the technique of echolocation to detect the distance and they can also identify the difference between the target and the walls.
2. Bat can fly accidentally along with the velocity and position for a static frequency that may vary in wavelength and loudness for searching the target. They can modify the wavelength automatically with respect to their pulse depending on the target.
3. Bat's loudness can vary in more number of ways ranging from large positive to minimum value.

Based on three assumptions, the algorithm produces a group of solutions randomly for the problem and afterward looks through the ideal solution by cycle and make stronger the nearby analysis during the time spent of searching. By providing the optimal solution randomly, bat algorithm discovers the global optimal solution to their problem. Some of the applications of bat algorithm are image processing, clustering, classification, data mining, continuous optimization, problem inverse and estimation of parameter, combination scheduling and optimization, and fuzzy logic.

1.5.1.4.14   Binary Bat Algorithm

Binary bat algorithm (BBA) is an approach utilized for solving discrete problems which was introduced by Nakamura. BBA is implemented in the problem of classification and selection of feature. It is a binary version of bat algorithm with the modification of velocity and position. In other version like continuous of bat algorithm, bat travels through the search place of target with the help of velocity and position parameters. In position, it shifts between 0's and 1's which act as the binary space to reach the target.

1.5.1.4.15   Cuttlefish Algorithm

The cuttlefish algorithm (CFA) is inspired by the color changing behavior of cuttlefish to identify the optimal solution of the problem. The set of patterns and hues found in cuttlefish are created by reflection of light from various types cells layer like chromatophores, iridophores, and leucophores which are stacked together, and it is a combination of specific cells on the double that permits cuttlefish to have such a huge selection of pattern and hues.

Cuttlefish is a sort of cephalopods which is distinguished for its capacities to change its shading either to apparently vanish into its condition or to deliver magnificent presentations. The pattern and hues found in cephalopods are created by various types and cell layers are stacked together including chromatophores, iridophores, and leucophores.

Cuttlefish algorithm thinks about two major measures, namely, reflection and perceptibility. Reflection process is referred to reproduce the light reflection system utilized by these three layers where the perceptibility is referred to putting on the perceptibility of coordinating example utilized by the cuttlefish. These two procedures are utilized for technique like searching to locate the optimal solution of the problem.

1.5.1.4.16   Grey Wolf Optimizer

Grey Wolf Optimizer (GWO) was introduced by Mirjalili, which is one of the mimicking of the management quality with leadership and hare coursing mechanism of grey wolves. Alpha, Beta, Delta, and Omega are the four types of grey wolves, which are used for mimicking the management quality with leadership. The technique of Grey Wolf like penetrating, surrounding, and attacking the target is used for mimicking the hare coursing for the implementation of optimization technique.

Grey Wolf has a place in a biological family named Canidae, which live in a pack of wolf. They have a severe social predominant chain of importance like Delta, Omega, Beta, and Alpha. Alpha that is referred to pioneer is a male or female which places a major role in making decision. The sets of the predominant wolf ought to be trailed by the pack. The Beta is referred as minor wolves that have ability to help the alpha in making decision. The beta is a guide to alpha for making decision and discipliner for the pack of wolf. Omega is referred as the lower positioning of grey wolf which needs to present all other predominant wolves. In the event that a wolf is neither an alpha or beta nor omega, it is called delta. Delta is referred as wolves that lead omega and report to alpha and beta.

The hare coursing strategies and the social progression of wolves are numerically displayed so as to create GWO and perform technique of optimization. The algorithm of GWO is established with the typical test mechanism that shows it has predominant investigation and utilization qualities than other techniques like swarm intelligent. When a wolf is not said to be alpha, beta, or omega, then it is called as minor or delta in certain cases. The categories of GWO are scouts, hunters, elders, caretakers, and sentinels, which have a place with this class. Scout wolves are referred as answerable for inspecting the limits of the section and threatening the pack if there should arise an occurrence of any threat. Hunter wolves are referred to as which help the alphas and betas when chasing prey and giving nourishment to the pack. Elder wolves are referred to as the proficient wolves that used to be alpha or beta. The caretaker wolves are referred to as answerable for thinking about the frail, sick, and injured scoundrels. Sentinel wolves are referred to as secure and ensure the protection of the pack.

Group coursing is also the mimicking behavior in count to the social behavior of grey wolves. Notwithstanding the social pecking order of wolves, bunch chasing is another fascinating social conduct of dim wolves. The algorithm of GWO is a moderately innovative populace-based technique of optimization that has the benefit of minimum parameter control, ability of robust optimization, and simple execution.

1.5.1.4.17   Elephant Herding Optimization

Elephant Herding Optimization (EHO) algorithm is one of the metaheuristic approach swarm-based search algorithms that is utilized to explain various problems of optimization and also utilized benchmark, localization based on energy, services selection in QOS web service compositions, appliance scheduling in smart grid identification, and PID controller tuning–based problems. The algorithm is inspired by the performance of group of elephant in the wild, in which elephants live in a group with a female elephant called leader matriarch, while the male are disconnected from the group when they are adulthood. The EHO algorithm is based on the models of collecting behaviors of elephants in two procedures. They are clan update and separation. Clan update is referred as updating the elephants and matriarch present location in every clan and separation is referred as enhancing the populace range in the subsequent phase of search.

Table 1.1 List of applications of various algorithms.

S. no.	Algorithm	Areas of application
1.	Memetic algorithm	Multi-dimensional knapsack problem, pattern recognition, feature/gene selection, training of artificial neural networks, clustering of gene expression profiles, traveling salesman problem, Robotic motion planning
2.	Genetic algorithm	Allocation of document for a distributed system, PC robotized plan, server farm/server center, code breaking, criminological science, robot behavior, PC design, Bayesian inference, AI, game hypothesis
3.	Ant colony optimization algorithm	Problems of generalized assignment and the set covering, classification problems, Ant Net for organized directing and multiple knapsack Problem
4.	Particle swarm optimization algorithm	Combination with a back engendering calculation, to prepare a neural system framework structure, multi-target optimization, classification, image clustering and image clustering, image processing, automated applications, dynamic, pattern recognition, image segmentation, robotic applications, time frequency analysis, decision-making, simulation, and identification
5.	Harmony search algorithm	Power systems, power systems, transportation, medical science and robotics, industry and signal and image processing

(Continued)

Table 1.1 List of applications of various algorithms. (*Continued*)

S. no.	Algorithm	Areas of application
6.	Artificial bee colony algorithm	Problem of medical pattern classification, network reconfiguration, minimum spanning tree, train neural networks, radial distribution system of network reconfiguration, and train neural networks
7.	Firefly algorithm	Semantic web composition, classification and clustering problems, neural network, fault detection, digital image compression, feature selection, digital image processing, scheduling problems, and traveling salesman problem
8.	Bat algorithm	Image processing, clustering, classification, data mining, continuous optimization, problem inverse and estimation of parameter, combination scheduling and optimization, and fuzzy logic

The working of EHO is based on that every elephant in clan is updated by utilizing group data through clan by the procedure of updating, and afterward, the poorest elephant is supplanted by randomly produced elephant individual through the procedure of updating. EHO can discover much improved solutions on more problems of benchmark. Problems of benchmark are a lot of different types of problem of optimization that comprises of different kinds of aptitudes that utilized in testing and the estimation is verified and described. Then, the execution of estimation enhances the algorithm under various ecological conditions.

Table 1.1 lists the various applications of NIC algorithms.

References

1. Siddique, N. and Adeli, H., Nature-Inspired Computing: An Overview and Some Future Directions. *Cognit. Comput.*, 7, 706–714, 2015.

2. Wang, L., Kang, Q., Wu, Q.-d., Nature-inspired Computation — Effective Realization of Artificial Intelligence. *Syst. Eng. - Theory Pract.*, 27, 126–134, 2007, 10.1016/S1874-8651(08)60034-4.

3. Fan, X., Sayers, W., Zhang, S. *et al.*, Review and Classification of Bio-inspired Algorithms and Their Applications. *J. Bionic Eng.*, 17, 611–631, 2020, https://doi.org/10.1007/s42235-020-0049-9.

4. Nguyen, B.H., Xue, B., Zhang, M., A survey on swarm intelligence approaches to feature selection in data mining. *Swarm Evol. Comput.*, 54, 100663, 2020.

5. Neri, F. and Cotta, C., Memetic algorithms and memetic computing optimization: A literature review. *Swarm Evol. Comput.*, 2, 1–14, 2012, 10.1016/j.swevo.2011.11.003.

6. Albuquerque, I.M.R., Nguyen, B.H., Xue, B., Zhang, M., A Novel Genetic Algorithm Approach to Simultaneous Feature Selection and Instance Selection. *2020 IEEE Symposium Series on Computational Intelligence (SSCI)*, Canberra, ACT, Australia, pp. 616–623, 2020.

7. Ding, X. *et al.*, An Improved Ant Colony Algorithm for Optimized Band Selection of Hyperspectral Remotely Sensed Imagery. *IEEE Access*, 8, 25789–25799, 2020.

8. Xie, X.-F., Zhang, W.-J., Yang, Z.-L., Social cognitive optimization for nonlinear programming problems. *Proceedings. International Conference on Machine Learning and Cybernetics*, Beijing, China, vol. 2, pp. 779–783, 2002.

9. Pham, D.T., Afshin, G., Ebubekir, K., Sameh, O., Sahra, R., Zaidi, M., The Bees Algorithm - A Novel Tool for Complex Optimisation Problems. *Proceedings of IPROMS 2006 Conference*, 10.1016/B978-008045157-2/50081-X.

10. He, S., Wu, Q.H., Saunders, J.R., Group Search Optimizer: An Optimization Algorithm Inspired by Animal Searching Behavior. *IEEE Trans. Evol. Comput.*, 13, 5, 973–990, Oct. 2009.

11. Rabanal, P., Rodríguez, I., Rubio, F., Solving Dynamic TSP by Using River Formation Dynamics. *2008 Fourth International Conference on Natural Computation*, Jinan, pp. 246–250, 2008.

12. Li, J., Guo, L., Li, Y., Liu, C., Enhancing Elephant Herding Optimization with Novel Individual Updating Strategies for Large-Scale Optimization Problems. *Mathematics*, 7, 395, 2019, 10.3390/math7050395.

13. Almufti, S.M., Asaad, R.R., Salim, B.W., Review on Elephant Herding Optimization Algorithm Performance in Solving Optimization Problems. *Int. J. Eng. Technol.*, 7, 6109–6114, 2018, 10.14419/ijet.v7i4.23127.

14. Ma, L., Wang, R., Chen, Y., The Social Cognitive Optimization Algorithm: Modifiability and Application. *2010 International Conference on E-Product E-Service and E-Entertainment*, Henan, pp. 1–4, 2010.

15. Redlarski, G., Pałkowski, A., Dąbkowski, M., Using River Formation Dynamics Algorithm in Mobile Robot Navigation. *Solid State Phenom.*, 198, 138–143, 2013, 10.4028/www.scientific.net/SSP.198.138.

16. Kang, Q., Lan, T., Yan, Y., Wang, L., Wu, Q., Group search optimizer based optimal location and capacity of distributed generations. *Neurocomputing*, 78, 55–63, 2012, 10.1016/j.neucom.2011.05.030.

17. Liu, F., Xu, X.-T., Li, L.-J., Wu, Q.H., The Group Search Optimizer and its Application on Truss Structure Design. *2008 Fourth International Conference on Natural Computation*, Jinan, pp. 688–692, 2008.

18. Joong, K., Harmony Search Algorithm: A Unique Music-inspired Algorithm. *Proc. Eng.*, 154, 1401–1405, 2016, 10.1016/j.proeng.2016.07.510.

19. Yang, X.-S., Harmony Search as a Metaheuristic Algorithm. *Stud. Comput. Intell.*, 191, pp.1–14, 2010, 10.1007/978-3-642-00185-7_1.

20. Gao, X.Z., Govindasamy, V., Xu, H., Xianjia, W., Kai, Z., Harmony Search Method: Theory and Applications. *Comput. Intell. Neurosci.*, 1–10, Vol 2015, 10.1155/2015/258491.

21. Husseinzadeh Kashan, A., A new metaheuristic for optimization: Optics inspired optimization (OIO). *Comput. Oper. Res.*, 55, pp.99–125 2014, 10.1016/j.cor.2014.10.011.

22. Redlarski, G., Dabkowski, M., Pałkowski, A., Generating optimal paths in dynamic environments using River Formation Dynamics algorithm. *J. Comput. Sci.*, 20, 8–16, 2017, 10.1016/j.jocs.2017.03.002.

23. Doğan, B., A Modified Vortex Search Algorithm for Numerical Function Optimization. *Int. J. Artif. Intell. Appl.*, 7, 37–54, 2016, 10.5121/ijaia.2016.7304.

24. Sajedi, H. and Razavi, S.F., MVSA: Multiple vortex search algorithm. *2016 IEEE 17th International Symposium on Computational Intelligence and Informatics (CINTI)*, Budapest, pp. 000169–000174, 2016.

Applications of Hybridized Algorithms and Novel Algorithms in the Field of Machine Learning

P. Mary Jeyanthi[1]* and A. Mansurali[2]

[1]*Jaipuria Institute of Management, Jaipur, Rajasthan, India*
[2]*PSG Institute of Management, PSG College of Technology, Coimbatore, India*

Abstract

Algorithms are data specific. In machine learning, there is no IDEAL algorithm available. One algorithm can not suit the best for all the problems. In the current era, the data are very huge; The effort of connecting information as a competitive catalyst is driving firms to higher levels of cognizance about how data is managed at its most basic level.

Due to the usage of large metrics of data in day to day of e-era, the necessity of Hybridized algorithms and novel algorithms to handle the consistent increasing the data. Hybrid algorithms have been developed by combining two or more algorithms to improve or enhance overall efficiency to reach the optimization. Every scientists often try to use the benefits of every algorithms for the common good; at least that is the purpose in opinion. In practice, whether a hybrid can really achieve better performance is another matter, and finding ways to combine different algorithms to develop new algorithms is still an open problem. There are more than 40 other algorithms in the literature as reviewed in recent surveys and more algorithms are appearing.

Keywords: Genetic algorithm, artificial bear optimization, machine learning, novel algorithm, heuristic algorithm, data mining, market basket analysis, hybridized algorithms

2.1 Introduction of Genetic Algorithm

Nils Barricelli's work at Princeton on imitating the natural reproduction process in creating an artificial life through the software was the first genetic

---

**Corresponding author*: dr.maryprem@gmail.com; mary.jeyanthi@jaipuria.ac.in

S. Balamurugan, Anupriya Jain, Sachin Sharma, Dinesh Goyal, Sonia Duggal and Seema Sharma (eds.)
Nature-Inspired Algorithms Applications, (33–66) © 2022 Scrivener Publishing LLC

algorithm (GA) but not attempted at solving optimization problems [1] which were followed by many biologists in the decade of 1950–1960.

History of GAs is dated back to Holland's work on adaptive systems and getting the academic spotlight in 1975 with the publication of the book by Holland adaption of natural and artificial systems along with this team. By the 1980s, GAs have been earning prominence and used among many subject areas, and John Koza called it as genetic programming. The GA gained more prominence after the book "Genetic algorithms in Search, Optimization and Machine learning" in 1989 by David Goldberg, a graduate student of Holland [2].

The GA follows the genetics and natural selection principles in a path to achieve optimization through the search techniques. Optimization is, in general, about the best possible ways of inputs for the better output in the problem space. The GA is also famous for the reason of good enough than being fast enough [3]. The GA is also standing appropriate when the problem is more complex and also when no algorithmic solutions exist.

GA is an evolutionary algorithm inspired by Darwin's theory of human evolution and natural selection where the evolution characteristics such as inheritance, mutation, and crossover are present. A study by Kinnear, K. E., Langdon, W. B., Spector, L., Angeline, P. J., and O'Reilly, U. M. (eds.) [4] reiterates that the GA is an algorithm which is working under the concept of evolution and its computation.

The GA also works on the principle of search heuristic algorithm which was inspired by the natural evolution theory of Darwin where the fittest individual among the people are selected for the reproduction in the process of crossover and mutation. The GA which follows the principle of "Survival of Fittest" will help to solve both constrained and unconstrained problems of optimization [2]. The typical process of the GA can be understood in Figure 2.1.

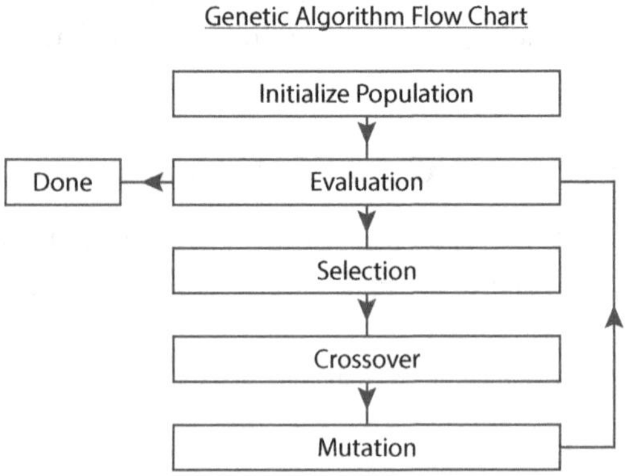

Genetic Algorithm Flow Chart

Figure 2.1 Genetic algorithm flow chart. Image source: Moustafa Alzantot [5].

The intuition behind the GA is very simple that it can be viewed as a black box technique, which can give an acceptable solution in terms of time involved and the quality of solution with the availability of multiple possibilities to us.

2.1.1   Background of GA

In this section, the detailed explanation of what is Natural Selection and why it is necessary to compare with Search Heuristic algorithm and gives the sequence of Genetic Algorithm and how it works.

2.1.2   Why Natural Selection Theory Compared With the Search Heuristic Algorithm?

Natural selection theory, in general, will exist by selecting the fittest of individuals from the population. Fittest individuals, in turn, involved in reproduction and produced the offspring with the inherited characteristics of parent and continue to pass the characteristics to the next generations to come. The process of reproduction among the fitted individuals is iterative in nature, and hence, the fitted individuals are present in the generations. Fitness characteristics of the parents will be present in the offspring's produced.

Above is the process which is also the working mechanism of search algorithms in general that the search space will consider a set of solutions in the process and select the best solutions out of it which can be attributed the natural evolution theory where the fitted individuals are selected [6].

2.1.3   Working Sequence of Genetic Algorithm

The stages of the GA as follows:

- Population
- Fitness among the individuals
- Selection of fitted individuals
- Crossover point
- Mutation

2.1.3.1   Population

By definition, the population can be termed as a group of individuals. Going with the theory of natural evaluation, every individual among the population could be the solution to the problem. An individual in the population can be understood by its parameters such as genes. Genes present in the individuals denoted by the binary characters such as 0 and 1, numbers such as 1, 2, and 3, or alphabets such as a, b, and c collectively called

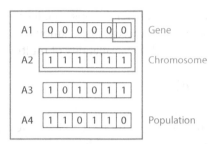

Figure 2.2 Definition of gene, chromosome, and population. Image source: Vijini Mallawaarachchi [6].

chromosomes. There are no hard and fast rules that the elements in the array need to be binary; it can also be continuous in nature (Figure 2.2). GAs generally work in the encoded space [7] like how the genes are represented in the diagram below. Encoding of the genes is not just binary; there are many encoding mechanisms that are used to represent such as octal encoding, hexadecimal encoding, gray encoding, permutation encoding, value encoding, and tree encoding. This encoding mechanism is more important in understanding the performance of the GA [8].

2.1.3.2   Fitness Among the Individuals

Like the theory of nature, not every individual is the same in their score of fitness. The fitness score of the individual decision will also help us to understand the individual's advantage over the others in the set. The best fitness individual in turn involved in the process of reproduction. Fitness score in the reproduction can be associated with the probability of the variables getting selected in the process of algorithmic modeling and it is generated from each generation until finding the best one [9].

2.1.3.3   Selection of Fitted Individuals

Based on the fitness score, fittest individuals among the population are selectees for reproduction and allowed to pass the genes of its own to the generations followed. Selected two fitted individuals who are parents in the cases are involved in the process and the high fitness scored involved will have a higher chance to be involved in the way of reproduction selection. Methods such as Roulette Wheel selection, random selection, rank selection, and tournament selection are all used in the process of selection. The selected fitted chromosomes based on the fitness score at each level will be taken to the next stage to reach the top which is hill climbing in the gradient descent algorithm from the local optimum [10].

2.1.3.4   Crossover Point

As it known, the parents who are selected individuals in the process of reproduction have the collection of genes in the respective positions (Figure 2.3). During the process of mating, the random selection point will be chosen among the positions of the genes which are known as crossover point that can be seen from the figure below. It is not necessary that the crossover will happen at only one point, crossover can happen in two-point, multi-point, uniform crossover, and arithmetic crossover methods.

Offspring will be developed as below and also genes will get exchanged in the positions till the crossover point as below (Figure 2.4).

2.1.3.5   Mutation

The mutation is the process of swapping genes among the offspring's post crossover. The swap in the mutations process happens for the reason of diversity and also to avoid the convergence of prematurity. The mutation also happens in the modes flipping, reversing other than interchanging or swapping modes (Figure 2.5).

First parent

| A | B | C | D | E |

Second parent

| F | G | H | I | J |

Figure 2.3 Crossover point. Image source: Patacchiola [11].

First child

| F | G | C | D | E |

Second child

| A | B | H | I | J |

Figure 2.4 Development of offspring. Image source: Patacchiola [11].

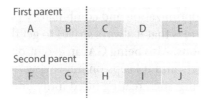

Figure 2.5 Mutation. Image source: GeneHunter.

Above are the sequential steps of GA in reproducing the offspring's and process will get terminated in the case of not producing the significant different offspring compared to the previous generations. In an algorithmic process, it is known as the stage of convergence which means that the solutions for the problem in the search space are already found. The algorithmic process will end its iterative process if maximum generations achieved, the time elapsed, stall of generations and time limit, and, more specifically, if there is no change in fitness.

2.1.4   Application of Machine Learning in GA

If the problem at hand is a genetic representation problem such as genes and the collection of genes, then those problems can be solved with the help of a GA.

2.1.4.1   *Genetic Algorithm Role in Feature Selection for ML Problem*

The machine learning algorithms can be made more efficient by the feature selection and feature engineering process and most, fortunately, GAs help largely in the process of feature selection. Selecting the right variable is always looked up as optimization and combinatory problem [12].

GA's working nature is that it always strives to get the best solution from the list of prior solutions. Also being GA, an evolutionary algorithm, selection happens iteratively and it keeps on improving over the time periods. In a process of selecting and creating fitted individuals, a solution arrived by GAs is selecting the best genes which are the process applied in machine learning to select the variables (genes in the case of GAs). GA's role is not just limited in the variables selection; it can also be extending to the tuning parameters, optimization function such as maximization or minimization problem (fitness function in the case of GAs), and also the search space which is a procedure in GA that can help the architecture of the neural network.

A most important characteristic of GAs which helps machine learning is GA's consideration of genes (variables) that are always as a whole and not against the target variable which is also the machine learning mechanism that the handling of variable as a whole group together against the problem at hand. In the world of massive databases, traditional data analysis methods are not sufficient to find out the patterns in the data and also to discover knowledge out of it. Sikora, R. and Piramuthu, S. [13] in their study used a GA-based data mining techniques which used the adaptive method for the feature selection using Hausdorff distance measure.

2.1.4.2   Traveling Salesman Problem

A traveling salesman is one of the classic problems in the area of optimization. Optimization here in the case is to identify the shortest possible route to visit the cities and returning back to the city of origin, given the list of cities and the distance between every pair in the city list. As like any optimization problem, traveling salesman problem also has some constraints such as the city needs to be visited only once and the salesman needs to return to the city of origin [14] (Figure 2.6).

GA has also been successfully implemented to solve the problem of a traveling salesman. Here in the case of traveling salesman problem, route to a city is considered as chromosome and the coordinates of the city say X and Y are considered as a gene. As the single route is a chromosome, a complete list of routes is as population. Two routes which are creating a route combined with each other considered as parents and the mating pool are represented by a group of parents who are the collection of routes involved in creating a new set of routes. The shortest distance which is the prominent objective of the problem is achieved through the fitness score, and the fitted individual is passed to the next process that is the shortest route chosen by a salesman.

The usage of GAs to solve the travel time optimization problem of UPS drivers in delivering a package and also helping the company from a loss

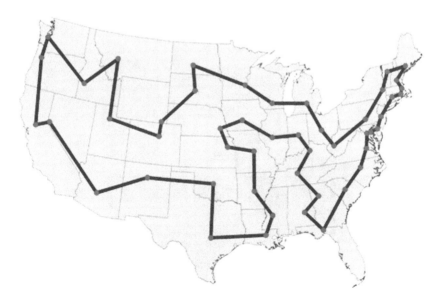

Figure 2.6 Traveling salesman problem. Image source: Jessica Yu (2014)—Traveling Salesman Problem.

of 30 million dollars given the locations to be delivered and the distance between the locations.

2.1.4.3   Blackjack—A Casino Game

GA helps in crafting a strategy for the casino game known as blackjack game or Game 21. Strategy for the game can be understood as the guide for a player which helps in minimizing the loss or maximizing the winning for the player. Blackjack is game with a soft hand and hard hand logic, whereas the soft hand is having an Ace counting as 1 or 11 and hard hand is the remaining, together not exceeding the value of 21. The dealer or the host will have up the card and the player will have a pair of soft and hard hands. Based on the move, the game will result in a hit or stand or double down or split each denoted by S, H, D, and P. The typical strategy of the game table is as follows [15]. GAs begin with random solutions and find a solution in an iterative process.

To arrive at a better solution, GAs compare all the candidate models and solutions based on the fitness score. GA's connection to the blackjack is in relation to the fitness score, more specifically the positive fitness score

Blackjack Basic Strategy Chart
4/6/8 Decks, Dealer Hits Soft 17

Dealer Upcard										
Hard Total	2	3	4	5	6	7	8	9	10	A
5-7	H	H	H	H	H	H	H	H	H	H
8	H	H	H	H	H	H	H	H	H	H
9	H	D	D	D	D	H	H	H	H	H
10	D	D	D	D	D	D	D	D	D	D
11	D	D	D	D	D	D	D	D	D	D
12	H	H	S	S	S	H	H	H	H	H
13	S	S	S	S	S	H	H	H	H	H
14	S	S	S	S	S	H	H	H	H	H
15	S	S	S	S	S	H	H	H	R	R
16	S	S	S	S	S	H	H	R	R	R
17	S	S	S	S	S	S	S	S	S	RS
Soft Total	2	3	4	5	6	7	8	9	10	A
A,2	H	H	H	D	D	H	H	H	H	H
A,3	H	H	H	D	D	H	H	H	H	H
A,4	H	H	D	D	D	H	H	H	H	H
A,5	H	H	D	D	D	H	H	H	H	H
A,6	H	D	D	D	D	H	H	H	H	H
A,7	DS	DS	DS	DS	DS	S	S	H	H	H
A,8	S	S	S	S	DS	S	S	S	S	S
A,9	S	S	S	S	S	S	S	S	S	S

(Pairs are listed on back of card.)
by *Kenneth R Smith* © 2008–2016 Bayview Strategies, LLC

Figure 2.7 Blackjack—a casino game.

which helps in minimizing the loss, as the host will have a strategy for you to lose which is like a fitness score of player will be mostly negative.

Post the fitness function, the selection is the next step of GA process which is picking N random cards or candidates (parents) for the play (reproduction in the case of GA). A cell in each table of the blackjack game is considered as a child from a parent as in GA based on the fitness score (Figure 2.7).

2.1.4.4 Pong Against AI—Evolving Agents (Reinforcement Learning) Using GA

The game and problem at the hand are very simple: the input for the neural network is pixels in the image or search space, and the agent's role or output is to move up, down, or do not move. The role of the reinforcement learning here is to find the weights and biases of the neural network which maximizes the win or getting more rewards that are hitting the ball back [16].

What GA does it here? And how it helps? The answer is straight forward. Agent in the game is an organism, the parameter of the agent in learning is genes and the rewards are nothing about the fitness score. The algorithm will start working with multiple agents in the beginning, as a process move fittest agents are selected for the iteration, tuning of parameters is been implemented in the go, and the best agent learns and obviously hits hard (Figure 2.8).

2.1.4.5 SNAKE AI—Game

Snake game is one of the most popular games in the early days of mobile in the market and it is still famous in the game market to solve the snake game using deep learning neural network along with the principle of GA.

As the theory of evolution reveals that the populations used to adapt the environments on basis of evolutionary mechanism, snake game solving also goes in with the same line as the objective of the game is making snake adapt its environment in a way to learn to avoid the obstacles and get the

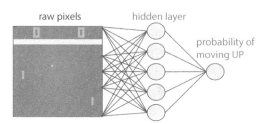

Figure 2.8 Pong against AI—evolving agents. Image source: Pong using pixels—Andrej Japathy (2016).

Figure 2.9 Snake AI—game. Image source: Greg Sharma (2018)—Via Siltherin.

fruits or eat it which is in GA's language as maximization of fitness score [17]. Also, it resembles the concept of "Survival of Fittest". How GA has been implemented to solve the same? It is quite simple. Chromosome in the GA has been considered as a vector of values in the neural net algorithmic model in which each value in the vector has been considered as gene (weights for neural net), and undoubtedly, the collection of chromosomes is a population; here in the case, it is a list of vectors. The output of the neural net gameplay has been considered as the fitness value. Snake's observation over the environment is an input to the model and predicted action in the environment is iteratively progress and the process gets stopped when the snake dies (Figure 2.9).

2.1.4.6   *Genetic Algorithm's Role in Neural Network*

Neural networks are largely used efficient algorithms used in machine learning and deep learning today, but it also has some limitations and the most important elements in selecting the hyperparameters or in understanding which hyperparameter makes the learning better in the network [18]. Fortunately, the same problem can be solved with the help of a GA that helps in selecting the best hyperparameters to be included in the model of neural network using the process of fitness function and its score among the parameters using the process as below in the figure. In same way, weights for the parameters also can be obtained using GA.

Kim, M.-J., and Han, I. [19] in their research attempt to discover the quantitative bankruptcy knowledge from financial databases tried neural networks and inductive learning methods. The researchers have used the

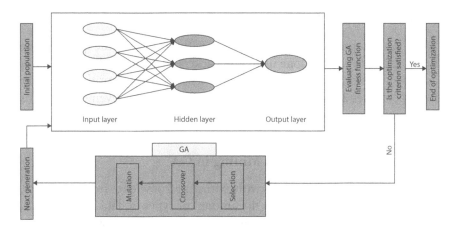

Figure 2.10 Genetic algorithm's role in neural network. Image source: Suryansh [18].

GA to discover decision rules from an expert's decision process and proved that GA is more efficient than many other data mining models (Figure 2.10).

2.1.4.7 Solving a Battleship Board Game as an Optimization Problem Which Was Initially Released by Milton Bradley in 1967

A problem that can be expressed in the form of genetic representation says a collection of arrays containing 0's and 1's, whereas the binary elements of the array are considered as gene and the array together as chromosome helps in devising board problem using GA. Here in the battleship board, squares filled by ships are expressed as genes in the binary noted of 0 and 1 related to occupied and unoccupied [20].

2.1.4.8 Frozen Lake Problem From OpenAI Gym

In frozen lake problem, search space looks like a grid in surface map, whereas the objective is to move from the starting point to the goal-reaching state but the surface is frozen, and the moves might end up in falling into the lake and also the planned moved by an individual can go another way round as the space is slippery. Frozen lake problem has been solved using the GA by considering the space as an array of 16 values with the values as 0, 1, 2, and 3 as possible moves on sixteen different positions on the surface. Being the problem devised using a GA, it will generate multiple solutions using an iterative process in terms of selection, mutation, and crossover. The algorithmic execution has yielded 85 scores while attempted by [5] which is better than the previous performance of 75 executed using the Markov chain process.

2.1.4.9   N-Queen Problem

The N-Queen problem, which is playing with the help of the queen in the board game, is usually done using the backtracking method in the field of gaming it works, but the efficiency of the backtracking algorithm is slower if the N crosses 25. But using the GA, the efficiency of movement in terms of seconds is very high compared to the backtracking solver [21].

2.1.5   Application of Data Mining in GA

Data mining is a field that deals with extracting knowledge from databases, without putting restrictions on the amount or types of data in a database. It is a process that starts with data and ends with previously unknown patterns and knowledge. The Knowledge Discovery in Databases (KDD) process is the process of analyzing data from different perspectives and summarizing it into useful insights. This raw data is selected and analyzed during the steps to reveal patterns and create new knowledge. The GA is used in data mining which is one of the five steps of the KDD process.

Freitas, A. A. [22] briefly discussed that the reason for using a GA in the data mining is because of its robustness and also because of its ability of adaptive search techniques which does the global search in the solution space. He also mentioned about the GAs that are applied in the data mining tasks such as clustering, classification, and attribute selection.

If an optimization problem to be solved is more complex and needs more memory, GAs can be run in two types, say parallel and distribution technique. The parallel algorithm is about multiple models run parallel in the process of selecting the best and the best out of the best is selected, whereas the distribution system is about running in parallel (different) machines itself unlike it runs in the same machine in the parallel technique [23].

2.1.5.1   Association Rules Generation

The GA also has its application in the education sector in many ways. For example, [24] applied GA in the data mining problem which involved the web-based educational data and created a set of association rules which will improve the performance of the system and individual.

Berkani, L., Chebahi, Y., and Betit, L. [25] highlighted the usage of data mining algorithms and GAs together in the path of creating association rules. The model proposed by the authors has adopted the GA in creating the optimal set of rules which are an output of the traditional algorithms and the process as follows.

2.1.5.2 Pattern Classification With Genetic Algorithm

This problem discusses the chrome differentiation using a GA in N-dimensional space. There are two types of pattern classification methods as classification with learning and classification without learning. The problem deals with the implementation of a new generic search strategy called GACD (GA with chrome differentiation) of n dimensions, where the decision boundaries are now approximated by hyperplanes.

In GACD, the chromosomes are distinguished into two classes, M and F (00—F class bits; 01, 10—M class bits), thereby constituting two separate populations. These are initially generated in such a way that the Hamming distance between the two is maximized. The results of GACD are applied to the GA-based classifier which improves the performance. GACD converges the optimal string as the number of iterations tends to infinity provided the probability of going from any population to the one containing the optimal string is greater than zero (Figures 2.11 and 2.12).

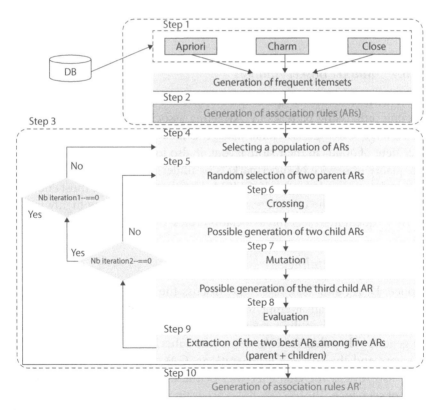

Figure 2.11 Association rules generation. Image source: Berkani, L., Chebahi, Y., and Betit, L. [25].

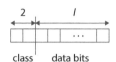

Figure 2.12 Structure of a chromosome in GACD. Image source: Sanghamitra Bandyopadhyay [26].

2.1.5.3   Genetic Algorithms in Stock Market Data Mining Optimization

The generation of technical trading rules in a stock market is a more prominent research area in a decision to buy or sell the shares. The trading rule's success or correctness is largely depending upon the parameters and its combination chosen. Selecting the best combination of parameters is always the toughest task in the rule generation which is solved by the use of GAs. The GA does the same in two steps: firstly by subsetting the parameters followed by near-optimal value achievement in the subset using the fitness score in a short span of time [27].

2.1.5.4   Market Basket Analysis

Market basket analysis is one of the data mining methods focusing on discovering purchasing patterns by extracting associations or co-occurrences from a large store's transactional data. This analysis is done to manage the placement of goods in their store layout. It also focuses on improving profit and quality of service of supermarkets by understanding the daily transactions and customer behavior. K-GFISM algorithm (GA) is the most effective algorithm among the other algorithms resulted in generating highly informative frequent item sets and association rules for the supermarket [28].

2.1.5.5   Job Scheduling

Koonce, D. A., and Tsai, S. C. [29] discuss the application of data mining algorithms in an attempt to understand the data patterns by a GA involved in the scheduling operation which executes the rule set using the genetic scheduler. As GAs reveal the inherited characteristics in the survivors and the successful generations, GA's application in job scheduling also reveals the characteristics of the operations executed and the order of sequence. The job scheduler program which uses a GA reproduces the solution (dispatcher rule) in case if the similar problems encountered before as like GA does in the process of reproduction.

2.1.5.6   Classification Problem

Marmelstein, R. E. [30] in his research on "Data Mining applications to the genetic algorithm" discussed the importance of GA in the field of data mining jobs such as classification and clustering. KNN is a classifier algorithm used to classify the classes or class of interest using the value of K which determines the number of neighbors to be compared to arrive at the classification class. KNN, because of its non-parametric nature, results in more error but it can be improved by feature extraction which is used to tune the attribute weights and distance calculation. The role of GA comes here which helps in determining the weights for the parameter (fitness score). GA derives the optimal weight for the set of features and each feature in the fitness set is considered as chromosomes. By this process, GAs select the most important vectors and features based on its optimal weights which will improve the type of the problem of KNN such as accuracy in classification.

2.1.5.7   Hybrid Decision Tree—Genetic Algorithm to Data Mining

The decision tree's role in data mining is to create a set of rules which help in predicting the data point of its class belonging. In data mining, the set of rules are considered as logical disjuncts. Small disjuncts cover only a few examples and also it is prone to error. Typical decision tree algorithms can cover larger disjuncts and the larger sets of examples, at the same time, the smaller disjuncts need to be addressed which causes the error. A hybrid approach of combining both decision trees and GAs can address this, especially GAs will handle small disjuncts and help the model perform better and fewer errors [31].

2.1.5.8   Genetic Algorithm—Optimization of Data Mining in Education

Michigan State University predicted the final grade of the students using the features extracted from their web-based system dataset. Multiple classifiers which are logged from the dataset are used for classification. The performance of the classification such as accuracy and classification has been improved with the help of GA by weighting the values for features [32].

2.1.6   Advantages of Genetic Algorithms

It can be understood from the applications that the power and usage of GAs are in general. The following bulletin points list the major advantages of the GA in a brief.

- The GA can be used when no algorithm or heuristics available for a problem or a solution to be achieved.
- GA is one of the important optimization algorithms, which finds the best solution in the problem space [33].
- Though the GA is an optimization algorithm, it does not use the function of derivatives which is the usual way to find the minima.
- Typical optimization algorithms have a high chance of getting stuck in the local minima while attempting to find the global minima which is not the case in genetics algorithm which is making GA more significant [34].
- The GA can accommodate nonlinear objectives and constraints which are not accommodated by traditional algorithms.
- The GA does not have a problem of local minima as the GA search is from multiple points unlike other optimization algorithms start from a single point [35].
- GA working principle of parallelism helps in saving the memory.
- GA uses simple operands and operations for solving a complex problem.
- The GA is easy to implement unlike gradient descent which needs more information about the problem and solution space.

2.1.7 Genetic Algorithms Demerits in the Current Era

Although GAs find its application in the fields of robotics, business, automation, design, games, and many more domains, there are some limitations that affect the process of adopting GAs in these fields, some are as follows.

- While implementing these algorithms, it is difficult to identify and select a fitness function, since the accuracy of the model depends on the fitness function that we need to spend a lot of time in determining these fitness functions. Also, there is no standard technique which is readily available to select these fitness function; this adds one more layer of complexity in identifying the best fitness function.
- Since GA is efficient for the reason of its iterative process to calculate the fitness score leads to the problem of expensive computation.
- The success of the GAs solely depends upon the user, and to ensure the success, the user is required to have select

appropriate parameters and fitness function with respect to the problem that he/she is trying to address.

- GA is also a stochastic process which is a random process that will not have guaranteed the quality of the solution arrived.
- GAs are usually slow and more time is consumed for convergence of the algorithm. So, these algorithms are computationally expensive [36].
- Diversity is one the key objective of the GAs which are affected when the premature convergence of algorithm happens, which leads to the loss of the diversity in the population under study [37].
- The outcome of the algorithm depends on parameters that are being used to model and selection of these parameters plays a critical role in the success of these techniques.
- GAs cannot be scaled to the domains that the algorithm is not trained upon. Even if it is a small change in the domain, the algorithm requires a lot of data that is required across various parameters to train it before deploying in that domain. This process of retraining and deploying the models for even minor changes in the input condition makes the model time consuming for deploying [38].
- If the model is scaled even moderately by increasing the parameters or by increasing the length of the chromosome, then we need a lot of data to train the model given the permutation and combination of different gene combinations that are possible. This makes the model consume more time for decoding and converging to fit a value.
- To check the fitness of the solution, the quality and quantity of data are important; in some cases, it may require an entire database of the organization to check for the fitness of the models.
- Since GAs look to fit the parameters for each chromosome, it is blind to the optimization and fails to know what the value of fitness obtained actually means. As a result, the model cannot explain why it has arrived at a particular solution.
- When multiple chromosomes represent the same solution, GAs suffer the problem of degeneracy. Degeneracy leads to inefficient solutions since the same pattern occurs repeatedly.
- Sometimes, it may have more than one feasible solution; in such cases, it is the responsibility of the user to select the one good solution.

- Shaked Zychlinski [39] in his research attempted to highlight whether the selection of the GA of the sample is better than random sampling and concluded that the random sample is doing better than the GA.
- GAs have a limitation in addressing if problem nature is simple and when the derivative information of the problem is visible and available.
- Though there are many terminations criteria are available, the one best termination criteria are not been advocated yet.
- The performance of GAs turns best during the solution vectors to get binary.
- While the problem remains along with more than 1 variable, the coding under multi-variable gets constructed with concatenating becoming several coding with single variables as the number of variables gets in the problem.
- Each problem in real life is dynamic; hence, their behaviors remain much complex, and serious weakness is suffered by genetic programming.
- The performance of GA gets best during the solution vectors to get binary. The problem gets multiple solutions.
- The population gets considered for evolution that should be suitable or moderate 1 for the concerned problem (generally 20–30/50–100).

2.2   Introduction to Artificial Bear Optimization (ABO)

Every algorithm for meta-heuristic is inspired by nature. Hence, before this gets applied along with the existing algorithm for meta-heuristic, the algorithms are required to be satisfied with the below given questions for proceeding along with those respective methodologies:

- Does the concerned functionality for the algorithm provide a solution to the problem?
- Though it provides the solution, do we require checking the solution as given along the complex functions that help for understanding and deriving the functionality?

In the implementation of the concerned NEW algorithm along with inspiration for nature, that remains differed from smelling the sense of

BEAR to the dynamic and optimal systems for decision-making under the current business world. The concerned question that remains with designing the meta-heuristic of the problems for dynamic optimization is what the information requires during the concerned search which must get memorized and how the information gets used toward the guide in searching and maintaining the adaptability toward changes. Along with several optimization problems, concerning environmental variables or the decision variables get subjected or perturbed that changes after the final solution gets implemented and obtained for the concerned problem. Thus, for solving the problem, it is required to be taken into account which the solution requires to be acceptable along with the respect with slight changes for the values of the decision variable.

Bears sustain a sense of smell due to the area of the along with their brain which manages the concerned sense of smell, known as the olfactory bulb, remains to be five times larger than the similar areas along human brains being the bear's brain is one-third the size. The bears can smell much better than any of the animals on earth, due to the region of olfactory bulb present in the brain. The sense of smell that the bear has remains 2,100 times much better than humans. The acute sense of smell they have helps them to track their concerned cubs, in finding food, mates along with keeping a tab on the other competing bears. Hundreds of tiny muscles along with their nose help them to control smell.

The skull of the bear showed the higher cavity or nasal for the grizzly bear, along the cavity of nasal similar to honeycomb-like that has the vast network of tissue. The concerned tissues get created along the immense amount of the surface area under the processing of the scent information. The bears are generally robust and bulky animals having relatively shorter legs. The eyes of the bears along with ears are usually small being a bigger animal. But the snout and nose of the bear are large. Grizzlies depend on their concerned sense of smell in finding the food. Smelling remains to be bear's one of the sharpest senses. The grizzly bear often smells the flesh or carrion of the dead animal, from distant places. Some scientists described that the bears can smell the carrion from a distance of 18 miles away. The grizzlies are about and out during both day and night. They often seem to become more active during dusk or dawn, however. Along with this, the places with people around, the bears remain to be nocturnal.

The adult bear usually has individual territory. The part of the territory remains to be the exclusive domain of the bear, but it gets shared with the other bears. These territories usually comprised of varied smaller areas being food source as connected with travel lanes. Generally, the

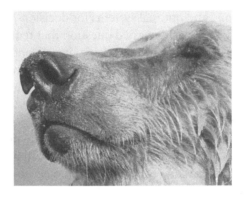

Figure 2.13 Grizzly bear.

female bears have the home ranging between 6.5 and 26 square kilometers, while the males normally have the home range being 26 to 124 square kilometers. Their acute sense of smell usually helps them in tracking their cubs, finding food, and mating along with keeping a tab on the competing bears. The bears can often detect the dead animal at a distance of 20 miles, thanks to the keen smelling power they have. The bears can smell often better than the other animal on earth, due to the region of the olfactory bulb. This remains to be surprised where the size of the brain is just one-third of humans. Hence, if you ever visit nature parks for camping, it remains difficult to keep the bears away from the food. The smelling power of the bear is around 2,100 times much better than that of humans.

The bears are often thought to be one of the best animals having the smelling power animal on earth (Figure 2.13). For instance, the average of the smelling power of the dogs remains to be 100 times much better than humans. The bloodhound remains better than 300 times. The bears usually have higher developed noses that contain 100 of the tiny muscles and let them manipulate them along with similar dexterity similar to people's fingers. The concerning surface area as inside their nine inches noses has around 100 times more of the surface area and receptors than that of human's.

2.2.1   Bear's Nasal Cavity

It is believed that Grizzly bears possess a strong smelling sense, which is stronger than the human by 100,000 times. The skull of the bear (Figures 2.14 and 2.15) shows that the nasal cavity has a wide tissue network which

Figure 2.14 Bear's nasal cavity. https://grizzlybearblog.wordpress.com/2010/11/10/grizzly-bear-nasal-cavity/.

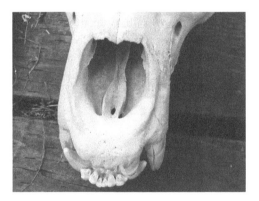

Figure 2.15 Top view of a grizzly bear skull. https://in.pinterest.com/ericgreb/grizzly-bear-skull/?autologin=true.

makes it look like a honeycomb. These well-knit tissues develop a huge area to process information regarding the scent.

Grizzly bears utilize their smelling sense to find the clams hidden under the sand, which makes the bears an expert in digging clam. Their smelling ability is acute which makes them find the fish under the water.

- Smell receptors would collect and transmit information about the smell.
- The olfactory bulb area of the brain acts and processes the data regarding the smell.
- The vast amount of network in the nasal cavity offers information about the smell.

2.2.2 Artificial Bear ABO Gist

Algorithm:

Step 1: Collect the "n" number of data about the smell in a given area.
Step 2: Evaluate the data about the smell (decide on which smell is needed and evaluate it from the rest of it).
Step 3: To arrive at the data regarding the value of fitness for each smell [i.e., f(n)].
Step 4: To remember the best smell data through its fitness value and store it in the given area S(n).
Step 5: Repeat steps 3 and 4 again, until the data regarding the smell is complete.
Step 6: Exchange the data of smell in the given area [S(n)] to determine the optimal decision-making (Figure 2.16).

Figure 2.17 represents the overall application that has been proposed to find the optimal population. GA, Ant Colony Optimization (ACO), and Artificial Bee Colony (ABC) algorithms are implemented and find the result database to set and evaluate the performance with Receiver Operating Characteristic (ROC) curve.

Pseudo Algorithm:

- Initializing of population; x_i = 1, 2, …, n.

Figure 2.16 ABO gist. https://www.ijser.org/researchpaper/Business-Intelligence-Artificial-Bear-Optimization-Ap-proach.pdf.

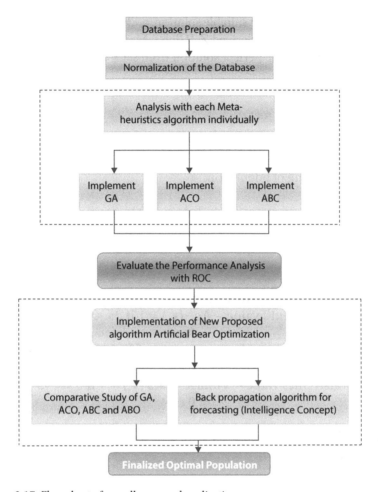

Figure 2.17 Flow chart of overall proposed application.

- Determine the fitness function with the help of constraints or objective function (y_j)

$$f(x_i) = \Sigma f(y_j) \text{ where } j = 1, 2, 3$$

- Cycle = 1

  - Compare between x_1 and x_2; if $f(x_1) > f(x_2)$, then $f(x_1)$ must be considered as the best solution [Local Maxima]. Similarly, $f(x_1)$ must be compared with the remaining population.

- Determine the suitable solution, and the perfect set of the population is derived Z_i [Global Maxima].
- Remove the perfect solution from set x_i.

- Cycle = cycle +1

Until all the needs are met.

Implementation:

- Initializing of population:

$$X_i = 1, 2, 3, ..., 200$$

- Calculation of Fitness:

Let us assume,

No. of constraints = 3

1st constraint's value – Age (y_1) = 1 if $25 <= y1 <= 45$
= 0 or

2nd constraint's value – Income (y_2) = 1 if $25,000 <= y2 <= 60,000$
= 0 or

3rd constraint's value – Vintage years (y_3) = 1 if $3 <= y3 <= 5$
= 0 or

When there are three constraints for a customer, then the level of fitness is maximum.

$$f(x_1) = 3$$
$$f(x_2) = 2$$
$$f(x_3) = 0$$
$$f(x_4) = 1$$
$$f(x_5) = 3$$
. . . .
. . . .
. . . .
$$f(1,000) = 2$$

Compare between $f(x_1)$ and $f(x_2)$ and the respective values are 3 and 2.
To maximize $f(x_1) = 3$:
Compare between $f(x_1)$ and $f(x_3)$ and the respective values obtained are 3 and 0.

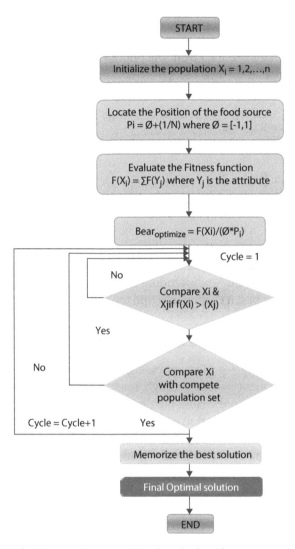

Figure 2.18 Artificial bear optimization: Pseudocode algorithm.

To maximize $f(x_1) = 3$:

Compare between $f(x_1)$ and $f(x_4)$ and the respective values obtained are 3 and 1.

To maximize $f(x_1) = 3$:

Compare between $f(x_1)$ and $f(x_5)$ and the respective values obtained are 3 and 3.

To maximize $f(x_1) = 3$ and $f(x_2) = 3$:

Similarly, compare the local maxima values up to 1,000.

Remember the final set population:

$Z_i = f(x_1)$ and $f(x_5)$.

Deduct the $f(x_1)$ and $f(x_5)$ from the population set x_i.

Now, the population is x = 2, 3, 4,................,1,000.

Compare between $f(x_2)$ and $f(x_3)$ and the respective values derived are 2 and 0.

To maximize $f(x_2)$ = 2:

Compare between $f(x_2)$ and $f(x_4)$ and the respective values derived are 2 and 1.

To maximize $f(x_2)$ = 2

Likewise, compare the local maximum values up to 1,000.

Remember the final set population:

$Z_i = f(x_1)$, $f(x_5)$, $f(x_2)$

Subtract the $f(x_2)$ from the population set x_i.

Finally, we would derive the new population set Z_i. The new population set would be fitness value in descending order from maximum to minimum. Then, find out the best n customer to find the valued customer (Figure 2.18).

2.2.3   Implementation Based on Requirement

Before implementing a project, assessing the business need and futuristic thinking on business benefit through implementation is another critical thing to be done due to the close relationship with the senior management. Sometimes, the implementation needs and benefits are determined by competition and to achieve a market advantage. Acquiring other organizations, which actually increase the original organization's size, is another reason to implement the BI in a business-driven approach. This merging can be beneficial for the implementation of DW or BI to create much better oversight.

2.2.3.1   Market Place

Business intelligence vendors are many in number whom can be categorized into consolidated "Megavendors", which entered the market through BI industry current acquisitions trend, and the remaining "pure-play" independent vendors.

2.2.3.2   Industry-Specific

Sensitivity for specific needs must be a part of industry-specific solutions, which must be flexible enough to customized requirements and ready to adopt new regulations as per the changes in existing laws.

2.2.3.3   Semi-Structured or Unstructured Data

Merrill Lynch mentions that 85% of the total business information exists in the form of information called as *semi-structured* or *unstructured* data, which comprises of news, web-pages, e-mails, memos, presentations, notes from call-centers, user groups, marketing material and news, video-files, chats, and image-files. Gartner projected that around 30%–40% of the time is being

Table 2.1 Factor analysis [40].

Factors	Component					Squared loadings % of variance
	1	2	3	4	5	
Profession	0.815					
Years of familiarity	0.758					
Aliment details	0.732					64.5%
Additional asset info	0.645					
Rental or owned residence		0.789				
Standard quarterly balance ought		0.654				69.5%
Cheque does not return		0.582				
Verification of the last six-month wage credited			0.856			
Motor vehicle details			0.785			72.3%
Place				0.756		
Family reliant				0.696		75.4%
Age					**0.764**	
Income					0.654	80.3%

Table 2.2 Performance evaluation of ABO for banking customer profile and cancer [40].

Dataset	Precision	Recall	F-measure
Banking Customer profile	0.83296	0.76951	0.79998
Cancer	0.87611	0.82299	0.84872

spent by the white-collar workers to search or find or assess the unstructured data. According to a particular decision, a project or simply a task could influence the poorly informed decision-making when the unstructured or semi-structured data is not drawn by the organizations because of practical difficulties in searching, retrieving, and assessing these data from the huge information database and accommodating the exact problems that are correlated with semi-structured, unstructured, as well as structured data whenever the business intelligence/DW solution is designed (Tables 2.1 and 2.2).

2.2.4 Merits of ABO

- It can eradicate the chances of guessing within the firm.
- To respond faster to initiate changes in the financial sector and the preferences of the customer.
- To initiate quick decision-making through quick action, the right information before the competitors in the business would do to offer the best performance than the rest.
- Perform clickstream data analysis to boost the strategies of eCommerce.
- Initiate more rates of profit for insurance premiums.
- To determine the objectives to optimize the business quickly with a low amount of risk, low cost, and effective strategy of information.
- Improve the power of decision-making and enhance productivity and efficiency through the environment where timely data which is accurate, reliable, and actionable is offered to track and enhance the performance.
- To be flexible and agile.
- To prevent the manual processes that are prone to errors.
- To gain the maximum advantage of loyalty economics by boosting the retention.
- It lowers the risk.
- Perform action-oriented and accurate decisions faster.

The below table provides the results of the factor analysis and a detailed description of each item for each of the five main factors.

2.3   Performance Evaluation

Any of the assessment for diagnostic performance seemed with the requirement of some comparisons for the diagnostic decisions along with "truth". The performance remains to be the test's ability incorrectly identifying the negative and positive cases.

The above table represents the Precision, Recall, and F-Measure for the ABO technique of cancer dataset. The below table shows that the customer profile dataset had poor precision, recall, and F-measures. The same was depicted in Figure 2.19.

The analytical results showed that the ABO algorithm showed good (excellent) discriminatory power (0.74) and had higher precision, recall, and F-measure values of 0.83%, 0.76%, and 0.79%, respectively, and this algorithm works better than the manual decision-making method. The decision-making of the performance of the proposed technique was visualized by implementing it in MATLAB. Experimental results on real-life datasets proved that the decision-making tool using the GA is not effective than manual decision-making.

As per Table 2.3, it is shown that the precision value of the banking customer profile obtained from the ABO approach is sophisticated than the precision values of clusters in the GA approach.

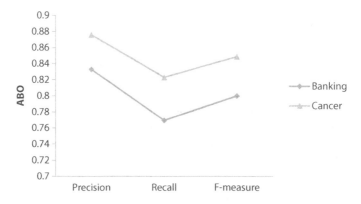

Figure 2.19 Performance evaluation of ABO for banking customer profile and cancer.

Table 2.3 Performance evaluation of GA and ABO for banking customer profile and cancer [40].

Dataset	Analysis variables/ techniques	GA	ABO
Banking Customer profile	Precision	0.49574	0.83296
	Recall	0.48302	0.76951
	F-measure	0.4893	0.79998
Cancer	Precision	0.43333	0.87611
	Recall	0.54082	0.82299
	F-measure	0.48115	0.84872

2.4 What is Next?

Research of the applications of the neural network will increase with significance in the future based on the publication rates of the past and its increase of interest in a particular area. The main purpose of the research is to find out how much is the algorithm proposed is capable of providing the best classifier with the low tuning of the parameter. It is very important to select an algorithm that can produce the best classifier with a better accuracy level with the help of better parameters. It must also have the possible disadvantages of experiencing poor results when the care is taken is much lower. In this backdrop, the current study features a new algorithm with the help of the attributed of bear technique.

The study was held in various stages and according to our sources; this is a unique study as many studies were conducted to create an algorithm to maximize the database of the customer specified in the bank applications. Even today, most of the banks make use of excel or other applications of lower end level to find out about the best customer. This study would throw light upon the issue where the proposed algorithm would be utilized as an application for those bankers to make use of decision-making on day-to-day basis.

The researchers involved in the study created an algorithm that took in to account the limitations of those ANN or genetic models of the current scenario. Also, the proposed model was developed with a sense of smell of the bear. To maintain discipline about the strategic financial model, the implementation of meta-heuristic algorithms and forecasting strategies was done. The results of the experiments show the manual decision-making view and the meta-heuristic algorithm and ABO algorithm proposal.

References

1. Simon, D., *Evolutionary optimization algorithms*, John Wiley & Sons, Hoboken, New Jersey, 2013.
2. Goldberg, D.E., *Genetic Algorithms in Search, Optimization, and Machine Learning*, Addison-Wesley, Reading, MA, 1989.
3. De Jong, K.A., Spears, W.M., Gordon, D.F., Using genetic algorithms for concept learning. *Mach. Learn.*, 13, 2–3, 161–188, 1993.
4. Kinnear, K.E., Langdon, W.B., Spector, L., Angeline, P.J., O'Reilly, U.M. (Eds.), *Advances in genetic programming*, vol. 3, MIT press, Cambridge, Massachusetts, London, England, 1994.
5. Alzantot, M., *Episode 1 - Genetic Algorithm for Reinforcement Learning*, 2017, June 16, https://becominghuman.ai/genetic-algorithm-for-reinforcement-learning-a38a5612c4dc.
6. Mallawaarachchi, V., *Introduction to Genetic Algorithms - Including Example Code*, 2020, March 1, https://towardsdatascience.com/introduction-to-genetic-algorithms-including-example-code-e396e98d8bf3.
7. Yokota, T., Gen, M., Li, Y.X., Genetic algorithm for non-linear mixed integer programming problems and its applications. *Comput. Ind. Eng.*, 30, 4, 905–917, 1996.
8. Mitchell, M., *An introduction to genetic algorithms*, MIT press, Cambridge, Massachusetts, London, England, 1998.
9. Koza, J.R., Introduction to genetic programming, in: *Proceedings of the 9th annual conference companion on Genetic and evolutionary computation*, 2007, July, pp. 3323–3365.
10. Steeb, W.H., *The nonlinear workbook: Chaos, fractals, cellular automata, genetic algorithms, gene expression programming, support vector machine, wavelets, hidden Markov models, fuzzy logic with C++*, World Scientific Publishing Company, Singapore, 2014.
11. Patacchiola, M., Dissecting Reinforcement Learning-Part.5, 2017, March 14, https://mpatacchiola.github.io/blog/2017/03/14/dissecting-reinforcement-learning-5.html.
12. Casas, P., *Feature Selection using Genetic Algorithms in R*, 2019, April 8, https://towardsdatascience.com/feature-selection-using-genetic-algorithms-in-r-3d9252f1aa66.
13. Sikora, R. and Piramuthu, S., Efficient genetic algorithm based data mining using feature selection with Hausdorff distance. *Inf. Technol. Manage.*, 6, 4, 315–331, 2005.

14. Stoltz, E., *Evolution of a salesman: A complete genetic algorithm tutorial for Python*, 2018, July 17, https://towardsdatascience.com/evolution-of-a-salesman-a-complete-genetic-algorithm-tutorial-for-python-6fe5d2b3ca35.

15. Sommerville, G., *Winning Blackjack using Machine Learning*, 2019, February 12, https://towardsdatascience.com/winning-blackjack-using-machine-learning-681d924f197c.

16. Chopra, P., *Reinforcement learning without gradients: evolving agents using Genetic Algorithms*, 2019, January 7, https://towardsdatascience.com/reinforcement-learning-without-gradients-evolving-agents-using-genetic-algorithms-8685817d84f.

17. Surma, G., *Slitherin - Solving the Classic Game of Snake with AI (Part 3: Genetic Evolution)*, 2019, January 21, https://towardsdatascience.com/slitherin-solving-the-classic-game-of-snake-with-ai-part-3-genetic-evolution-33186e6be110.

18. Suryansh., S., *Genetic Algorithms Neural Networks = Best of Both Worlds*, 2018, September 20, https://towardsdatascience.com/gas-and-nns-6a41f1e8146d.

19. Kim, M.-J. and Han, I., The discovery of experts decision rules from qualitative bankruptcy data using genetic algorithms. *Expert Syst. Appl.*, 25, 4, 637–646, 2003.

20. Dick, *Understanding Genetic Algorithms*, 2019, June 27, Retrieved from https://towardsdatascience.com/understanding-genetic-algorithms-cd556e9089cb.

21. Babayan, H., *Genetic algorithm vs. Backtracking: N-Queen Problem*, 2019, May 24, https://towardsdatascience.com/genetic-algorithm-vs-backtracking-n-queen-problem-cdf38e15d73f.

22. Freitas, A.A., A review of evolutionary algorithms for data mining, in: *Data Mining and Knowledge Discovery Handbook*, pp. 371–400, Springer, Boston, MA, 2009.

23. Ivan, *Parallel and distributed genetic algorithms*, 2019, November 3, https://towardsdatascience.com/parallel-and-distributed-genetic-algorithms-1ed2e76866e3.

24. Romero, C., Ventura, S., De Castro, C., Hall, W., Ng, M.H., Using genetic algorithms for data mining in web-based educational hypermedia systems, in: *Workshop on Adaptive Systems for Web-based Education*, 2002, May.

25. Berkani, L., Chebahi, Y., Betit, L., Using Data Mining Techniques and Genetic Algorithm, in: *Proceedings of the International Conference on Learning and Optimization Algorithms: Theory and Applications*, 2018, May, pp. 1–6.

26. Bandyopadhyay, S. and Pal, S.K., Pattern classification with genetic algorithms: Incorporation of chromosome differentiation. *Pattern Recognit. Lett.*, 18, 2, 119–131, 1997.

27. Lin, L., Cao, L., Wang, J., & Zhang, C., The Applications of Genetic Algorithms in Stock Market Data Mining Optimisation. 10. *WIT Trans. Info. Comm. Tech.*, 33, 8, 2004.

28. Kumar, A., Market Basket Data Analysis Using A Novel Genetic Frequent Itemset Mining Algorithm by Partitional Clustering Approach. Paripex – *Indian J. Res.*, 6, 4, 2017. https://www.worldwidejournals.com/paripex/recent_issues_pdf/2017/ April /April_2017_1493648113__160.pdf.

29. Koonce, D.A. and Tsai, S.C., Using data mining to find patterns in genetic algorithm solutions to a job shop schedule. *Comput. Ind. Eng.*, 38, 3, 361–374, 2000.

30. Marmelstein, R.E., Application of genetic algorithms to data mining, in: *Proceedings of 8th Midwest Artificial Intelligence and Cognitive Science Conference (MAICS-97)*, E. Santos Jr. (Ed.), pp. 58–65, AAAI Press, 1997.

31. Carvalho, D.R. and Freitas, A.A., A hybrid decision tree/genetic algorithm method for data mining. *Inf. Sci.*, 163, 1–3, 13–35, 2004.

32. Minaei-Bidgoli, B. and Punch, W.F., Using genetic algorithms for data mining optimization in an educational web-based system, in: *Genetic and evolutionary computation conference*, Springer, Berlin, Heidelberg, pp. 2252–2263, 2003, July.

33. Lazovskiy, V., *Travel Time Optimization With Machine Learning And Genetic Algorithm*, 2018, June 27, https://towardsdatascience.com/travel-time-optimization-with-machine-learning-and-genetic-algorithm-71b40a3a4c2.

34. Haupt, R.L. and Ellen Haupt, S., *Practical genetic algorithms*, A John Wiley & Sons Inc, Hoboken, New Jersey, 2004.

35. Bartu, C., *Continuous Genetic Algorithm From Scratch With Python*, 2019, October 30, https://towardsdatascience.com/continuous-genetic-algorithm-from-scratch-with-python-ff29deedd099.

36. Thomas, D., *Disadvantages of Genetic Algorithm (GA)*, 2019, October 21, https://www.quora.com/What-are-the-disadvantage-of-genetic-algorithm.

37. Faizan, A., *Introduction to Genetic Algorithm (GA)*, 2019, October 21, http://engineerexperiences.com/introduction-to-genetic-algorithm-ga.html.

38. Rao, A.V., Rao, G.R., Rao, M.V.B., Coping and limitations of genetic algorithms. *Orient. J. Comp. Sci. Technol.*, 1, 2, 137–141, 2008.

39. Zychlinski, S., *Are Genetic Models Better Than Random Sampling?*, 2018, June 22, https://towardsdatascience.com/are-genetic-models-better-than-random-sampling-8c678002d392.

40. Jeyanthi, M.S. and Karnan, M., A comparative study of genetic algorithm and artificial bear optimization algorithm in business intelligence. In *International Conference on Mathematics in Engineering & Business Management (ICMEB 2012)*, 2012.

3

Efficiency of Finding Best Solutions Through Ant Colony Optimization (ACO) Technique

K. Sasi Kala Rani* and N. Pooranam†

Department of Computer Science and Engineering, Sri Krishna College of Engineering and Technology, Coimbatore, India

Abstract

In the modern era, moving from place to another is a difficult task when it comes to the word traffic. The traffic can be of any thing like climate and road accident. To identify the situation and solution, this chapter will briefly explain with different case studies. This chapter addresses the challenges of tourism in which the family is planned for making a trip for a place, and if any obstructions like climatic condition found in the path, an optimal solution is generated using heuristic value and ACO algorithm in which continuous orthogonal ant colony (COAC) method helps in solving real-world problems. In general, searching and tracking an object are computerized visually by routing charts. While traveling from one place to another, the GPS tracking system provides the entire detail about route which is visualized as a graph. When GPS system starts on the vehicle, a continuous value is recorded both on path and shortest distance, and this is established as a searching algorithm. Consequently, the purpose of this chapter is to deliver a summary of how tracking is carried out even after any obstacle which stops the tracking process; this is improved by calculating probability value of path cost and using ACO algorithm and plot optimized solution. The experiments are made with real-time applications, and results were discussed in this chapter.

Keywords: Climatic condition, tracking, shortest distances, heuristic value, continuous orthogonal ant colony, ant colony optimization

Corresponding author: sasikalaranik@skcet.ac.in
†*Corresponding author*: pooranamn@skcet.ac.in

S. Balamurugan, Anupriya Jain, Sachin Sharma, Dinesh Goyal, Sonia Duggal and Seema Sharma (eds.) *Nature-Inspired Algorithms Applications*, (67–88) © 2022 Scrivener Publishing LLC

3.1   Introduction

Optimization is an important method in the field of science and analysis. The entire focal point is to optimize the solution to evaluate the design process of a system; the constraints may be on the resource or the cost of design [1]. The practical engineering problems are more complex in solving the appropriate solutions. The major modeling process is to optimize the cost and designing material and minimize processing time, to maximize profit, to simplify the productivity, to improve the efficiency, etc. The decision-making process to find an effective solution needs many alternative methods and techniques, which frequently compare with different standards.

In this chapter, ACO algorithm plays a foremost process which deals with finding the shortest path from the current location by evaluating the heuristic value. The ACO algorithm is a model which combines both local and simulated ant techniques to sort numerous charts to find the optimal solution in routing. Our objective is to find the shortest route in the graph by evaluating the frequent visit route at optimal solution. The COAC mechanism helps in solving the practical difficulties in finding the routes [2].

In case of computational problems in computer science, the computational cost of the algorithm increases gradually by increasing the input size which is to be executed on a computer, when the computational cost gets more than the expected value, then the implemented model is ineffective for both smaller inputs and also for larger once [3]. Hence, problems become unsolvable in specified time. In such cases, optimization techniques can be used.

Optimization algorithms are considered to be a verdict variable by finding effective standards for the given heuristic function, which meets some of the objective(s) that excellent changes in best abuse of the constraints specified. Term "optimization" refers to the process of choosing the best solution from some set of available solutions. In this chapter, it deals with overall work that is going to be carried out through normal ant species to find the shortest path of each trip. Though ants move from place to place, if any ant is missing, then the ant can find the place where other ants are present, while pheromone dissipated in the environment, other ants can also find it easy and finding food for their growth can also be done by similar process. There are several applications which relates ACO algorithm as a best search technique.

The ACO algorithm is one of the swarm Intelligence algorithms where the system will be designed in such a way that probability of each evaluation function is generated. In this chapter, the proposed method uses

ACO algorithm to define the problem to find the best solution on shortest path in the given problem. In the discussion, researchers can able to find the workings of ACO algorithm and how each case study is using ACO to find best solution for the problem defined. In each case study, the evaluation function is generated using proposed method to solve computational problem. ACO algorithm is used to find the shortest path in an optimized way; the technique uses real-time ant behavior to find their food and also easy path to their place [4]. The ant will dissipate phenomena which help other ant to follow the same path to find their source easily then if the probability is high that decided the best shortest path.

The phenomena is generated in each move of ant and probability value is calculated to find phenomena level; all other ants follow the highest phenomena level path to reach the destination; this mechanism is used in all the engineering and technology fields for optimized methodology. In this chapter, many fields are defined and described with case studies which help researchers to get more knowledge on ant colony optimization technique. There are some general applications using ACO; they are as follows:

- Traveling salesman problem
- Network routing process
- Graph coloring
- Bus routing
- Scheduling problem
- Assembling parts in mechanical engineering
- Digital processing
- Delivery process

These are some applications which use ACO for optimized solution, though there are similar applications which describes as case study in this chapter.

3.1.1 Example of Optimization Process

Example: Locate the most extreme estimation of $r = 3p1 + 5p2$, where $p1 \leq 0$ and $p2 \geq 0$, subject to the accompanying imperatives

$$-p1 + p2 \leq 9$$

$$p1 + p2 \leq 26$$

$$3p1 + 4p2 \leq 85$$

In the given example, the neutral gathering is r = 3p1 + 5p2. The resolution variables are p1 and p2 and the neutral is to find the values of p1 and p2 that maximizes r.

The Calculation for convolution is to find efficiency on solving difficult problem is given using O(n) symbolization, which shows the asymptotic time important to take care of the issue when it includes "n" occurrences of the choice factors and the issue size is controlled by the quantity of these choice factors. A calculation of request O(n) will burn through a processor season of n*c where "n" refers to the number of instances of the decision variable and "c" is a constant. The period essential to resolve the difficulty depends on the number of instances and the constant "c". The value of "c" depends on the CPU power and the programming environment, i.e., "c" value can be decreased by increasing the CPU power. The best way to decrease "c" is to use a better algorithm. A polynomial calculation of request O(nk) will devour c*nk, where k is a steady explicit for the issue or calculation.

3.1.2   Components of Optimization Algorithms

The components of optimization algorithms are as follows:

- Optimization goal: The enhancement objective is to limit (or boost) a target work from a bunch of arrangements accessible, fulfilling determined limitations. The target work is a capacity used to assess the nature of a produced arrangement.
- Search space: It denotes to a range of decision variables that will be searched to find solution during optimization.
- Solution: It alludes to the estimations of the choice factors indicated by an advancement issue with a target work subject to requirements. A solution to optimization problem may be feasible, near optimal, or optimal.
  - o A feasible solution satisfies all the specified constraints.
  - o A close ideal arrangement is attainable and gives a prevalent target work esteem, yet not really the best.
  - o An ideal arrangement is doable and gives the best target work esteem.

3.1.3   Optimization Techniques Based on Solutions

- Arrangement-based enhancement issues manage issues where an ideal arrangement must be browsed a limited (or some of the time countable) number of potential outcomes. The improvement issue may have a few arrangements relying upon whether the target work must be boosted or limited. In case of multiprocessing, limited number of processes may be available and the processors have to be assigned to different processes. Here, processors have to be allocated to different processes, i.e., CPU has to be scheduled in such a way that the average waiting time of processes has to be minimized and the average through-put has to be maximized [5].

• Consider a capacity with a target may be to discover the incentive for x where f(x) arrives at its most elevated worth. Worldwide optima are the ideal arrangement among every conceivable arrangement, not only those in a specific neighborhood of qualities. Worldwide and nearby optima are shown graphically in Figure 3.1. In the figure, xB alludes to worldwide ideal as it yields the most noteworthy generally speaking an incentive for the goal work, though xA and xC are neighborhood optima.

The solution-based optimization problems may be divided into two groups:

    a. Resolutions encoded with separate variables.
    b. Resolutions encoded with real-valued variables.

Combinatorial optimization problems refer to the problems with solutions encoded in discrete variables. Combinatorial optimization can be applied in the field of designing like plan and examination of information organizations, VLSI-hardware plan and testing, the format of circuits to limit the region committed to wires, via aircraft organizations to timetable and value their flights, by huge organizations to choose what and where to stock in their distribution centers, by conveyance organizations to choose

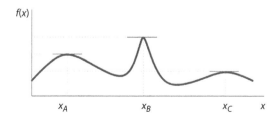

Figure 3.1 Global and local optima for f(x).

the courses of their conveyance trucks, by Netix to choose which motion pictures to suggest you, by a GPS guide to concoct driving bearings, and by word processors.

3.1.3.1 Optimization Techniques Based on Algorithms

This category uses algorithms (predefined procedure) to solve optimization problems. Algorithms that are used to solve optimization problems may be classified into two categories:

1. Exact algorithms
2. Approximate algorithms

3.1.3.1.1 Exact Algorithms

Exact algorithms are ensured to locate an ideal arrangement and to demonstrate its optimality for each case of a streamlining issue. In this class, one can locate the accompanying traditional calculations like dynamic programming, and branch and X group of calculations (branch and bound, branch and cut, branch and cost). The pursuit space is investigated by progressively fabricating a tree whose root hub addresses the issue being tackled and all others address search space.

The pruning of the inquiry tree depends on a jumping capacity that prunes or kills the subtrees that do not contain any ideal arrangement.

Limitation writing computer programs is a language worked around ideas of tree search and coherent ramifications. Improvement issues in imperative writing computer programs are displayed by methods for a bunch of factors connected by a bunch of limitations. The factors take their

Table 3.1 Size of instances that can be solved by exact algorithms.

S. no	Optimization problems	Size of instances
1	Quadratic assignment	40 objects
2	Flow-shop scheduling	100 jobs, 30 machines
3	Graph coloring	1,000 nodes
4	Capacitated vehicle routing	50 clients

qualities on a limited area of numbers exposed to the predetermined limitations. Just little or respectably measured occasions can be for all intents and purposes tackled utilizing accurate calculations. Table 3.1 shows for some well-known improvement issues and the size of the cases that can be addressed precisely by best in class accurate calculations.

3.1.4 Characteristics

i. **Generation of new solutions:** A deterministic standard, an irregular conjecture, or a mix of both can be utilized to create arrangements. Be that as it may, they do not ensure an ideal arrangement.

ii. **Treatment of new solutions:** The heuristic optimization methods not only consider the new arrangements that may prompt quick improvement yet additionally the arrangements that were discovered substandard. The second rate arrangements might be incorporated when the arrangement is not a long way from the ideal arrangement or may be given less weight (need). The new arrangements are positioned dependent on their distance to the ideal arrangement and simply the best arrangements are viewed as further.

iii. **Limitations of the search space:** At the point when the pursuit space is tremendous, the new arrangements can be found via looking inside a specific neighborhood of an inquiry specialist's present arrangement or inside the promising populace. A few strategies prohibit the areas to maintain a strategic distance from cyclic hunt ways and costly calculation.

iv. **Prior knowledge:** Earlier information can be utilized for the decision of starting arrangements and search measure. Earlier information can henceforth decrease the pursuit space and speed up. It might likewise prompt second rate arrangement when guided off course or when the calculation has issue in beating nearby optima. Thus, earlier information is utilized in just set number of heuristic techniques.

v. **Flexibility for specific constraints:** Some heuristic techniques are customized to specific kinds of imperatives and are accordingly hard to apply to different classes of advancement issues.

vi. **Computational complexity:** The intricacy of a technique relies upon the expense for assessing per up-and-comer arrangement, number of cycles, populace size, and cost of overseeing the populace. For the most part, the computational intricacy of heuristic streamlining strategies is low.

vii. **Convergence speed:** The CPU interval is used to associate different heuristic optimization processes. When reasonable time is not exceeded, there is no need to differentiate local or global optimum.

viii. **Reliability:** Significant heuristic strategies hypothetically meet toward worldwide ideal with adequate time and fitting decisions. For all intents and purposes, there is a trade-off between union speed and the possibility that the worldwide ideal is missed.

3.1.5   Classes of Heuristic Algorithms

i. **Strategies run in polynomial time, however, give no assurance as far as arrangement quality:** The class contains basic need rule–based heuristics with a low request of intricacy and modern heuristics with higher request of intricacy have a place with the class. Simple heuristics can solve complex problems in short period but with compromised quality of the solution. Complex heuristics produce quality results but consumes a lot of time.

ii. **Strategies that give no deduced ensure regarding arrangement quality and computational time:** This class basically comprises of neighborhood search heuristics which iterates through a set of available solutions. Neighborhoods through which the iterations continue depend on the current solution.

iii. **Methods can be solved in polynomial time with guaranteed rate of approximation**

Advantages

- They are universally useful techniques which are generally simple that can be adjusted to a solid streamlining issue.
- It is useful when solving issues that do not require a formula.

The underlying populace for this situation is haphazardly produced (or made with an avaricious calculation) and afterward upgraded through an iterative cycle. At every age of the interaction, the entire populace (or a piece of it) is supplanted by recently created people (frequently the best ones). The main individuals from this class are transformative calculations (EA) and the calculations dependent on swarm intelligence. Transformative calculations (EA) emulate the standards of characteristic development. EAs work on a set or populace of arrangements and utilize two systems to look for great arrangements:

- The recombination of those arrangements into new ones, utilizing particular administrators that join the ascribes of at least two arrangements.
- After recombination, new arrangements are reinserted into the populace, expecting them to fulfill conditions like plausibility or least quality requests, to supplant bad quality arrangements.

3.1.6   Metaheuristic Algorithms

Metaheuristic algorithms can be used to resolve the difficulties through multiple goals. Heuristics intend to discover or to find by experimentation. Metaheuristic calculations guide the search process.

Heuristics are normally customized to perform best on a particular issue type, i.e., heuristics remain problem-dependent. On the other hand, metaheuristics refer to a general skeleton of an algorithm for problem solving. Metaheuristics are more generic and can be applicable to variety of problems with little modifications and hence problem-independent.

3.1.6.1   *Classification of Metaheuristic Algorithms: Nature-Inspired vs. Non-Nature–Inspired*

The grouping depends on the cause of the calculation. There are nature-propelled calculations, such as genetic algorithms, and ant algorithms, and non-nature–enlivened ones, for example, Tabu search and iterated local search.

3.1.6.2   *Population-Based vs. Single-Point Search (Trajectory)*

The order depends on the quantity of arrangements utilized simultaneously. Calculations chipping away at single arrangements are called direction strategies and include nearby pursuit-based metaheuristics, similar to Tabu Search, iterated local search, and variable neighborhood search.

Memory use can be characterized into present moment and long haul. The first ordinarily monitors as of late performed moves, visited arrangements or, by and large, choices taken. The second is normally a collection of engineered boundaries about the inquiry.

3.1.7   Data Processing Flow of ACO

In Figure 3.2, the initial process, all the variables are assigned to respective values, each iteration the pheromone value is updated, and intermediate

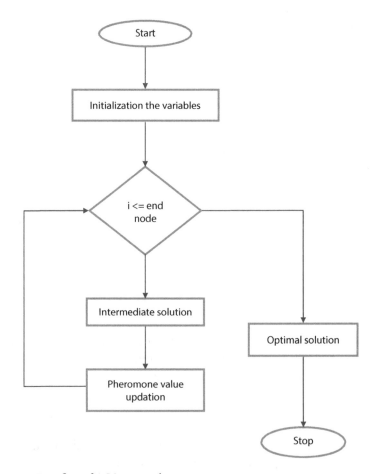

Figure 3.2 Data flow of ACO approach.

values are added in each iteration if suppose i <= final empty node, final output is obtained and the process is stopped.

3.2 A Case Study on Surgical Treatment in Operation Room

In real time, health is a more important parameter in life without which other essential things cannot be done properly. The researchers can able to find and analyze about swarm intelligent system as an efficient algorithm helps in real-world problem statement. In this chapter, the optimized solution using best algorithm is defined and described. In hospitals, each patient is treated in three different categories when they are in to a surgery at operation room, first and foremost is setting up for a surgery in which the patients are treated with initial process to undergo surgery. Second stage is surgical operation is carried out for some timestamp and here the proposed method will be implemented for efficiency. The last and final stage is recovery of patient after surgery, then after completion of each stage timestamp is generated. In general, one surgery gets over the room should be cleaned and then only remaining persons will be allowed for next surgery. The ACO algorithm helps in scheduling the surgical treatment in the hospital; each process should be demonstrated with a timestamp which will be updated as a centralized data processing.

Figure 3.3 describes the entire surgical process in which dataset is created based on entire details of hospital and the surgical process that is carried out in each timestamp; the specialists and patients' detail will be stored in the centralized database to access the data in efficient way; in any emergency,

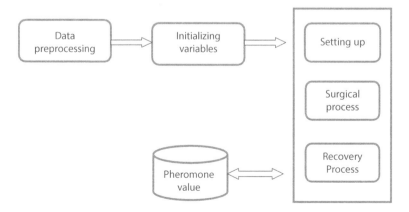

Figure 3.3 Work flow of surgical process.

each time, data cannot be searched; it is centralized but secured, where all patient details are confidential with other persons. Figure 3.4 shows detail about the hospital and each person will be identified with unique id as patient id or customer id through which the data of those patients will be taken, and each time, diagnosing process will be carried out on their sufficient days or observations. The process of any changes in surgery, scheduled for a patient the details, will be updated in the database; another few data will be notified by doctors and individual patients. The surgical process is carried out as discussed earlier; those data will also be updated for future purpose. Each schedule is made by ACO algorithm which deals with new or old data processing through frequent data process; it finds more effective solution for many scheduling and searching process. Location of each data will be maintained using hash value for indexing those data.

The graph describes the waiting time and the completion time for a surgical treatment of a particular hospital through which the efficiency of each schedule is determined using ant colony optimization technique; each scheduling is done by giving priority for emergency surgery [8]. When waiting time increases, the completion time will be increased; it is directly propositional to data processing system. Figure 3.5 shows waiting time and completion time of each scheduled process. Throughput for each process varies accordingly to find efficient schedule method [9] and to calculate that efficiency of each patient's critical condition is taken and verified for future purpose. Classical data interference is obtained for finding deviation between the time changes; although it is dynamic problem, solving those in real time is a challenge for each task. Final change is done with cause of the emergency period of each individual schedule.

	Type	X2	UPRN	XTKEYVAL	ADDRESS	POSTCODE	MAP_EAST	MA
6	Doctors	26	47069624	3.33000e+12	69 Park Parade Whitley Bay Tyne And Wear NE26 1DN	NE26 1DN	435216	
4	Doctors	27	47227766	2.82000e+12	Marine Avenue Health Centre Marine Avenue Whitley…	NE26 3LW	434744	
5	Doctors	29	47059156	2.82000e+12	49 Marine Avenue Whitley Bay Tyne And Wear NE26 …	NE26 1NA	435172	
3	Doctors	8	47058443	2.79000e+12	2 Manor Walk Benton NEWCASTLE UPON TYNE NE7 7XX	NE7 7XX	427093	
2	Doctors	31	47045958	2.22000e+12	Beaumont Park Surgery Hepscott Drive Whitley Bay T…	NE25 9XJ	433708	
0	Doctors	13	47044826	2.17000e+12	Appleby Surgery Hawkeys Lane Health Centre Hawk…	NE29 0SF	434811	
1	Doctors	14	47044827	2.17000e+12	Collingwood Surgery Hawkeys Lane Health Centre H…	NE29 0SF	434811	
9	Doctors	2	47041206	2.03000e+12	Village Green Surgery The Green Wallsend Tyne And …	NE28 6BB	430213	
8	Doctors	30	47040981	2.01000e+12	Wideopen Medical Centre Great North Road Wideope…	NE13 6LN	424093	
7	Doctors	5	47028086	1.35000e+12	Garden Park Surgery Denbigh Avenue Wallsend Tyne…	NE28 0PP	432210	
6	Doctors	24	47105302	1.06000e+12	Wellspring Medical Practice Killingworth Health Centr…	NA	427959	

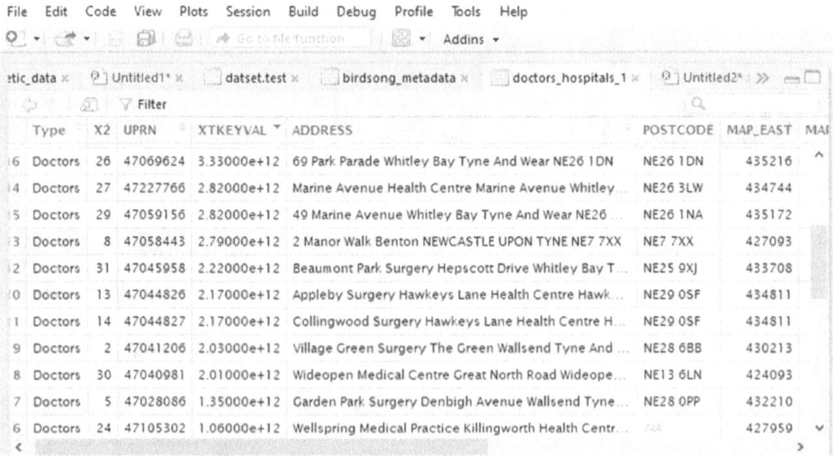

Figure 3.4 Hospital dataset.

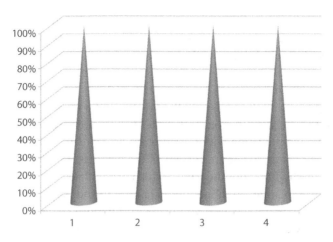

Figure 3.5 Waiting time and completion time.

In this, the representation is a matrix format to find an efficient solution of scheduling.

	[.1]	[.2]	[.3]	[.4]	[.5]
[1,]	47	48	49	50	51
[2,]	52	53	54	55	56
[3,]	57	58		60	61
[4,]	62	63	64	47	48

It can be of infinite scheduling process; when an empty plot comes, it defines that particular operating room is not in use. Utilization of each resource is done in an efficient way though overall locations represented in the matrix are easy way to schedule.

	[.1]	[.2]	[.3]	[.4]	[.5]
[1,]	47	48	49	50	51
[2,]	52	53	54	55	56
[3,]	57	58	□	60	61
[4,]	62	63	64	47	48

Evaluation function deals with all the possible combinations of resources, usage of its data availability, and combination of both features [8]. The value is updated in each stream of data capturing though it is difficult to complete but frequent evaluation of heuristic function can help in producing the overall process rate in an increasing manner. ACO algorithm will find in two different fames: one is done by evaporation of pheromone content and without evaporation so that estimation time gets faster and data gets diverge for improving process iteration [10].

The important components with the overall swarm intelligence can be estimated using heuristic function, and clustering methods are used to incorporate the data manipulation with classification data streams; individual data is clustered with some constraints where all the data has been taken as parameters of heuristic function; the values which are initiated with variables will update their maximum likelihood for data mining and preprocessing to estimate those things; each data is verified with timeslot [11]. Essential process here is done by efficiency of value creation on time without any delay. The calculated value is used for scheduling real-time problem; this intelligence system will monitor the overall process for the fine tune process dynamically.

3.3   Case Study on Waste Management System

In this case study, the researcher can able to understand the optimization technique used to deposit the waste in a particular area where it is recycled and to

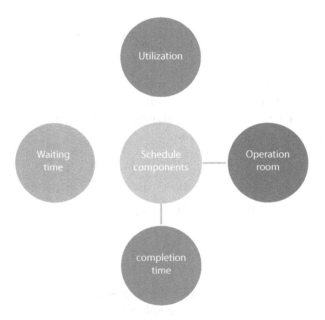

Figure 3.6 Components for scheduling.

reduce the pollution of carrying waste is routed using ACO algorithm [6]. In this, shortest path has been scheduled to driver mobile where person will be guided with efficient path to reach the designation in quick and safe mode. In Figure 3.6 shows the general scheduling components for processing the data. All the garbage collection will be node and connecting points will be edges of the node; each path cost is calculated using path cost algorithm to find efficient move; at the same time, cost of disposal is proposed as combination, and it defines overall deposit that is used for recycling process for future purpose.

In this graphical representation, each number plot represents the waste segregation, and in the node 6, the overall collection of waste is disposed and it is recycled. Each collection of waste is segregated using ACO evaluation, and the shortest path is matched with the smart system for safe and security purpose though the tones of weight have to be disposed efficiently to maintain cost; it helps in finding each turn and shortest path that will be decided based on the value generated in each cycle. The routing system will be exposed only to the drives of the waste collecting vehicles; after all, the waste is collected; it is disposed at the final recycle system for future purpose [7]. This approach is a massive one for streams of data collection and maintenance.

3.4   Working Process of the System

Each feature extraction is assigned with suitable variables; phenomenon of ant is suspected in all spaces; the values are generated accordingly; heuristic function

	DATE	MONTH	TYPE	TOTAL (IN TONS)
6	10/31/2013	October	Asphalt Debris	5000
7	10/31/2016	October	Yard Waste	900
8	03/31/2015	March	Recycled Tires	12
9	06/30/2014	June	Misc. Garbage	226
10	01/31/2017	January	Yard Waste	1000
11	12/31/2017	December	Bottle Bill	317
12	01/31/2017	January	Bottle Bill	317
13	11/30/2016	November	Bottle Bill	317
14	03/31/2016	March	Sidewalk Debris	0
15	03/31/2014	March	Scrap Metal	336
16	02/28/2016	February	Misc. Garbage	1026

Showing 6 to 16 of 1,140 entries

Figure 3.7 Dataset waste management.

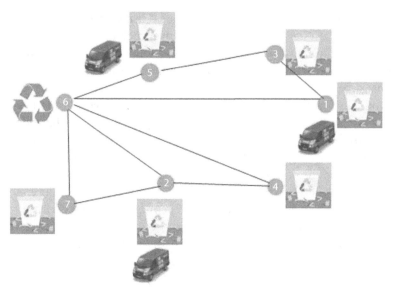

Figure 3.8 Routing systems for waste collection.

is established with all possible data; and the probability of each space is identified with absolute. Generated value is less than the phenomenon value iterate for heuristic function else obtained optimal solution for the problem to be solved.

At the same time, as discussed in the previous sections, values are generated with dataset collected annually. Dataset of waste collection is shown in Figure 3.7; each collected value is compared with the existing cluster of phenomenon value; graphical representation is discussed here though each value in the cluster is differed from other; the mapping is made for an easy understanding of work flow. The workflow diagram of waste collection is shown in Figure 3.8 to identify each step of waste collection process. Examined data says that, when extracted value is less than the cluster data, find a new data for that value; when it is greater than the cluster data, it is to be finalized for solving the problem with the heuristic value. If any changes are made in dataset, then values will be changed so the particular process can alone be repeated so that the evaluation cost reduced and optimized solution is generated. The flow of data will ever be changed for any reason because change in value will change entire solution.

3.5   Background Knowledge to be Considered for Estimation

The trends will explore traveling tourists who will benefit finding their destination as it's shortest path. This section will demonstrate how the plots can be used when an obstacle is found in the path; the GPS tracking will stop when vehicle stops to avoid this situation; the intelligent process is carried out to find some other path from the current state. If the obstacle is based on climatic condition, then the problem will be sorted out by finding the condition and the heuristic value is found for each nearby path and the values will be explored. General flow of the working model is given in Figure 3.9.

Next, the demonstration is on exploring the path using ACO algorithm to find nearest path so that the data processing will occupy only minimum memory and will display the plots as graph.

3.5.1   Heuristic Function

The function is to find the optimal among all possible solutions in a search space that can be referred to as heuristic search algorithms. They calculated

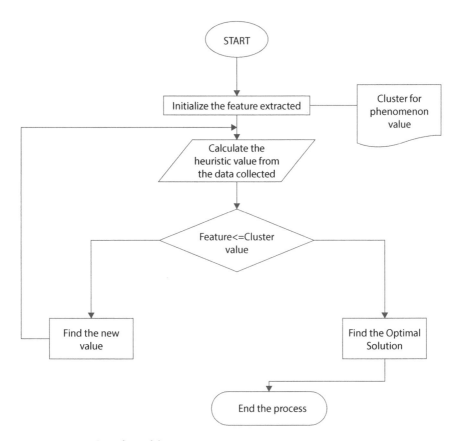

Figure 3.9 Working flow of the system.

for solving many problems than some other classical problems which is too slow. These functions may not provide the best outcome rather used to find a good and optimal solution in an efficient computational cost. This is achieved through compromising optimality, entirety, accuracy, or precision for speed. Heuristics which provides the result individually or group can be a base for the optimization problem. Heuristic methods find with more or less random solutions; the repeated process generates new solutions and rules which ultimately find best solution established during the search technique. Figure 3.10 shows the comparison of heuristic value with phenomenon value. The implementation of repeated searches halts when one of the following conditions is met:

- The found solution is good enough.
- There is no auxiliary enhancement overall known counts of repetitions.
- If the in-house variables expires during computational process.
- Valid candidate solutions are exhausted.

Some of the heuristic search algorithms are majorly on the informed search strategies and uninformed search strategies mainly on A* algorithm and the evaluation function of BFS.

Traveling sales man problem can be defined as pursues: Given with some list of cities and the heuristic values between those cities, evaluate the shortest possible routes which visits all the cities exactly once. The heuristic evaluation uses an easy solvable approach through NN approach or greedy approach.

This approach is optimal because unaccountable steps are evaluated during the selection process. For instance, the NN approach implements with 25% of outcome when compared with other solutions.

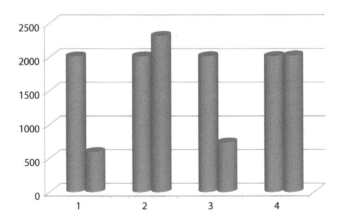

Figure 3.10 Comparison of heuristic value with phenomenon value.

3.5.2   Functional Approach

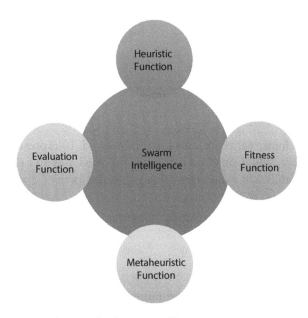

Figure 3.11 Functional approach of swarm intelligence.

3.6   Case Study on Traveling System

In this study, when a family or an individual is going for a trip, they will travel from different location, in which, nowadays, the location can be shared via different media; while traveling from one place to another place, finding shortest path is difficult while there are plenty of ways. In this case, the ant colony optimization technique can be used for finding the best and optimal solution for the real-time problem. Figure 3.11 describes the functional approach of swarm intelligence to find a optimal solution. Here, one major difference is that, while there is any obstacle, the ACO algorithm will help in such condition and provide a different solution. Some new formulation helps in finding phenomenon value where it is dissipated in the path traveled where climatic condition is also considered as obstacle [12].

Consider the following example for better understanding; in ACO algorithm, each data is represented as graphical way and also in matrix format for finding a better solution using heuristic value estimation.

Consider the following for examples.

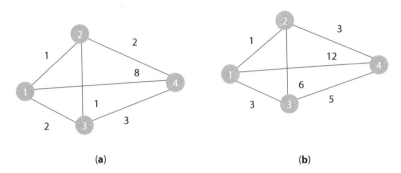

(a)   (b)

The above figure (a) represents pheromone and (b) represents cost, and the matrix representation of each graph is followed; it is an easy method to find the probability of values by evaluating in the form of matrix.

0	1	2	8
0	0	1	2
2	1	0	3
8	2	3	0

0	1	3	12
1	0	6	3
3	6	0	5
12	3	5	0

(a)   (b)

The above is the matrix representation of same graph shown after this step; pheromone and cost have been calculated using some computational method which is an easy method to find the solution, and at last, probability is estimated for each node.

In (c), if the pheromone value is a unit, it is represented as 1.

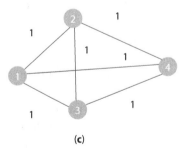

(c)

The calculation is done by two ways: one is by considering vaporization and another one is without vaporization. The value is obtained directly without any constant value; the new value is generated accordingly as initialized value.

$$\sum_{n=1}^{x} \Delta \tau i^{n}$$

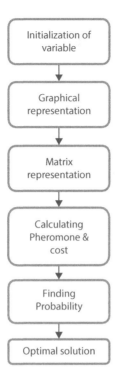

Figure 3.12 Process flow.

The probability is estimated using the above equation, and the numerical value is calculated till x variable gets infinity from which heuristic value tends to be efficient. According to the above equation, the change in the location is taken into account for evaluation purpose. The probability and optimal solution is calculated with given process flow which is shown in Figure 3.12. It is an easy way to find the probability for an efficient algorithm used to find the shortest path. Then, the location is lively shared to their circles for the purpose of tracking which is an efficient way of dealing with cost and pheromone values.

3.7 Future Trends and Conclusion

While the heuristic value calculation is processed, the outcome of the process is efficient in such a way that each process is carried out separately and final solution is calculated at the end of the process. The result of this plan will be a graph plot to improve the route finding process in an efficient way. The chapter concludes with a summary of efficient way of finding the routes for traveling to different location by considering the climatic change as obstacle and by helping in reaching the destination in a shortest distance also on time. This can be further a research to develop an API using deep learning techniques.

References

1. https://developers.google.com/maps/documentation/
2. https://www.tavant.com/sites/default/files/download-center/Tavant_Manufacturing_White_Paper_Google_Maps_Business_Final.pdf
3. https://pdfs.semanticscholar.org/0bdf/934ce6d16b17b6b81d6f670bf44fc3e8135 6.pdf
4. https://ieeexplore.ieee.org/document/5446141/
5. Bigano, A., Hamilton, J.M., Tol, R.S., The impact of climate change on domestic and international tourism: a simulation study, in: *Fondazione Eni Enrico Mattei (FEEM) > Climate Change Modelling and Policy Working Papers,* 2006. DOI 10.22004/ag.econ.12018.
6. Nazif, H., Operating Room Surgery Scheduling with Fuzzy Surgery Durations Using a Metaheuristic Approach. *Adv. Oper. Res.,* 2018 in the journal Advances in Operations Research is a peer-reviewed, Open Access journal, Volume 2018 |Article ID 8637598 | https://doi.org/10.1155/2018/8637598.
7. Jin, H., Wang, W., Cai, M., Wang, G., Yun, C., Ant colony optimization model with characterization-based speed and multi-driver for the refilling system in hospital. *Adv. Mech. Eng.,* 9, 8, 1687814017713700, 2017.
8. Ning, J., Zhang, C., Sun, P., Feng, Y., Comparative study of ant colony algorithms for multi-objective optimization. *Information,* 10, 1, 11, 2019.
9. Dorigo, M. and Blum, C., Ant colony optimization theory: A survey. *Theor. Comput. Sci.,* 344, 2–3, 243–278, 2005.
10. Akhtar, A., Evolution of ant colony optimization algorithm–a brief literature review, in: *arXiv: 1908.08007,* 2019.
11. Zhong, J.P. and Fung, Y.F., A Theoretical Proof and Case Study of Ant Colony Optimization Improved Particle Filter Algorithm Conference Proceeding, vol. 2, pp. 705–707. 2006.
12. Hlaing, Z.C.S.S. and Khine, M.A., Solving traveling salesman problem by using improved ant colony optimization algorithm. *Int. J. Inf. Educ. Technol.,* 1, 5, 404, 2011.

4

A Hybrid Bat-Genetic Algorithm–Based Novel Optimal Wavelet Filter for Compression of Image Data

Renjith V. Ravi[1*] and Kamalraj Subramaniam[2]

¹Department of Electronics and Communication Engineering, MEA Engineering College, Vengoor, Pattikkad PO, Malappuram, Kerala, India
²Dept. of Electronics and Communication Engineering, Faculty of Engineering, Karpagam Academy of Higher Education, Coimbatore, India

Abstract

In the past two decades, significant advances have been made in the fields of image cryptography and compression, motivated by a growing demand for visual information storage and transmission. However, including both compression and encryption in a single algorithm can be significant research which can reduce the computation overhead and also improve the security in transmission. In this paper, a novel optimal wavelet filter bank based on hybrid bat-genetic algorithm for image compression is proposed. Initially, a novel optimization algorithm based on hybridizing the techniques of bat algorithm and genetic algorithm is developed, and further, an optimal wavelet filter bank is derived from the hybrid bat-genetic optimization algorithm. This filter bank is then used for wavelet-based image compression of images taken from unmanned vehicle, and then, the compressed image is encrypted using chaos theory–based encryption. The strategy involves three modules, namely, optimized transformation module, compression and encryption module, and receiver module. Initially, the input image is sub-band coded using hybrid bat-genetic algorithm–based optimized DWT. Subsequently, the encoding using SPIHT and chaos-based encryption is carried out. In receiver module, the received signal from the AWGN channel is demodulated, decrypted, and decompressed to have the estimated image. From the results, we can infer that the use of proposed filter and the technique has produced better image quality when compared to existing techniques.

Corresponding author: renjithravi.research@gmail.com

S. Balamurugan, Anupriya Jain, Sachin Sharma, Dinesh Goyal, Sonia Duggal and Seema Sharma (eds.)
Nature-Inspired Algorithms Applications, (89–136) © 2022 Scrivener Publishing LLC

Keywords: Optimal wavelet coefficients, DWT, hybrid genetic bat algorithm, chaos theory, encryption, compression, SPIHRT, QASK, AWGN

4.1   Introduction

In computer applications, digital images are commonly used. Digital images without compression require considerable bandwidth and storage capacity. With the recent development of data intensive and multimedia-based web applications, efficient image compression solutions are becoming more critical. The compression of data aims to decrease the amount of data needed for a certain amount of information. Transform coding is a popular and commonly used image compression technique [1, 2]. The transition aims at generating decorrelated coefficients and reducing redundancy.

In both spatial frequency areas, several rapid and powerful image compression processors were proposed. Compression of images is divided into lossy and lossless compression. We sacrifice image information with lossy compression. Mostly in web browsing, photography, picture processing, and printing, for very small storage, the form of lossy compression is used. JPEG is an appropriate method for image compression for lossy compression. There are, on the other side, some imaging applications (medical, satellite, remote, and forensic) that did not involve a pixel difference between an original and a reconstructed image; therefore, some lossless applications are required [3, 4].

Image compression reduces the number of bits required by the deletion of redundant information to represent an image. Psychovisual redundancy is used to ignore certain data by the human eyes, to code redundancy, to present statistics of the original data, while interpixel redundancy examines the fact that certain pixels in an image have equal or almost equal value. Psychovisual redundancy image compression is widely classified into two categories, namely, lossy and lossless, depending on whether a compressed image can recover the original image with complete mathematical precision [5, 6].

In the digital world, security of digital images/videos is increasingly important since digital products are increasingly communicated over the network. Since a compression module to minimize the transmitted bit rate typically comes with the video digital transmission system, cryptographic techniques must be carefully configured to prevent possible adverse effects on compression effectiveness and on the functionality offered by the compression format. Cryptography, a modern encryption technology, including mathematical processes involving formula implementation (or algorithms), was historically developed to protect military and diplomatic communications discretion. A new creative field for cryptographic technologies has stimulated with the rapid growth of information technology and encryption. Cryptography is characterized as the subdivision of encryption/decryption algorithms for the purpose of ensuring data protection and authentication. Cryptographic coding techniques for multi-media applications should be researched and developed for potential internet applications on the wireless networks, besides sources and channel coding techniques. In this article, we are concentrating on joint compression and encryption of images [7, 8].

Optimal wavelet–based compression employing hybrid genetic bat algorithm is proposed in this work. The technique comprises of three modules, namely, optimized transformation module, compression and encryption module, and receiver module. In optimized transformation module, the input image is decomposed to high frequency and low frequency components with the use of hybrid bat-genetic algorithm–based optimal wavelet filter coefficients. Afterward, in the compression and encryption module, the compression using SPIHT, chaos-based encryption, and QASK-based modulation is carried out. In receiver module, initially, the channel estimation is also carried out and then the received signal from the AWGN channel is demodulated, decrypted, and decompressed to have the estimated image.

The remainder of the article is structured as follows: Section 4.2 discusses the relevant works. Section 4.3 describes the existing safe transmission technique. Section 4.4 offers a brief overview of the methodology proposed with all the mathematical formulations and figures available. The findings and discussions are in Section 4.5. Section 4.6 will conclude the paper.

4.2 Review of Related Works

At this juncture, we set out to analyze certain works offered for image encryption in accordance with various renovation and encodings methods. Ibtisam a. Aljazaery [10] intelligently advocated a novel technique to encrypt the signals with one dimension and images (monochrome or colour images) in a shorter span of time than the duration required for encrypting these signals and images with their original dimensions. The innovative technique relies on mining the significant traits which distinguish these signals and images and thereby dispensing with them. The succeeding phase consists in encrypting the lowest dimensions of these data. Discrete wavelet transform (DWT) is employed as a trait mining method as it is a leading device for signal processing in view of its multi-resolution potentialities. The select data is encrypted with one of the traditional cryptographic technique such as the permutation algorithm after reducing its size by means of an appropriate encryption key. The encrypted data is

100% unidentified, and the decryption technique takes back the encrypted data to its original dimension effectively.

Somaya Al-Maadeed [11] has spent a tremendous amount of time and energy in setting up an effective technique for developing stable image-encryption methods. In fact, an innovative algorithm is the amalgamation of two powerful methods, such as encryption and compression. A wavelet transformation was used in the novel approach to decay the image and separate the pixels into approximation and detail parts. The approximation part is encrypted using a chaos-based encryption technique. The algorithm produces a test image code that has excellent diffusion and misunderstanding characteristics. The residual segments, *viz.*, the detail components, are compacted by means of a wavelet transform. The innovative method is corroborated to furnish a superior security level. An overall pattern for the algorithm is also furnished. Various test images are employed to illustrate the soundness of the novel technique. The captivating outcomes of various tests illustrate the fact that the innovative technique for image cryptosystems furnishes a proficient and safe method to concurrent image encryption and communication. Marcus Arthur *et al.* [12] were granted the name and fame of flagging a novel technique for automatic generation of orthophoto mosaics using the Scale Invariant Feature Transform (SIFT) method for automatic identification of key points and matching issues. Invariably, the workflow uses professional and robust algorithms to implement an acceptable methodology that is optimized to meet near-current requirements.

In light of the GA, by reducing the quadrant calculation of the error in the frequency band, the authors showed the optimal techniques for the 2D FIR digital filter [13] and developed real value measures in order to acquire filter coefficient with an evolutional algorithm. The adaptive GA approach in this document is built for 2D FIR filters, which can generate high response filters while reducing the error criteria and processor time considerably. The suitability and validity of the proposed solution have been shown by testing of various 2D filters. Also, this paper says a future work of hybridizing GA with other filters. Xin-She Yang and Xingshi He were brightly offered an opportune audit of the bat algorithm and its new variations in [14]. An extensive variety of various applications and contextual investigations are additionally evaluated and compressed quickly. Additionally compresses a few focal points of BAT algorithm, for example, frequency tuning, automatic zooming, and parameter control which demonstrates the predominance of BA over other swarm intelligence–based and metaheuristic algorithms. The contributors were magnificently green-signaled an algorithm formed by the combination of Random PSO

and DE, termed as Random PSODE (RPSODE) in [15]. In order to preserve diversity and explore the search field more effectively, the random
PSO algorithm is integrated into the DE algorithm. The use of hybrid optimization techniques ensures that all algorithms have the best practices and
that their design time. Fitness is also increased considerably as the hybridization helps to keep the particles stuck in the local minimum and thereby
leads them to the global solution.

4.3   Existing Technique for Secure Image Transmission

Multi-resolution decomposition is one of the most important features of
DWT [5]. The DWT consists of filters for degrading (analysis) and rebuild-
ing. Hair, Daubches, Bianorthogonal, Reverse Biorthogonal, Symlets,
Coiflets, and Discrete Mayer are the most popular wavelet filters. The 2D
low- and high-pass filters are considered and passed by an image and are
decomposed into high and low frequency components on a row and column
wisely. This procedure is called sub-band coding and filters are called analysis filters, resulting in four substrips. Then, the quantizer is given this decomposed image. The sampler approaches the continuous set of values with finite
values in image data. Then, additional compression may be encoded via
entropy code. The most popular wavelet-based image coding schemes are
EZW, SPIHT, SPECK, WDR, ASWDR, SFQ, CREW, EPWIC, EBCOT, and
SR. Among these, SPIHT [16] is the most effective one. The compressed data
is then encrypted using any of the encryption algorithms to ensure the security. This encrypted data is modulated and transmitted through the channel.

The data is demodulated and decrypted by the decryption technique in
the receiver. Next is the decoder which carries the process of decoding, i.e.,
the single bits of code sent instead of the data bits. The dequantizer quan-
tizes the decoded information bits and passes through the wavelet reconstruction filter. Conversely, the procedure is to extract the image data from
the collected image values. The entire process is depicted in Figure 4.1.

4.4   Proposed Design of Optimal Wavelet Coefficients for Image Compression

In this paper, optimal wavelet filter–based compression employing hybrid
genetic bat algorithm is proposed. The technique employ optimized DWT

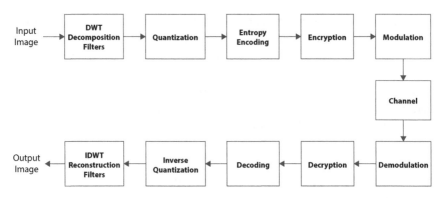

Figure 4.1 Existing technique for secure image encoding.

and chaos theory–based encryption. The technique comprises of three modules, namely, optimized transformation module, compression and encryption module, and receiver module. In optimized transformation module, the input image is transformed to wavelet domain with the use of optimal wavelet coefficient–based DWT. The optimality is brought about by the employment of hybrid bat-genetic algorithm. Subsequently, in the compression and encryption module, the compression using SPIHT and chaos-based encryption is carried out. QASK-based modulation is carried out in this section. In receiver module, the received signal from the AWGN channel is demodulated, decrypted, and decompressed to have the estimated image. Before the reception of the signal, the channel estimation is also carried out.

4.4.1   Optimized Transformation Module

This module transforms input images of unmanned vehicles into a wavelet domain through the utilization of optimized DWT. With the aid of the hybrid bat-genetic algorithm, the high-pass wavelength and low-pass filter coefficients are optimized. The block diagram of proposed technique is shown in Figure 4.2.

4.4.1.1   DWT Analysis and Synthesis Filter Bank

The execution of the discreet wavelet transform is shown in Figure 4.3. The input signal in this filter bank is processed by two single-dimensional digital FIR filters. One of them, H0, performs a high-pass filtering procedure and the other a low-pass H1 filtering procedure. A sub-sampling factor of 2 is added to each filtering process. At this stage, the signal is first reconstructed, filtered, and summarized by sampling.

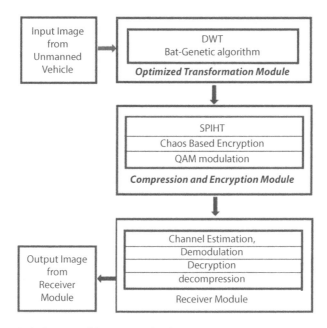

Figure 4.2 Block diagram of the proposed technique.

In order to perform a perfect reconstruction, the G0 and G1 synthesis filters must be adapted unique to the H0 and H1 analytical filters. With the z-transform of the filter bank shown in Figure 4.3, the relationship that these filters must have is not difficult to establish. After analysis, the two sub-bands are as follows:

$$\frac{1}{2}[H_0(z^{1/2})X(z^{1/2})+H_0(-z^{1/2})X(-z^{1/2})] \tag{4.1}$$

$$\frac{1}{2}[H_1(z^{1/2})X(z^{1/2})+H_1(-z^{1/2})X(-z^{1/2})] \tag{4.2}$$

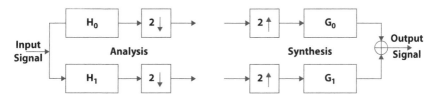

Figure 4.3 DWT analysis and synthesis.

The collective filter bank in z-domain is given by

$$\hat{Z}(z) = \frac{1}{2}[G_0(z)H_0(z) + G_1(z)H_1(z)]X(z) + \frac{1}{2}[G_0(z)H_0(-z) +$$
$$G_1(z)H_1(-z)]X(-z) \qquad (4.3)$$

With a specific end goal to dispose of the issues of aliasing and distortion, the accompanying conditions must be fulfilled:

$$G_0(z) = H_1(-z)$$

$$G_1(z) = H_0(-z)$$

The last filtering equation with the delay term by Smith and Barnwell is displayed as

$$\hat{Z}(z) = \frac{1}{2}z^{-N}[H_0(z)H_0(z^{-1}) + H_0(z)H_0(-z^{-1})]X(z) \qquad (4.4)$$

Figure 4.4 shows the Mallat decomposition of an image reconstruction of a high-pass and ow-pass filter image is shown in Figure 4.5. The progressive implementation of this decomposition into the LL sub-band results in a pyramid decomposition in which sub-images are contrasted with various resolution levels and introductions are shown in Figure 4.6.

There are four frequency bands, namely, Low-Low (LL), Low-High (LH), High-Low (HL), or High-High (HH) after one stage of decompression. The decomposition of the following level is only related to the LL band of the

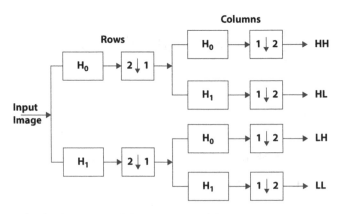

Figure 4.4 Filter bank structure of the 2D DWT analysis.

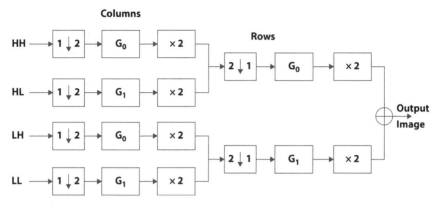

Figure 4.5 Filter bank structure of the 2D DWT synthesis.

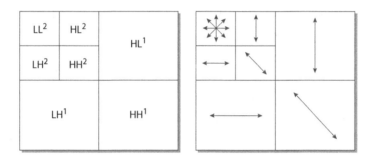

Figure 4.6 Image decomposition. Each sub-band has a natural orientation.

current decomposition point, which structures a recursive decomposition process. A decomposition at N level would therefore eventually involve 3n+1 separate frequency bands, containing 3n high frequency bands and only an LL frequency band.

4.4.1.1.1 Bat-Genetic Hybridization

The hybrid bat-genetic hybridization is formed by incorporating mutation and crossover operators into the bat algorithm. Bats are the only mammals endowed with wings which are also endowed with the advanced capability of echolocation. Insectivores are a big piece of micro-bats. Microbars typically use the so-called echolocation sonar to track the beasts, avoid obstacles, and find their roosting gaps in the darkness. Such bats emit an incredibly loud sound pulse and feel the echo from the objects around. Some of the echolocation characteristics of micro bats assist in the development of several bat-inspired algorithms or bat algorithms. The vital features connected with the bat algorithm are the velocity of the bats, the location of the bats and their loudness. Based on the features, the AI technique derived the bat algorithm for exploration and exploitation issues. Motivated by the characteristics of the bat algorithm, the proposed approach adopts the bat algorithm for optimizing the features listed in the feature list, which comprises countless irrelevant data, which are effectively filtered out by applying the bat algorithm on the feature list.

The virtual bats [9] are the data considered for the optimization process based on the bat algorithm. In the proposed technique, the wavelet coefficient is considered as the virtual bats. Based on the definition of bat algorithm, each virtual bat is assigned a velocity ve_j, a position po_j, and loudness lo_j.

In addition to guessing the difference between food and prey and background obstacle, it is expected that all bats still use the echolocation to sense space. Bats travel at a fixed frequency with velocity, specific wavelengths and loudness to locate a target. They can change the pulse emissions automatically depending on the closeness to their target and can change te pulse emissions rate.

Bat algorithm [9] consists of diverse steps such as initialization, creation of new solutions, local search, and generation of a new solution by flying randomly and finally ascertaining the current best solution. In the initialization process, all the elements are assigned arbitrary values in a specific range demanded by the problem definition. Once all the bats are being initialized, their fitness is estimated by means of a fitness function, which represents a ratio linking the velocity, position, and the loudness. As it is supposed that the virtual bats are moving over the space, it is certain that their velocity and position also will undergo change.

So, the updated velocity and position should be updated for the existing virtual bats. The new updated solutions can be defined as

$$fre_j = fre_{\min} + (fre_{\max} - fre_{\min})\beta$$
$$ve_j^t = ve_j^{t-1} + \left(po_j^t - po_{gb}\right) fre_j$$
$$po_j^t = po_j^{t-1} + po_j^t$$

where t is the time (iteration) in consideration, $\beta \in [0,1]$ is a random vector drawn from a uniform distribution, and po_{gb} is the current global best location (solution) which is located after comparing all the solutions among all the bats. Subsequently, the initial best solutions are found out. For the local search portion, a new solution is generated for each kit locally through a local random walk when a solution is selected from the current best solutions:

$$po_{new} = po_{old} + \Lambda Lo_t$$

where $\Lambda \in [-1,1]$ is a random number, while Lo_t is the average loudness of all the bats at the current time step. According this, all the virtual bats are updated their velocity and position till an end criterion.

The fitness function employed is the PSNR (peak signal–to-noise ratio) value. The best solutions obtained after the bat algorithm is then modified using genetic algorithm operators of crossover and mutation. Genetic algorithms (GAs, in essence), are adaptive heuristic search algorithms that have been extensively researched, tested, and applied to the incredible fields of engineers, based on the emerging principle of natural and genetic selection. Genetic algorithms are part of a broader evolutionary algorithm (EA), generating solutions to problems of optimization using naturally evolving technologies such as descent, mutation, selection, and crossover. Such a genetic algorithm, a chromosomal string population, is created to provide superlative solutions which code candidate solutions to an optimization problem.

In our case, we make use of only crossover and mutation operators from genetic algorithm. Crossover characterizes the convergence cycle between two separate individuals to produce better fitness solutions than every parent. The coefficients of the wavelet in our case are kin. In order to produce a new child, two parents are selected from the present population. A crossover likelihood is used to calculate the number of offspring chromosomes. Roulette wheel selection [20] is used in this relation for selecting the kin. For this operator, a two-point crossover is normally used. Probabilistically, mutations are disrupted to contribute to transition. Crossover cannot add new features since only the same characteristics of a new generation are joined together. It is probable that certain new features will disappear with changes in the chromosome using the mutation operator. Gaussian transformation is used to convert people. On the other hand, mutation is done based on the predicted likelihood of mutation. Table 4.1 shows the best chosen parameters for the hybrid bat-genetic algorithm.

After performing the crossover and mutation, the obtained solutions are compared with the earlier obtained solutions from bat algorithm and the best solutions are selected. The comparison is made by the use of fitness function. Finally, after all the iterations, the best solutions are found out which gives the optimized wavelet coefficients and making use of this coefficients decomposition and reconstruction is performed. The pseudo code of the algorithm is given below:

Table 4.1 The best chosen parameters for the hybrid bat-genetic algorithm.

Parameters	Parameters value
Population size	25
Loudness	0.9
Pulse rate	0.1
Minimum frequency	0
Maximum frequency	2
No. of iterations	100
Crossover	Two point crossover
Crossover rate	0.1
Mutation	Gaussian Mutation
Mutation rate	0.1
Parent selection	Modified Ranking

4.4.2   Compression and Encryption Module

In this module, the transformed image is then compressed using SPIHT, encrypted using chaos and finally QASK modulation so as to make it ready for the transmission.

4.4.2.1   SPIHT

The SPIHT [16] is a good compression method based on the wavelets. It splits the wavelet into Trees of Spatial Orientation. The SPIHT codes a wavelet sub-band by conveying information regarding the significance of a pixel. This is a tool for encoding and decoding an image after wavelet transformation. The algorithm first codes the most appropriate wavelet transforming coefficients and transmits bits so that you can slowly obtain a progressively finished copy of the original image. With the following strong image quality advantages, SPIHT generates a fully embedded coded format, is designed for progressive image transmission, and can be used for lossless compression.

After application of the wavelet transformation, the SPIHT algorithm partitions the decomposed wavelet into two partitions on the basis of the following function:

Pseudo Code of the Proposed Hybrid Bat-Genetic Algorithm
Input: High-pass and low-pass coefficients
Output: Optimized coefficients
Steps

Initialize the bat population with velocity ve_j, a position po_j
Initialize pulse frequency fre, pulse emission pe and loudness lo_j
All for iterations
    {
Update position and velocity using formulas:

$$fre_j = fre_{min} + (fre_{max} - fre_{min})\beta$$

$$ve_j^t = ve_j^{t-1} + (po_j^t - po_{gb}) free_j ; \quad po_j^t = po_j^{t-1} + po_j^t$$

Select initial best solutions
Generate a local solution around the best solution using:

$$po_{new} = po_{old} + \Lambda\, Lo_t$$

Generate new solution by flying randomly
Find the best solutions to form the bat best solutions
Perform cross over and mutation
Find the final best solutions by comparing to earlier bat solution
    }

$$\gamma_p(C) = \begin{cases} 1, \max imum_{(m,n)\in C}\{|q_{m,n}|\} \geq 2^p \\ 0, otherwise \end{cases}$$

Here, $\gamma_p(C)$ is the significance of a set of co-ordinates C and $q_{m,n}$ is the coefficient value at coordinate (i, j). The algorithm consists of two passes of sorting pass and refinement pass. The SPIHT makes use of three lists of LIP (List of Insignificant Pixels), LIS (List of Insignificant Sets), and LSP (List of Significant Pixels).

LIP includes individual coefficients that are less than thresholds in magnitude. LIS contains a set of coefficients of wavelets defined by the structures of the tree and found to be less than the threshold. LSP is a pixel list that is larger magnitude than the threshold.

The sorting pass is done on the three lists above. The maximum number of bits required for the largest coefficient in the tree of spatial orientation is obtained and shown by

$$p_{max} = [\log_2(\max_{m,n}\{|q_{m,n}|\}]$$

The coordinates of the pixels remaining in the LIP are evaluated by the above equation for their value during the sorting process. The result is sent to the source, which passes the relevant source and the sign bit output to the LSP. Sets in the LIS will also be checked and excluded and separated into subsets if found to be highly significant.

Subsets with only one coefficient are removed and split into subsets that are considered to be significant. Subsets which have only one coefficient and have been shown to be important are included in the LSP. The pth MSB of LSP coefficient is the final output of the refinement pass. The decreased LIS value and the sorting and refining passes are again used. Both passes continue until either the optimal rate is reached or the output of all nodes in the LSP is achieved. Lastly, the reconstruction was almost exact because all of the coefficients were fully processed. As the output generated is single bit and the algorithm can be completed at any time, the bit rate can be exactly regulated with the Spitz algorithm.

4.4.2.2   Chaos-Based Encryption

The compressed image is then encrypted using chaos technique [7]. The technique comprises of four processing stages: decomposition, shuffle, diffusion, and combination. The decomposition decomposes the original image, namely, plain-image, to sub-image, namely, component image or components. For each component, the shuffle displaces the positions of the pixels and the diffusion diffuses the values of the pixels which are mentioned ass position and values mask, respectively. The combination combines all the components to final encrypted image.

The component that comes from decomposition is a two-dimension matrix. Each element of this array is an element or pixel in component images. It can stand for any of types such as grey scale, colour component, bit-plane, or the part of the original image. For example, a RGB image before encrypted can be decomposed three components which are called red, green, and blue components.

Shuffle is to mask original organization of the pixels of the image. Specifically, it permutes all the pixels of the image without changing their values. For this purpose, chaotic map is employed which is defined by

$$\begin{bmatrix} x_{m+1} \\ y_{m+1} \end{bmatrix} = \begin{bmatrix} 1 & c \\ d & cd+1 \end{bmatrix} \begin{bmatrix} x_m \\ y_m \end{bmatrix} \mathrm{mod}\, W$$

where c and d are two positive integers and W is the width or height of the image. An image encryption algorithm only has the shuffle, and its security is weak because the cat map is an invertible discrete map without mixing the pixels' values. In other words, the map does not change the statistical properties of the plain-text such as the intensity distribution of the pixels. Diffusion is aimed at overcoming this drawback and logistic map is employed which is defined as

$$x_m + 1 = \alpha x_m (1 - x_m)$$

where α is a parameter, $x_m \in (0,1)$ and $m = 0,1,2,\ldots.$ two logistic maps are used to improve security given by

$$x_{m+1}^{odd} = \alpha\, x_m^{odd} \left(1 - x_m^{odd}\right); x_{m+1}^{even} = \alpha\, x_m^{even} \left(1 - x_m^{even}\right)$$

The chaotic sequence is digitized by amplifying it with a proper scaling and sampling. The output of encryption can be generated by the formula:

$$En(j) = t(j) \oplus pi(j) \oplus En(j-1)$$

where $\oplus$ is bitwise OR, $pi(j)$ is the currently operated pixel, and $En(j-1)$ is the previously output cipher-pixel, the initial condition $En(0)$ is equal to $t(0) \oplus pi(0)$.

After the completion, we have the cipher component image. Subsequently, the combination is carried out. The combination is carried out by placing entire cipher component image to a cipher image in their original order. Security is enhanced by use of permutation of the cipher component images sequence.

Let the input component image sequence be represented by $\{1,2,3,\ldots,M\}$ and then its permuted output $\{PER_1\ PER_2, PER_3,\ldots,PER_M\}$ is given by

$$PER_i = ((Fc(j) + \rho).i) \mathrm{mod} Fc(j + 1)$$

Here, $Fc(j)$ is the Fibonacci sequence, j is the index location, and ρ is minimal integer constant. Hence, the compressed image is encrypted and is subsequently modulated QASK modulation.

4.5 Results and Discussion

In this section, results obtained for our proposed topics are discussed. In Section 4.5.1, experimental setup and the evaluation metrics employed are discussed. The simulation results obtained are given in Section 4.5.2, and comparative analysis is made in Section 4.5.3.

4.5.1 Experimental Setup and Evaluation Metrics

The technique is implemented in MATLAB on a system having 8 GB RAM and 3.2 GHz Intel i-7 processor. The setup for QASK modulation is shown below in Table 4.2.

Figure 4.7 shows frame used for QASK modulation. There are 256 number of sub-channels among which 224 are data sub-channels and 32 are pilot channels. Copies of first 64 bits of data are used as guard bits to avoid the interference. A 1 bit of pilot is added after every data bits.

The metrics used to evaluate the performance of the system include PSNR [17, 22] and mean squared error (MSE) between the original image and the

Table 4.2 QASK modulation setup.

Total Number of Sub-Channels	256
Total Number of Data Sub-Channels	224
Total Number of Pilots	32
Pilot Position Interval	8
Guard Interval Length	64

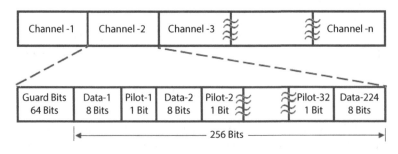

Figure 4.7 QASK data frame.

decompressed image. MSE gives the average of the squares of the errors which is the difference between the original and what is estimated. PSNR is described as the ratio of the maximum possible power of the signal (original data) to the noise power (error introduced by compression) that affects the fidelity of the signal. PSNR is employed as evaluation metrics in wide range of applications and is frequently used in compression techniques [23]. A lower esteem for MSE implies lesser error and higher estimation of PSNR is great as it means the degree of sign to commotion is higher PSNR can be defined as

$$PSNR = 10 \log_{10} \frac{P_{max}^2}{MSE}$$

where P_{max} is the maximum intensity is the image and E is the MSE of the signal and is defined as

$$MSE = \frac{1}{MN} \sum_{i=0}^{M-1} \sum_{j=0}^{N-1} [I(m,n) - I'(m,n)]$$

Other parameters that we have considered are least absolute difference (LAD) and L2 norm between the original image and the decompressed image. Norm [18, 19] measures indisputably the separation between the pixels of the original and the corrected image. LAD is also called least absolute errors (LAE) or L1-norm. It is fundamentally, minimizing the sum of the absolute difference between the input image I(m, n) and the evaluated output image I'(m, n).

Formula for the LAD or L1 norm is

$$LAD = \sum_{i=0}^{M-1} \sum_{j=o}^{N-1} abs(I(m,n) - I'(m,n))$$

L1 norm is very basic among the norm gang. It has numerous name and numerous forms among different fields, to be specific Manhattan norm is its moniker. In the event that the L1 norm is figured for a distinction between two vectors or matrices, so it is called LAD.

L2 norm is also called least squares. It is essentially minimizing the entirety of the square of the differences between the input image I (m, n) and the output image I'(m, n)

$$L2\,\text{Norm} = \sum_{i=0}^{M-1} \sum_{j=o}^{N-1} (I(m,n) - I'(m,n))^2$$

L2 norm is exceptional as a Euclidean norm that is used as a basis for calculating a difference in vectors. The MSE calculation, which is used to estimate a similarity, a consistency, or a correlation between two signals or images, is the most popular method in the field of signal processing. The test images used are shown in Figure 4.8 and all other test images mentioned in the results are standard test images.

Compression ratio and compression rate are the two parameters used here for evaluating the performance of image compression. Among these, compression ratio is a measure to quantify the execution of an image compression system. It is nothing but the redundancy of data between the original image (OI) and compressed image (CI) and is given by the following equation:

$$Compression\,Ratio\,(CR) = \frac{Number\,of\,bits\,in\,the\,OI}{Number\,of\,bits\,in\,the\,CI}$$

The compression ratio CR is connected to the compression rate that is utilized to estimate the normal number of bits required to signify a single pixel. It is characterized by the following equation:

$$Compression\,Rate = \frac{Number\,of\,bits\,per\,pixel\,in\,the\,OI}{CR}$$

Its units are bits/pixel and bits/second.

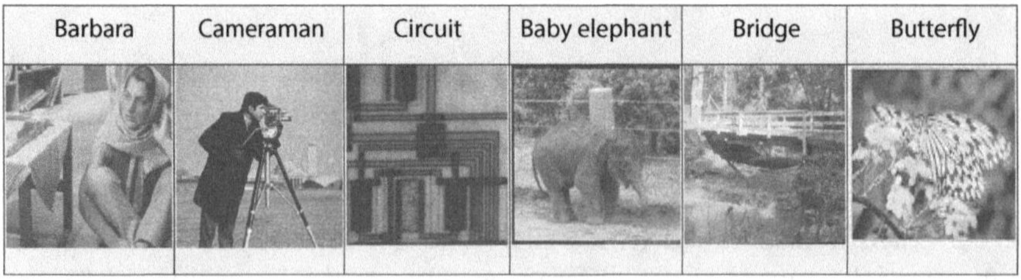

Barbara	Cameraman	Circuit	Baby elephant	Bridge	Butterfly

Figure 4.8 Input images.

4.5.2   Simulation Results

4.5.2.1   *Performance Analysis of the Novel Filter KARELET*

After successful iteration of hybrid bat-genetic algorithm, the coefficients for four optimum FIR filters are obtained, where Lo_D and Hi_D are the low-pass and high-pass decomposition filters and the low-pass and high-pass reconstruction filters are denoted as Lo_R and Hi_R, respectively. We have assigned a name "KARELET" for the novel filter bank.

The optimal filter coefficients for the proposed KARELET filter are given Table 4.3 and are plotted in Figure 4.9.

Table 4.4 shows the performance analysis of the novel filter based on energy and correlation coefficient. Ea, Eh, Ev, and Ed are the percentage of energy retained in the approximation, horizontal, vertical, and diagonal components, respectively. The sum of energy is 100 in all cases that mean there is no any loss of energy due to decomposition. Also the correlation coefficient between original image and reconstructed image is unity that means there is no any difference between these two.

Table 4.3 Filter coefficients of the proposed filter bank "KARELET".

Lo_D (H_1)	Hi_D (H_0)	Lo_R (G_1)	Hi_R (G_0)
0.00043141	0.00011404	−0.00011404	0.00043141
0.037562	−0.063221	−0.063221	−0.037562
−0.029353	0.037165	−0.037165	−0.029353
−0.10699	0.41179	0.41179	0.10699
0.3818	−0.77856	0.77856	0.3818
0.85906	0.4246	0.4246	−0.85906
0.37253	0.032395	−0.032395	0.37253
−0.11395	−0.066452	−0.066452	0.11395
−0.022964	0.0013942	−0.0013942	−0.022964
0.036085	3.7704e-06	3.7704e-06	−0.036085

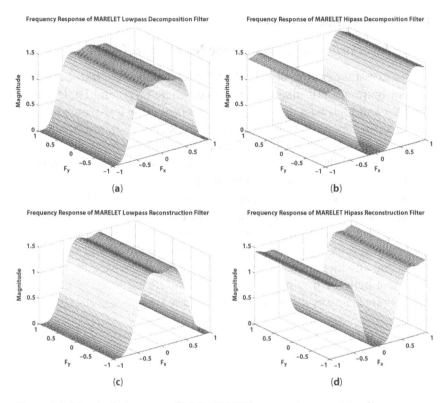

Figure 4.9 Magnitude Response of (a) KARELET low-pass decomposition filter, (b) KARELET high-pass decomposition filter, (c) KARELET low-pass reconstruction filter, and (d) KARELET high-pass reconstruction filter.

4.5.3   Result Analysis Proposed System

Simulation results obtained for our proposed technique as well as for the exiting standard techniques such as for Haar, Db4, Bior4.4, RBior4.4, Coif4, and Sym4 are shown in Figure 4.10. Figure 4.11 gives the corresponding decompressed image obtained by various techniques for three standard images.

In this section, the results obtained for the proposed technique is given. The evaluation metrics employed are PSNR and MSE. The comparison is also made with respect to the Bior4.4, RBior4.4, and Db4, Haar, Sym4, and Coif4.

Table 4.4 Properties of KARELET filters.

Sl. no.	Information	Low-pass decomposition filter	High-pass decomposition filter	Low-pass reconstruction filter	High-pass reconstruction filter
1	Filter Length	10	10	10	10
2	Filter Order	9	9	9	9
3	Stable	Yes	Yes	Yes	Yes

Figure 4.10 Original image before decomposition and reconstruction.

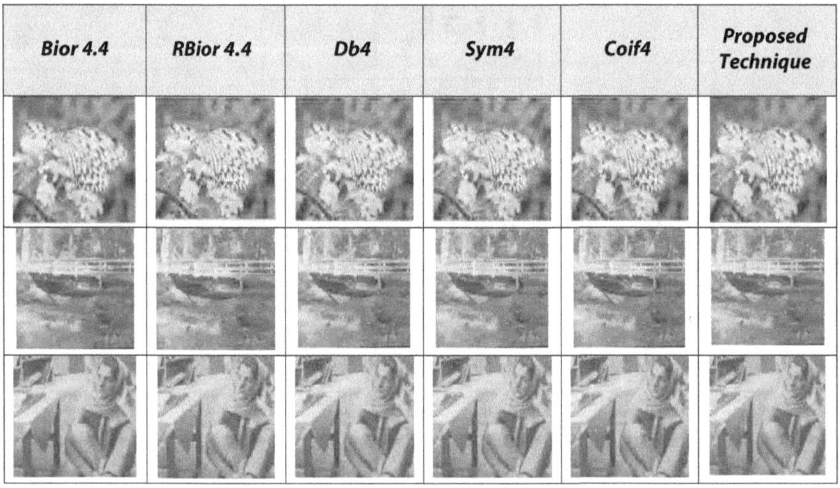

Bior 4.4	RBior 4.4	Db4	Sym4	Coif4	Proposed Technique

Figure 4.11 Simulation results.

From Table 4.5 and Figures 4.12 to 4.14, we can infer that the obtained results for the proposed technique were better than existing techniques. Among existing techniques, Bior4.4 gave the best results, followed by Db4 and RBior.

Table 4.5 Percentage of energy retained after KARELET decomposition and coefficient of correlation.

Sl. no.	Image	Ea	Eh	Ev	Ed	Sum of percentage of energy	Correlation coefficient b/w original and reconstructed images
1	Barbara	99.4275	0.1351	0.2756	0.1618	100	1.00
2	Cameraman	99.3776	0.1917	0.3671	0.0636	100	1.00
3	Bridge	98.8672	0.5932	0.3947	0.1449	100	1.00
4	Butterfly	97.6677	1.0761	0.9347	0.3215	100	1.00
5	Circuit	99.9031	0.0371	0.0544	0.0054	100	1.00
6	Baby Elephant	98.0348	1.0469	0.7694	0.1489	100	1.00

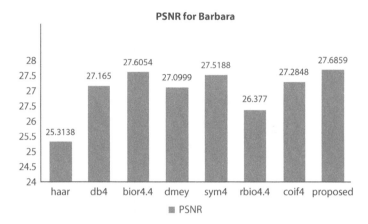

Figure 4.12 PSNR comparison for different wavelets for Barbara.

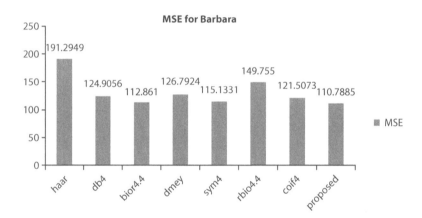

Figure 4.13 MSE comparison for different wavelets for Barbara.

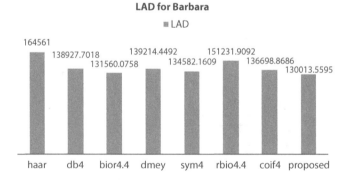

Figure 4.14 LAD comparison for different wavelets for Barbara.

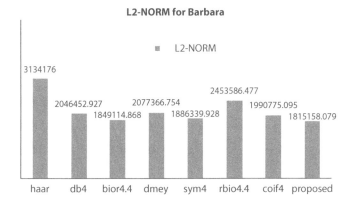

Figure 4.15 L2 norm comparison for different wavelets for Barbara.

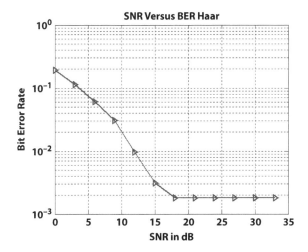

Figure 4.16 SNR vs. BER plot while using Haar.

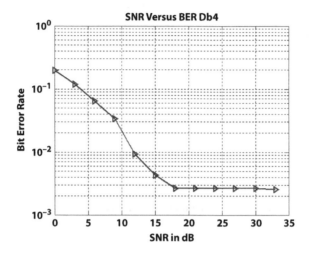

Figure 4.17 SNR vs. BER plot while using Db4.

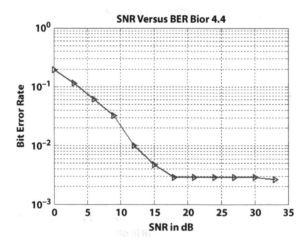

Figure 4.18 SNR vs. BER plot while using Bior4.4.

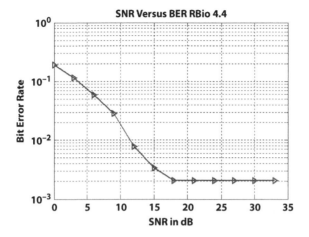

Figure 4.19 SNR vs. BER plot while using RBio4.4.

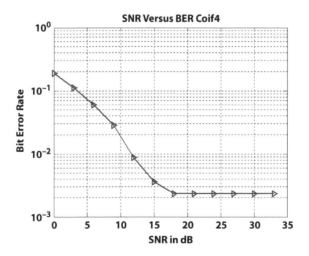

Figure 4.20 SNR vs. BER plot while using Coiflet 4.

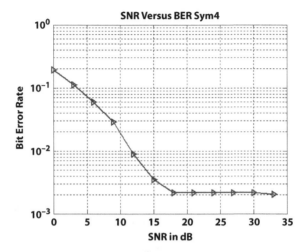

Figure 4.21 SNR vs. BER plot while using Symlet 4.

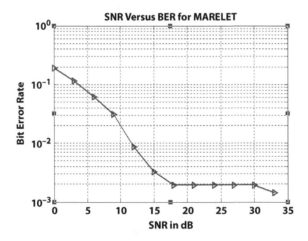

Figure 4.22 SNR vs. BER plot while using KARELET.

Table 4.6 Results obtained.

S. no.	Image	Wavelet filter name	Comp. rate	MSE	PSNR	LAD	L2-NORM
1	Barbara	Haar	0.5	191.2949	25.3138	164561	3134176
		Db4	0.5	124.9056	27.165	138927.7	2046453
		Bior4.4	0.5	112.861	27.6054	131560.1	1849115
		RBio4.4	0.5	149.755	26.377	151231.9	2453586
		Sym4	0.5	126.7924	27.0999	139214.4	2077367
		Coif4	0.5	121.5073	27.2848	136698.9	1990775
		KARELET	**0.5**	**110.7885**	**27.6859**	**130013.6**	**1815158**

(Continued)

Table 4.6 Results obtained. (*Continued*)

S. no.	Image	Wavelet filter name	Comp. rate	MSE	PSNR	LAD	L2-NORM
2	Cameraman	Haar	0.5	105.9313	27.8806	106606	1735579
		Db4	0.5	106.626	27.8522	116327.7	1746960
		Bior4.4	0.5	88.5417	28.6593	106081.7	1450667
		RBio4.4	0.5	120.188	27.3322	122600.9	1969161
		Sym4	0.5	99.9596	28.1326	112896.1	1637737
		Coif4	0.5	107.4723	27.8178	118026.9	1760826
		KARELET	**0.5**	**88.1432**	**28.6789**	**106600.4**	**1444138**

(*Continued*)

Table 4.6 Results obtained. (*Continued*)

S. no.	Image	Wavelet filter name	Comp. rate	MSE	PSNR	LAD	L2-NORM
3	Circuit	Haar	0.5	90.8389	28.5481	121137	1488304
		Db4	0.5	78.5924	29.177	115745.9	1287657
		Bior4.4	0.5	68.1202	29.798	105547.8	1116081
		RBio4.4	0.5	84.1374	28.8809	119170.8	1378507
		Sym4	0.5	75.6062	29.3452	112795.8	1238732
		Coif4	0.5	75.7769	29.3354	112936.5	1241528
		KARELET	**0.5**	**67.9052**	**29.8118**	**104834.3**	**1112558**

(*Continued*)

Table 4.6 Results obtained. (*Continued*)

S. no.	Image	Wavelet filter name	Comp. rate	MSE	PSNR	LAD	L2-NORM
4	Baby elephent	Haar	0.5	206.412	24.9835	177684	3381854
		Db4	0.5	166.4256	25.9186	160279.7	2726717
		Bior4.4	0.5	165.1617	25.9517	159724.1	2706009
		RBio4.4	0.5	181.0287	25.5533	167150.8	2965973
		Sym4	0.5	160.946	26.064	158198.3	2636939
		Coif4	0.5	159.176	26.112	157532.4	2607940
		KARELET	**0.5**	**164.2229**	**25.9765**	**159462.9**	**2690628**

(*Continued*)

Table 4.6 Results obtained. (*Continued*)

S. no.	Image	Wavelet filter name	Comp. rate	MSE	PSNR	LAD	L2-NORM
5	Bridge	Haar	0.5	226.8196	24.574	190279	3716213
		Db4	0.5	193.3353	25.2677	176937.6	3167606
		Bior4.4	0.5	194.0487	25.2517	175604.2	3179295
		RBio4.4	0.5	225.9994	24.5897	190355	3702774
		Sym4	0.5	195.4451	25.2206	177278	3202172
		Coif4	0.5	193.1527	25.2737	176856.8	3163211
		KARELET	**0.5**	**193.0671**	**25.2718**	**175394.7**	**3164614**

(*Continued*)

Table 4.6 Results obtained. (*Continued*)

S. no.	Image	Wavelet filter name	Comp. rate	MSE	PSNR	LAD	L2-NORM
6	Butterfly	Haar	0.5	503.4828	21.111	277532	8249062
		Db4	0.5	290.6425	23.4972	210438.4	4761886
		Bior4.4	0.5	260.0679	23.9799	196477.1	4260953
		RBio4.4	0.5	344.6692	22.7568	227808	5647060
		Sym4	0.5	267.7359	23.8537	200808.5	4386585
		Coif4	0.5	263.0519	23.9304	198081.8	4309842
		KARELET	**0.5**	**258.9234**	**23.9991**	**195859.7**	**4242201**

(*Continued*)

Table 4.6 Results obtained. (*Continued*)

S. no.	Image	Wavelet filter name	Comp. rate	MSE	PSNR	LAD	L2-NORM
7	Concordorthophoto	Haar	0.5	248.4949	24.1776	199956.5	4071341
		Db4	0.5	208.7023	24.9355	184403.5	3419378
		Bior4.4	0.5	200.852	25.102	180911.5	3290760
		Coif4	0.5	200.6672	25.106	182072.6	3287732
		Sym4	0.5	206.788	24.9756	183865.1	3388014
		RBio4.4	0.5	229.812	24.5171	194050.1	3765240
		KARELET	**0.5**	**198.3677**	**25.1561**	**179637.3**	**3250056**

(*Continued*)

Table 4.6 Results obtained. (*Continued*)

S. no.	Image	Wavelet filter name	Comp. rate	MSE	PSNR	LAD	L2-NORM
8	Westconcordorthophoto	Haar	0.5	561.9664	20.6337	299013	9207257
		Db4	0.5	402.1393	22.087	256605.8	6588651
		Bior4.4	0.5	385.9956	22.265	251490.6	6324152
		Coif4	0.5	393.1115	22.1856	255087.5	6440738
		Sym4	0.5	405.8956	22.0467	258374.3	6650193
		RBio4.4	0.5	481.8915	21.3013	281402.9	7895310
		KARELET	**0.5**	**383.7261**	**22.2906**	**250733.9**	**6286969**

(*Continued*)

Table 4.6 Results obtained. (*Continued*)

S. no.	Image	Wavelet filter name	Comp. rate	MSE	PSNR	LAD	L2-NORM
9	Gantrycrane	Haar	0.5	103.7931	27.9691	106011	1700546
		Db4	0.5	97.3013	28.2496	116259.6	1594184
		Bior4.4	0.5	88.7796	28.6477	110084.8	1454565
		Coif4	0.5	92.496	28.4696	112789.4	1515454
		Sym4	0.5	88.0339	28.6843	107858.6	1442348
		RBio4.4	0.5	119.8065	27.346	126730.5	1962910
		KARELET	**0.5**	**87.1297**	**28.7291**	**108859.2**	**1427532**

(*Continued*)

Table 4.6 Results obtained. (Continued)

S. no.	Image	Wavelet filter name	Comp. rate	MSE	PSNR	LAD	L2-NORM
10	Greens	Haar	0.5	553.8847	20.6966	300845	9074847
		Db4	0.5	458.37	21.5186	275332.4	7509934
		Bior4.4	0.5	443.0537	21.6662	270513.2	7258993
		Coif4	0.5	452.5143	21.5745	273223.5	7413994
		Sym4	0.5	460.6685	21.4969	276056.2	7547593
		RBio4.4	0.5	529.9332	20.8886	296403.8	8682425
		KARELET	**0.5**	**438.2528**	**21.7136**	**268753.7**	**7180334**

(Continued)

Table 4.6 Results obtained. (*Continued*)

S. no.	Image	Wavelet filter name	Comp. rate	MSE	PSNR	LAD	L2-NORM
11	Hestain	Haar	0.5	220.3376	24.6999	184698	3610012
		Db4	0.5	153.7077	26.2638	157956.8	2518346
		Bior4.4	0.5	143.7219	26.5556	153399.9	2354739
		Coif4	0.5	144.775	26.5239	153360.9	2371993
		Sym4	0.5	150.6577	26.3509	156956.1	2468375
		RBio4.4	0.5	177.3966	25.6414	168791.4	2906466
		KARELET	**0.5**	**143.4323**	**26.5643**	**153192.1**	**2349996**

(*Continued*)

Table 4.6 Results obtained. (*Continued*)

S. no.	Image	Wavelet filter name	Comp. rate	MSE	PSNR	LAD	L2-NORM
12	M83	Haar	0.5	115.0874	27.5205	128688.3	1885592
		Db4	0.5	102.398	28.0279	122929.4	1677689
		Bior4.4	0.5	100.0386	28.1291	120880.5	1639032
		Coif4	0.5	102.0988	28.0406	122047.2	1672787
		Sym4	0.5	102.0954	28.0407	122276.1	1672731
		RBio4.4	0.5	109.185	27.7492	127131.3	1788888
		KARELET	**0.5**	**99.6785**	**28.1448**	**120729.7**	**1633133**

(*Continued*)

Table 4.6 Results obtained. (*Continued*)

S. no.	Image	Wavelet filter name	Comp. rate	MSE	PSNR	LAD	L2-NORM
13	Office4	Haar	0.5	133.1926	26.886	135547	2182227
		Db4	0.5	136.4603	26.7807	142149.3	2235766
		Bior4.4	0.5	120.0181	27.3383	132824.9	1966377
		Coif4	0.5	126.7976	27.0997	136894.8	2077453
		Sym4	0.5	126.974	27.0937	136031.8	2080342
		RBio4.4	0.5	146.7039	26.4664	146122.7	2403596
		KARELET	**0.5**	**119.1085**	**27.3714**	**131179.2**	**1951473**

(Continued)

Table 4.6 Results obtained. (*Continued*)

S. no.	Image	Wavelet filter name	Comp. rate	MSE	PSNR	LAD	L2-NORM
14	Rise	Haar	0.5	251.5712	24.1242	175392.5	4121742
		Db4	0.5	149.6937	26.3788	153440.5	2452582
		Bior4.4	0.5	139.075	26.6983	149081.4	2278605
		Coif4	0.5	137.7485	26.7399	149558.3	2256871
		Sym4	0.5	149.9276	26.372	153538.5	2456413
		RBio4.4	0.5	182.7449	25.5123	170549.2	2994093
		KARELET	**0.5**	**136.3608**	**26.7839**	**146744.5**	**2234136**

(*Continued*)

Table 4.6 Results obtained. (*Continued*)

S. no.	Image	Wavelet filter name	Comp. rate	MSE	PSNR	LAD	L2-NORM
15	Tire	Haar	0.5	157.4072	26.1606	136907.5	2578959
		Db4	0.5	93.994	28.3998	115966.5	1539998
		Bior4.4	0.5	81.8739	28.9993	110084.2	1341423
		Coif4	0.5	91.8776	28.4987	117728.8	1505323
		Sym4	0.5	98.3824	28.2016	119169.4	1611897
		RBio4.4	0.5	117.287	27.4383	127990.9	1921630
		KARELET	**0.5**	**80.8633**	**29.0533**	**108817.8**	**1324865**

(*Continued*)

Table 4.6 Results obtained. (*Continued*)

S. no.	Image	Wavelet filter name	Comp. rate	MSE	PSNR	LAD	L2-NORM
16	Toysnoflash	Haar	0.5	134.3838	26.8473	131465	2201745
		Db4	0.5	107.4553	27.8185	126821.5	1760548
		Bior4.4	0.5	96.4495	28.2878	120690.6	1580228
		Coif4	0.5	104.6544	27.9332	125740.5	1714658
		Sym4	0.5	105.444	27.9006	124969.8	1727594
		RBio4.4	0.5	127.8363	27.0643	137278.6	2094469
		KARELET	**0.5**	**95.3214**	**28.3389**	**120247.2**	**1561745**

(*Continued*)

Table 4.6 Results obtained. (*Continued*)

S. no.	Image	Wavelet filter name	Comp. rate	MSE	PSNR	LAD	L2-NORM
17	Trees	Haar	0.5	137.9124	26.7348	133547	2259557
		Db4	0.5	91.4361	28.5196	118067	1498088
		Bior4.4	0.5	83.5399	28.9119	112058.1	1368717
		Coif4	0.5	85.3223	28.8202	114804	1397920
		Sym4	0.5	87.5801	28.7068	115007	1434912
		RBio4.4	0.5	112.0339	27.6373	128019.4	1835564
		KARELET	**0.5**	**82.2656**	**28.9786**	**110809.8**	**1347840**

Here, the BER value is calculated and plotted for SNR values of 0 to 35 db. Compared to Figures 4.15 to 4.20, we can see that in Figure 4.21, the bit error rate (BER) value starts decreasing when the signal-to-noise ratio (SNR) reaches at 30 db and its increases. Figure 4.22 shows the PNSR vs. iteration curve for the proposed hybrid bat-genetic algorithm while inputting the trained image. In Table 4.6, it is observed that the algorithm gives the highest PSNR value as increases with the iteration and reaches saturation when iteration count reaches more than 30. The maximum PSNR reached is 25.751.

4.6   Conclusion

Optimal wavelet filter–based compression employing hybrid genetic bat algorithm is proposed in this paper. The technique makes use of optimized DWT and chaos theory–based encryption and QASK modulation. The technique consists of three modules, namely, optimized transformation module, compression and encryption module, and receiver module. The technique is evaluated using PSNR, MSE, LAD and L2 norm values, and BER. The proposed technique is compared with Haar, *Daubechies* 4, Biorthogonal 4.4, Coiflet 4, Symlet 4, and Reverse Biorthogonal 4.4. The simulation results show that the proposed technique has obtained better evaluation metric values than all other existing wavelet-based systems in the case of all these parameters. Further, the performance in decomposition and reconstruction using the proposed filter named KARELET in terms of energy retained in sub-bands and coefficient of correlation. The percentage of sum of energy retained in all sub-bands in all cases is 100%, and thus, there is no loss in decomposition. The coefficient of correlation between the reconstructed images is unity in all cases. This shows that the proposed filter gives perfect decomposition and reconstruction. From all these results, we can infer that the proposed technique shows better performance when compared to existing techniques [21].

Figure 4.23 shows the iteration curve obtained for the hybrid bat-genetic algorithm. In this curve, the PSNR is taken in the X-axis and number of iteration is taken in the Y-axis.

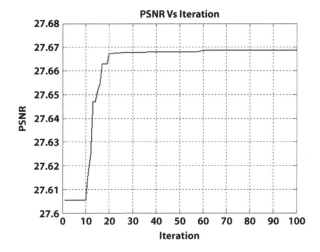

Figure 4.23 PSNR vs. iteration curve (for proposed hybrid algorithm on train image).

References

1. Usevitch, B.E., A tutorial on modern lossy wavelet image compression: 365 Fundations of JPEG 2000. *IEEE Signal Process. Mag.*, 18, 5, 22–35, 2001.
2. Gargour, C., Gabrea, M., Ramanchandran, V., Lina, J.M., A short intro-to wavelets and their applications. *IEEE Circuits Syst. Mag.*, 9, 2, 57–68, 2009.
3. Ansari, and Anan, Recent Trends in Image Compression and Its Application in Telemedicine and Teleconsultation. *National Systems Conference*, pp. 59–64, 2008.
4. Naor, M. and Shamir, A., Visual cryptography, in: *Advances in Cryptology, Eurpocrypt'94, Lecture Notes in Computer Science*, vol. 950, Springer, Germany, pp. 1–12, 1995.
5. Grgic, S., Grgic, M., Zovko-Cihlar, B., Performance Analysis of Image Compression Using Wavelets. *IEEE Trans. Ind. Electron.*, 48, 3, 682–695, June 2001.
6. Loganathan, and Kumaraswamy, Medical Image Compression Using Biorthogonal Spline Wavelet with Different Decomposition. *Int. J. Comput. Sci. Eng.*, 02, 09, 3003–3006, 2010.
7. Al-Maadeed, S., Al-Ali, A., Abdalla, T., A New Chaos-Based Image-Encryption and Compression Algorithm. *J. Electr. Comput. Eng.*, 2012, 11, 179693, 2012.
8. Daamouche, A., Hamami, L., Alajlan, N., Melgani, F., A wavelet optimization approach for ECG signal classification. *Biomed. Signal Process. Control*, 7, 4, 342–349, July 2012.
9. Yang, X.S., A New Metaheuristic Bat-Inspired Algorithm, in: *Nature Inspired Cooperative Strategies for Optimization (NISCO 2010)*, vol. 284,

J.R. Gonzalez and *et al.* (Eds.), pp. 65–74, Studies in Computational Intelligence, Springer, Berlin, 2010.

10.   Aljazaery, I.A., Encryption of Images and Signals Using Wavelet Transform and Permutation Algorithm. *Orient. J. Comp. Sci. Technol.*, 7, 1, 125–137, 2014.

11.   Al-Maadeed, S., Al-Ali, A., Abdalla, T., A New Chaos-Based Image-Encryption andCompression Algorithm. *J. Electr. Comput. Eng.*, 2012, 179693, 1–11, 2012.

12.   Arthur, M., Barbados, R.A.-T., Davis, D., Rapid Processing of Unmanned Aerial Vehicles Imagery for Disaster Management. *FIG Working Week*, pp. 1–10, 2012.

13.   Boudjelaba, K., Prisme Lab., Polytech'Orleans, Orleans, France, Ros, F., Chikouche, D., Adaptive genetic algorithm-based approach to improve the synthesis of two-dimensional finite impulse response filters. *IET Signal Proc.*, 8, 5, 429–446, July 2014.

14.   Yang, X.-S. and He, X., Bat algorithm: literature review and applications. *Int. J. Bio-Inspir. Com.*, 5, 3, 141–149, 2013.

15.   Vasundhara, Mandal, D., Ghoshal, S.P., Kar, R., Digital FIR Filter Design Using Hybrid Random Particle Swarm Optimization with Differential Evolution. *Int. J. Comput. Intell. Syst.*, Taylor & Francis, 6, 5, 911–927, September, 2013.

16.   Said, A. and Pearlman, W.A., A new fast and efficient image codec based on set partitioning in hierarchical trees. *IEEE Trans. Circuits Syst. Video Technol.*, 6, 3, 243–250, 1996.

17.   Huynh-Thu, Q. and Ghanbari, M., Scope of validity of PSNR in image/video quality assessment. *Electron. Lett.*, 44, 13, 800–801, 2008.

18.   Zibulevsky, M. and Elad, M., L1-L2 Optimization in Signal and Image Processing. *IEEE Signal Process. Mag.*, 27, 3, 76–88, 2010.

19.   Fu, H., Ng, M.K., Nikolova, M., Barlow, J., Ching, W.-k., Fast Algorithms for l1 Norm/Mixed l1 and l2 Norms for Image Restoration, in: *Lecture Notes in Computer Science*, vol. 3483, pp. 843–851, Springer, Berlin, Heidelberg, 2005.

20.   Zhang, L., Chang, H., Xu, R., Equal-Width Partitioning Roulette Wheel Selection in Genetic Algorithm. *Proceedings of Conference on Technologies and Applications of Artificial Intelligence (TAAI)*, pp. 62–67, Nov. 2012.

21.   Friedenberg, H. and Naik, S., Hitless Space Diversity STL Enables IP+Audio in Narrow STL Bands. *National Association of Broadcasters Annual Convention*, vol. 1, 2005.

22.   Vitthaladevuni, P.K. and Alouini, M.-S., A Recursive Algorithm for the Exact BER Computation of Generalized Hierarchical QAM Constellations. *IEEE Trans. Inf. Theory*, 49, 1, 297–307, January 2003.

23.   Cherifi, M., Lahdir, M., Ameur, S., Sorted run length coding-application to Meteosat image compression. *Proceedings of the 2014 International Conference on Environmental Engineering and Computer Application (ICEECA*, Taylor & Francis Group, pp. 159–163, 2014.

5

A Swarm Robot for Harvesting a Paddy Field

N. Pooranam[1*] and T. Vignesh[2†]

[1]Department of Computer Science and Engineering, Sri Krishna College of Engineering and Technology, Coimbatore, India
[2]Department of Mechatronics Engineering, Sri Krishna College of Engineering and Technology, Coimbatore, India

Abstract

Indian farmers lead their life by cultivating the crops and fresh vegetables. After the crop cultivation, they yield money in selling it in a profitable way. The main process in crop cultivation is harvesting which is a human behavior to cultivate the product. This chapter addresses to improve the human behavior in a fine way that the PSO swarm intelligent algorithm helps in searching and optimizing the process. The harvesting process has several steps; the first is reaping (cutting), threshing (separating process), and cleaning (removing non grain material from grains). The PSO algorithm will find the positions of all robots to start harvesting and crusted based PSO will help in improving the optimization. As a result, the aim of the episode is to give a summary on harvesting the crop in agriculture field; the main process is orienting the paddy. The simple mathematical operation optimizes the process of harvesting.

Keywords: Harvesting, PSO algorithm, crop cultivation, paddy field

5.1 Introduction

The swarm intelligence (SI) will position themselves in the environment; they are going to do the task or process. The swarm-based optimization is a nature-inspired, popular algorithm which has some robust solution in the branch of science of Artificial Intelligence with a collative behavior on the social swarm algorithm. The existing process is on generating the

---

*Corresponding author: pooranamn@skcet.ac.in
†Corresponding author: vignesht@skcet.ac.in

S. Balamurugan, Anupriya Jain, Sachin Sharma, Dinesh Goyal, Sonia Duggal and Seema Sharma (eds.) *Nature-Inspired Algorithms Applications*, (137–156) © 2022 Scrivener Publishing LLC

distributed process of swarm robot that will help in optimizing single task. To do this, the PSO algorithms have a fitness evaluation to find the appropriate position of the robot and they have two main components: they are cohesion and separation, which is an important move in the SI. Moreover, the data captured in the process of harvesting will be collected in single process. The process will be grouped in a cluster so that the unused or unwanted cluster will be discarded in an efficient way.

A related case study is examined with some of the real time applications which help researches in finding a best way to implement their ideas in their domain. This chapter will discuss more about PSO algorithm implemented in different domain knowledge and different use cases.

5.1.1   Working Principle of Particle Swarm Optimization

PSO has many similar characteristics like genetic algorithms but it has no evolution operators like crossover and mutation.

The optimization technique will calculate candidate solution known as population elements where the solution space has many dimensions. Elements will have some action inside the solution space through which speed of each element will be generated for all the dimensions. The location of each element will be altered by adding some momentum value to present location. The improved positions can direct the actions of the swarm in a fine way. The progression is continued by repeatedly changing the solution and optimal outcome can be reached [1].

The major highlight of the PSO is the behavioral approach of each element through the communicational channel individually or with whole swarm, which leads to overall action of the swarm toward majority of area to distinguish the search space.

5.1.2   First Case Study on Birds Fly

The PSO algorithm is implemented in bird's dataset to find the different moment and new positions in their flying hobby. The dataset is taken from the known forum in which the prediction and classification to analyze the data, and some steps are followed in predicting the moves of the birds the PSO algorithm helps in estimating the overall throughput. Figure 5.1 explains more on the process of dataset and analysis.

5.1.3   Operational Moves on Birds Dataset

The implementation is done on dataset, simulated using data analytics tools and techniques which find it easier in measuring each moves of the

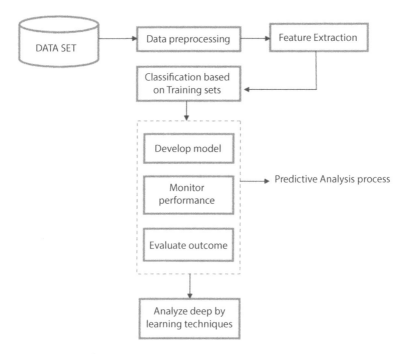

Figure 5.1 Process of dataset.

object; here, the object describes about the birds. The data is first trained using some basic concept like distance measure [4]. Then, test data is implemented using PSO algorithm through collective object monitoring. Each process in the PSO will focus on the evaluation function where the fitness value is estimated.

Figure 5.2 describes each row and column data estimates the overall details about individual object. The overall measure is calculated using fitness function through PSO algorithm. This is executed and a graphical representation finds the best and worst move by each object. New move is measured and the current move is updated as old move; the compassion is made on each best move.

The classical behavior of data is made use of processing unit. Data mining and data warehousing comes into picture for this type of application. Preprocessing data is important in finding the duplicated and will increase the performance measure of individual column data. Figure 5.3 shows the best move of bird to reach their designation.

The figure describes that most of the birds' moves follow similar path though they reach same place and their output measure differs. The classification is made to find the similar items; here, it defines based on PSO algorithm to estimate the measure of overall result of each object. Velocity

	file_id	genus	species	english_cname	who_provided_recording	country
1	132608	Acanthis	flammea	Common Redpoll	Jarek Matusiak	Poland
2	132611	Acanthis	flammea	Common Redpoll	Jarek Matusiak	Poland
3	35068	Acanthis	flammea	Common Redpoll	Sander Bot	Netherlands
4	82715	Acrocephalus	palustris	Marsh Warbler	Dougie Preston	United Kingdom
5	64685	Acrocephalus	palustris	Marsh Warbler	Dougie Preston	United Kingdom
6	64686	Acrocephalus	palustris	Marsh Warbler	Dougie Preston	United Kingdom
7	120664	Acrocephalus	schoenobaenus	Sedge Warbler	david m	United Kingdom
8	120666	Acrocephalus	schoenobaenus	Sedge Warbler	david m	United Kingdom
9	76767	Acrocephalus	schoenobaenus	Sedge Warbler	Richard Dunn	United Kingdom
10	124052	Acrocephalus	scirpaceus	Eurasian Reed Warbler	david m	United Kingdom
11	124053	Acrocephalus	scirpaceus	Eurasian Reed Warbler	david m	United Kingdom
12	27999	Acrocephalus	scirpaceus	Eurasian Reed Warbler	Stuart Fisher	United Kingdom
13	113082	Aegithalos	caudatus	Long-tailed Tit	Timo Roeke	Netherlands
14	101371	Aegithalos	caudatus	Long-tailed Tit	Krzysiek Deoniziak	Poland
15	128853	Aegithalos	caudatus	Long-tailed Tit	Alexandre Renaudier	Spain
16	123169	Alauda	arvensis	Eurasian Skylark	david m	United Kingdom
17	123170	Alauda	arvensis	Eurasian Skylark	david m	United Kingdom
18	158166	Alauda	arvensis	Eurasian Skylark	david m	United Kingdom
19	138979	Anthus	pratensis	Meadow Pipit	Fernand DEROUSSEN	Norway
20	30614	Anthus	pratensis	Meadow Pipit	Ruud van Beusekom	Netherlands
21	142431	Anthus	pratensis	Meadow Pipit	Erik Roels	Netherlands

Showing 1 to 23 of 264 entries

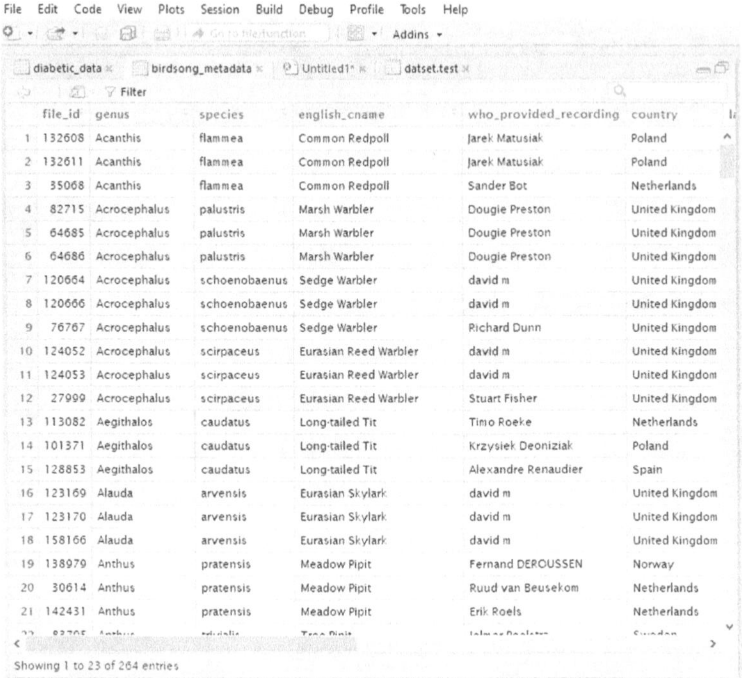

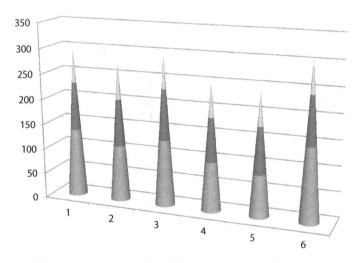

Figure 5.2 Data frame of birds.

Figure 5.3 Best move of birds.

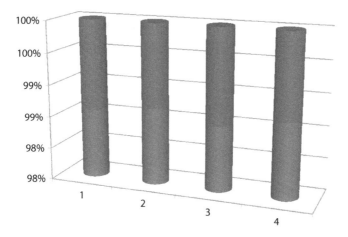

Figure 5.4 Performance measure of classification algorithm through trained data.

of each object is defined based on the source distance by which each data is determined using some evaluation function deals with overall measurement that estimates current position and new move, i.e., change in position. The cost estimation 1 of each data is obtained individually to find the exact measure of trained data (Figure 5.4) [5].

5.1.4   Working Process of the Proposed Model

The major steps involved in processing the data is preprocessing, extracting features from the data and sending those data into the classified model. The model is being developed by monitoring the data based upon the performance, evaluation and its outcome. These three main important processes are being defined as a predictive analysis process. The PSO algorithm helps in doing these steps in a behavioral approach. In this PSO algorithm the data collected over the swarm is being distinguished based upon the search space generated from the location of the element. Each data is classified based upon two different sets, one training set and another testing set. The final analysis is being collected from the training set and the testing set by making a deep learning technique.

Classification algorithm is applied on the trained and test data to examine the exact value that defines the most current position of each data measure. The value is best classifier that estimates all the parameter which deals with

POSITION	FITNESS VALUE
180	2.571429
186	2.431373
191	2.850746
192	2.543046

Figure 5.5 Objects move vs. fitness evaluation.

final selection of place. The PSO algorithm is then applied on selected data to optimize value on candidate solutions. Value generated is based on population, fitness evaluation, and so on (Figure 5.5). The generalization process is carried through many moves done on different object which deals with many massive approaches. The first and foremost processes in finding the moves of objects are measured through group of objects. The comparison is made on different evaluation scheme in the course of best moves; it is identified and verified using some generalized method of individual values obtained.

The example data estimated by PSO is shown below.

The comparative data is estimated through different data obtained from classical approach by which each process is carried on with different data frames. The case study of the above dataset is examined and done through PSO algorithm to obtain optimized throughput to handle many similar process.

5.2 Second Case Study on Recommendation Systems

The PSO examines in many forms; in this case study, the researcher can come for a conclusion that how the process is producing optimal result. In this study, the throughput for each process varies; here, all extracted processes are examined in different ways. The recommendation system helps the users in many ways; it is used to find the users interest where all the users' opinion is not same. The data flow process is shown in Figure 5.6 for decision making. It acts as a software tool to find the hidden experience of user. In each step, the recommendation system generates lots of different opinion to demonstrate that the optimality PSO algorithm will act as a bridge [8]. In this case study, recommendations can be generated in different domain; here, the

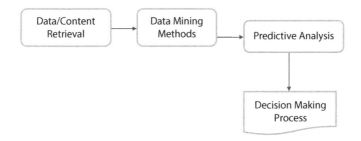

Figure 5.6 Data flow for decision process.

stock analysis is one of the applications, which deals with purchasing a best product in the market. Since PSO algorithm has the velocity and accuracy, it will use only the fitness function to estimate all the queries; it omits the crossover and mutation like genetic algorithm (GA) [6]. Here, data analysis does first phase and the remaining phase is carried out by PSO algorithm. In this phase, the velocity and finding new position is done by two different ways: one is evaluating fitness function, and next is finding the overall moves that all are best moves; these are so called global solution or global best move.

The preprocessing step for analysis process is done by data analytics tool which deals with some steps through which it leads to make a decision in an optimized way. Figure 5.7 shows the output for future recommendation system using data analytics tool.

The maximum likelihood estimates are defined through frequencies in the dataset. A frequent item in stock is measured by estimating all the data which have both trained and test data.

Figure 5.7 Preprocessing output for future recommendation system.

$$\hat{P}(m_j) = \frac{N(F = m_j)}{N}$$

$$\hat{P}(x_i \mid m_j) = \frac{N(X_i = x_i, F = m_j)}{N(F = m_j)}$$

Attributes are positions of data, values, or words; here, key value pair is defined for estimating throughput for each data in the dataset. Below equation evaluates all the maximum repeated data in trained dataset.

$$c_N = \underset{m_j \in C}{\operatorname{argmax}} P(m_j) \prod_i P(x_i \mid m_j)$$

$$= \underset{m_j \in C}{\operatorname{argmax}} P(m_j) P(x_1 = \text{"our"} \mid m_j) \cdots P(x_n = \text{"text"} \mid m_j)$$

Finally, the estimated trained data is passed to a block of data processing step that evaluated the cost of data and defines on recommendation system which helps users in finding the stock rate of each item using PSO algorithm [3]. Feature extraction is the most important step while processing trained or test data. There different stages that help in finding recommendation system. The following Figure 5.8 shows are the stages to find remanded rate.

Here, recommendation is based on different parameter on different iteration that leads to find maximum likelihood; in each iteration, the parameter precision increased due to stock comments taken from data forum. This case

Figure 5.8 Stages of recommendation rate.

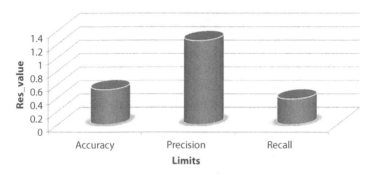

Figure 5.9 Graph representation of PSO.

study describes more about various methods and models implicated in cluster mining. These studies demonstrate much essential method like classification, analysis, and PSO [2]. The evaluation is prepared among special models and process for the effectiveness of high-dimensional data. There are similar methods which affect its own process to find the optimal SI using GA. This offers field information on different techniques on clustering analysis. In recommendation system, the process can be done in many ways: one is through collaborative filtering and another is based on the content-based analysis. In modern era, web users increase day by day to identify those dynamic platforms; the recommendation system plays an important part in the research where the end user can be found through similar likelihood and even similarity measure. This case study simulates such kind of demo.

Each iterative process is carried out through fitness function and SI techniques.

However, PSO algorithm is one such category which evaluates the optimal solution in each process; it helps in finding recommendation rate in an efficient method. The normal process of recommendation system is based on applying GA and fuzzy logic; these are common techniques used to find evaluation rate. This case study deals with PSO as shown in Figure 5.9; an intelligent method finds the significant swam optimization and finds the feature extractions through intelligent methods to make the clear iterations on data processing and another one which finds optimal solution on level indicator.

5.3   Third Case Study on Weight Lifting Robot

In modern evolution, most of the works are done by machines through control systems. This is to reduce the human resources, which has many essential things that have to be done on those humans. This study deals with intelligent system which reduces the time of work completion, and though human does the same work, the variation is mainly on time efficiency. Figure 5.10 shows a comparison between iterations made in the process flow and algorithms efficiency. The detailed description will discuss on how it works and how it helps the organization in work completion. In mechanical engineering, the machines are used to lift high end metals that are made by intelligent system and maintained over control system [7]. Though there are some ways to do the same, here, it describes on PSO algorithm which is one of the SI.

Standard process of design manufacturing is made automatic using many advanced systems; similarly, the industry made all the process automated and it is controlled over single system. For example, in industry, the heavy vehicle is automated to lift the racks using controller system. This process is made easy using SI process and the process flow is shown in Figure 5.11. The feature extraction is done based on process; it is grouped together to design and deliver it in an efficient way.

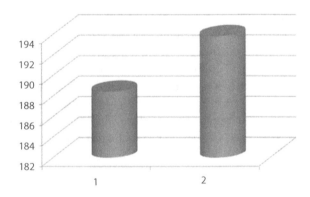

Figure 5.10 Comparison on iterations and algorithms.

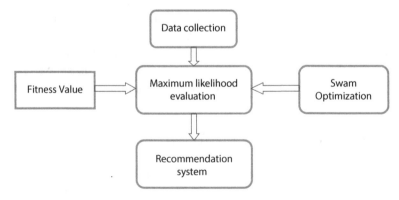

Figure 5.11 Process of case study.

Figure 5.12 process flow says that each machine will be manufactured through some constrain and each process has its own data format and procedure to make a final design; here, first design says about data collection or orientation that how final product is designed. A mining process will decide how should work, while it is equipped in a separator and at the last session, the conditions should be satisfied and the opinion is gathered for future purpose. The overall procedure is made through SI system which gives a best move for designing or for the working model which is incorporated in all stages of machine fabrication. Figure 5.13 describes the process flow in manufacturing and design.

The dataset is trained and tested under many extractions of features; here, the algorithm is genetic which creates population; among each evaluation, instead of crossover and mutation, the PSO algorithm helps in finding the optimal solution. In both weight estimation, the evaluation is done on

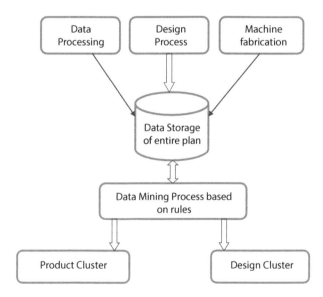

Figure 5.12 Process flow of machine design.

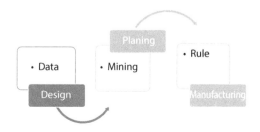

Figure 5.13 Flow of manufacturing and design process.

likelihoods of minimum and maximum widen. The stimulations are made to have an onsite of dataset through which swam intelligence will produce the optimal position of the weight. In Figure 5.14 shows the weight lifting data frame work. For example, AWS uses intelligence system to lift heavy weight machine or racks through which time is efficiency utilized and each position will produce an exact best move by velocity and accuracy [10]. The iteration is continued till it finds the best move of the process to examine each process fitness function that is evaluated for each clustered data. The final process of machine design is throughput of the associated rules on data to cluster each item and design fabrication. In some article, the author worked on ensemble methods and machine learning algorithms for sentimental analysis. The

	X1	user_name	raw_timestamp_part_1	raw_timestamp_part_2	cvtd_timestamp	new_window	num_window	r(
1	1	pedro	1323095002	868349	05/12/2011 14:23	no	74	^
2	2	jeremy	1322673067	778725	30/11/2011 17:11	no	431	
3	3	jeremy	1322673075	342967	30/11/2011 17:11	no	439	
4	4	adelmo	1322832789	560311	02/12/2011 13:33	no	194	
5	5	eurico	1322489635	814776	28/11/2011 14:13	no	235	
6	6	jeremy	1322673149	510661	30/11/2011 17:12	no	504	
7	7	jeremy	1322673128	766645	30/11/2011 17:12	no	485	
8	8	jeremy	1322673076	54671	30/11/2011 17:11	no	440	
9	9	carlitos	1323084240	916313	05/12/2011 11:24	no	323	
10	10	charles	1322837822	384285	02/12/2011 14:57	no	664	
11	11	carlitos	1323084277	36553	05/12/2011 11:24	no	859	v

Figure 5.14 Weight lifting data frame.

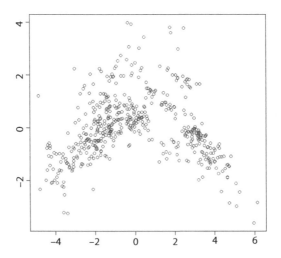

Figure 5.15 Weight estimation—minimum likelihood.

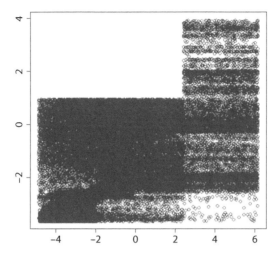

Figure 5.16 Weight estimation—maximum likelihood.

classification is mainly based on the combination of two models: one is deep feature and surface to unite several source of information into one source. They proposed a taxonomy which is used to classify the models. The classification is based on combinations of one or more dimensions; mainly, they answer for two things: one is how the prediction is made and how the learning process is finished. The weight estimation for both maximum and minimum likelihood is shown in Figures 5.15 and 5.16. The author discussed about many ensemble feature, meta ensemble models, and any model for classifying the output components to improve the high performance.

The above system diagram explains how it works in the environment through controller and storage. In each step, processed output is stored in open source environment through which the data is open to the authenticated user through the SI method. The program logic is essential to controlled through monitoring device and updation is needed throughout the process.

5.4   Background Knowledge of Harvesting Process

The innovation is based on intelligent work done by agent group. The section will demonstrate how the agricultural process collectively does the task using PSO algorithm. A harvesting process is a single task which contains some steps like the first is reaping (cutting), threshing (separating process), and cleaning (removing non grain material from grains); these steps will be done using SI system. Finally, the process will evaluate based on the cohesion and separation. There are some collective features to be extracted on different robots so that optimization is efficient [9]. In Figure 5.17 shows the working model of harvesting process.

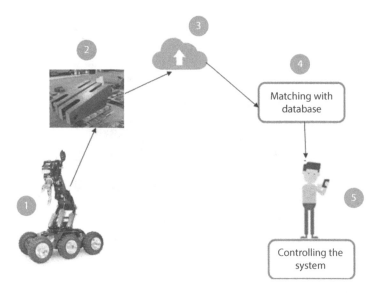

Figure 5.17 Working principle of the model.

5.4.1 Data Flow of PSO Process

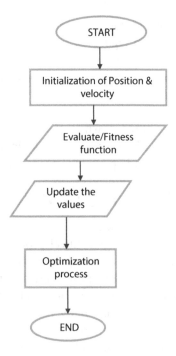

Figure 5.18 Dataflow diagram.

5.4.2   Working Flow of Harvesting Process

In the following session, the researcher can able to know how the harvesting is done through SI process. The model design is explained in the forthcoming sessions. In agriculture field, now, automation comes into picture where each process is controlled over device and some time stamp is maintained and it is visualized by the farmer. The data flow process of PSO algorithm is shown in Figure 5.18.

5.4.3   The First Phase of Harvesting Process

The above model describes how the SI will do the harvesting process in an optimized way. The design model for harvesting process is shown in Figure 5.19. Here, in this diagram, a sample of single swarm system is explained in brief manner. In each stage, the data is updated in an open source and fitness value is also updated in time stamp manner. A single change can make a huge difference in calculation of fitness function. Though PSO algorithm is used to find the best move using the velocity of the designed system, the farmer can easily identify the optimality in each move [11]. The first phase of harvesting process is shown in Figure 5.20.

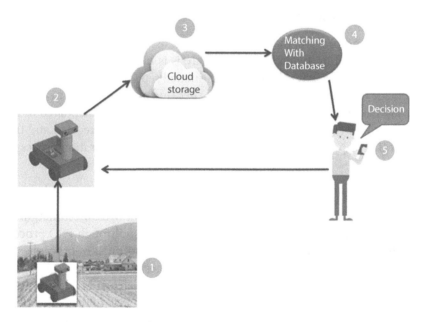

Figure 5.19 Design model for harvesting process.

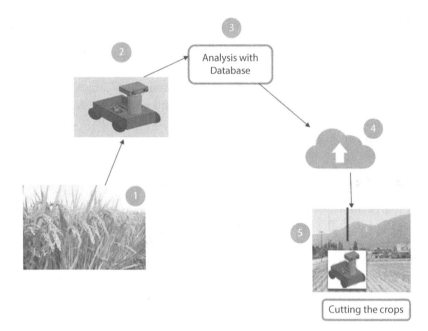

Figure 5.20 First phase—cutting the crops.

5.4.4 Separation Process in Harvesting

In the second process, the crop is harvested using machines and changed data is updated in the database. An analysis is made on each step carried out in the process. PSO algorithm is estimated separately comparisons that are made on both sets of data. The next checking process is done in the field through automated system after verification that process is updated in the existing dataset. Then, the quality is checked and it is segregated and this is so called separation process. Figure 5.21 shows the separation process.

5.4.5 Cleaning Process in the Field

In above model, the paddy is cleaned by checking overall estimation in dataset each time; best grain in the field is evaluated through PSO process and fitness function of each step though automation makes process easy, the grains and non-grains are cleaned and it is shown in Figure 5.22, the programming logic and working principle of each step is verified on time stamp process and data is examined till the final process of the paddy field.

The above diagram is the summary of overall estimation done on each category in paddy field; best move is evaluated over time stamp and data is

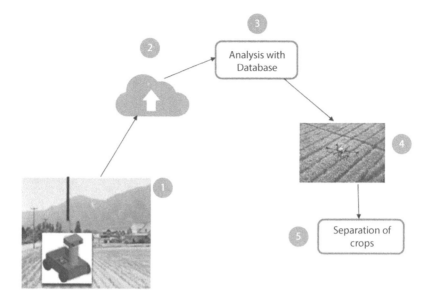

Figure 5.21 Separation process.

Figure 5.22 The grains and non-grains are cleaned.

verified though automation scheme. Figure 5.23 shows the entire process flow estimation.

The graphical representation shows balanced data that is evaluated through fitness function. Figure 5.24 shows the fitness evaluation of the established trained data. The overall data estimated is shown in which it

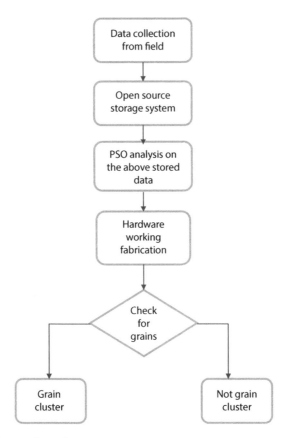

Figure 5.23 Process flow of entire estimation.

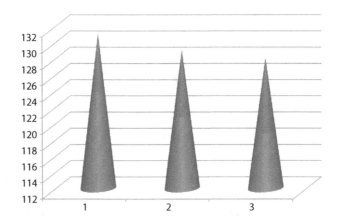

Figure 5.24 Fitness evaluation of the established trained data.

gradually increases over some time stamp, and through each time, it varies and values are evaluated through swam process. Instead, mutation generated using GA the fitness function is used to find the exact data of each field stored in the data base.

5.5   Future Trend and Conclusion

The fitness evaluation will choose the locality value and the optimization technique which initialize the position and the velocity of the swarm robot. After the evaluation process is over, the new updated value will be carried out. The adaptive velocity will be resulted in optimization. The chapter concludes with a summary, that the harvesting process will be very efficient. This clustering process will be helpful in performance measure of the quality process. This can be further a research to develop deep learning techniques.

References

1. http://www.knowledgebank.irri.org/step-by-step production/postharvest/harvesting
2. Grosan, C., Abraham, A., Chis, M., Swarm intelligence in data mining, in: *Swarm Intelligence in Data Mining*, pp. 1–20, Springer, Berlin, Heidelberg, 2006.
3. http://www.openarchives.org/OAI/openarchivesprotocol.html
4. Zedadra, O., Guerrieri, A., Jouandeau, N., Spezzano, G., Seridi, H., Fortino, G., Swarm intelligence-based algorithms within IoT-based systems: A review. *J. Parallel Distrib. Comput.*, 122, 173–187, 2018.
5. Amini, S., Javanshir, H., Tavakkoli-Moghaddam, R., A PSO approach for solving VRPTW with real case study. *Int. J. Res. Rev. Appl. Sci.*, 4, 3, 118–126, 2010.
6. Sibalija, T., Petronic, S., Milovanovic, D., Experimental optimization of nimonic 263 laser cutting using a particle swarm approach. *Metals*, 9, 11, 1147, 2019.
7. Kaloop, M.R., Kumar, D., Samui, P., Gabr, A.R., Hu, J.W., Jin, X., Roy, B., Particle Swarm Optimization Algorithm-Extreme Learning Machine (PSO-ELM) model for predicting resilient modulus of stabilized aggregate bases. *Appl. Sci.*, 9, 16, 3221, 2019.
8. Das, S., Mishra, B.S.P., Mishra, M.K., Mishra, S., Moharana, S.C., Soft-Computing based recommendation system: a comparative study. *Int. J. Innov. Technol. Exploring Eng. (IJITEE)*, 8, 8, 131–139, 2019.

9. Xiao, S., Wang, Y., Yu, H., Nie, S., An entropy-based adaptive hybrid particle swarm optimization for disassembly line balancing problems. *Entropy*, 19, 11, 596, 2017.

10. Alam, S., Dobbie, G., Riddle, P., Towards recommender system using particle swarm optimization based web usage clustering, in: *Pacific-Asia Conference on Knowledge Discovery and Data Mining*, 2011, May, Springer, Berlin, Heidelberg, pp. 316–326.

11. Zitzler, E., Deb, K., Thiele, L., Comparison of multiobjective evolutionary algorithms: Empirical results. *Evol. Comput.*, 8, 2, 173–195, 2000.

6

Firefly Algorithm

Anupriya Jain, Seema Sharma* and Sachin Sharma

Manav Rachna International Institute of Research and Studies,
Faridabad, India

Abstract

Data science community has been in continuous search for inspiration from nature and humans to solve various real-life problems. Machine learning itself is based on the way humans learn. Meanwhile, nature-inspired algorithms have gained popularity to solve complex optimization problems. These are termed as biology/nature-inspired algorithms. Researchers have found swarm intelligence algorithms that work on the principle of a swarm of bees, ants, etc. One of the most popular algorithms that use the behavior of fireflies, their light flashing patterns in order to find a global optimal solution is Firefly Algorithm (FA). In this chapter, we present the working principle of FA in detail with the algorithm explained and its implementation ready for the reference. In recent years, there has been the introduction of variants of FA to accommodate new problems. The hybrid or modified models have tremendously improved the performance of a standard FA. These special cases and applications of this meta-heuristic problem are discussed in detail. We also determine the need for FA over swarm optimization and why does FA works so well.

Keywords: Firefly Algorithm (FA), machine learning, swarm optimization, meta-heuristic problem

*Corresponding author: seema.fca@mriu.edu.in

S. Balamurugan, Anupriya Jain, Sachin Sharma, Dinesh Goyal, Sonia Duggal and Seema Sharma (eds.) *Nature-Inspired Algorithms Applications*, (157–180) © 2022 Scrivener Publishing LLC

6.1   Introduction

Optimization refers to finding the optimal, meaning the "best" or "most suitable" solution to the problem of interest. This optimal solution can be obtained by minimization or maximization of the objective function by choosing the values of variables involved in the equation wisely. There exist many real-world problems that require optimization. It may seem easy to find the solution manually for some. But the majority of them require heavy computation to reach the final result. For example, differentiating a simple mathematical equation to find maxima or minima is an easy task which takes a few minutes as there are finite possible solutions. But, if there is a sales company X that wants its salesperson to go around the city in each street for the purpose of marketing of their products, they need to figure out a path wherein the salesperson takes the shortest route and also does not keep on repeating any lane. This is the famous Traveling Salesperson Problem and can have infinite possible solutions. It is an optimization problem [26] that takes several iterations to solve and find the optimal path. In such situations, optimization algorithms [4] developed to date come to the rescue.

These optimization problems can be divided into two subsets based on variables involved in the objective function:

- Discrete: It is a combinatorial optimization problem having a finite discrete set of alternatives for the optimal solution.
- Continuous: It is a continuous optimization problem with either infinite possible alternatives or finite but very large. There are certain constraints and restrictions that are to be handled for finding the optimal solution.

Let us get a little familiar with the terminologies involved with an optimization algorithm and how it works. The following constitutes a general optimization algorithm:

- Objective function $f(x)$: the output of which we are trying to minimize or maximize.
- Variables $x1$, $x2$, $x3$, which are the inputs.
- Constraints, which limit the range of variables.

Finally, constraints place a limit on variables which, in turn, influence the outcome of the objective function. As shown in Figure 6.1 flowchart, an objective function is defined as per the problem statement with some

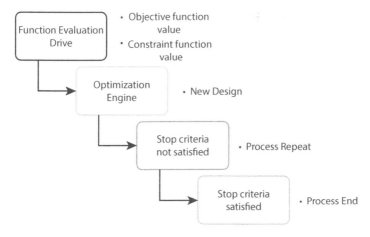

Figure 6.1 Flowchart of a general optimization algorithm.

constraints and variables. Then, a formal algorithm is designed which has the potential to solve the problem. The algorithm converges when the stop criteria are met and give the final output. Otherwise, it keeps going on repeat. These days, biologically inspired optimization algorithms are being widely researched for they are self-organized algorithms. They work on swarm behavior similar to ants and bees. They work on some educated heuristics to find the approximate solutions inspired by behavior of nature. Genetic Algorithm (based on Darwin's survival of fittest concept), Swarm Optimization, and Firefly Algorithm (FA) are all such metaheuristic algorithms. The primary focus of this chapter is getting into details of the FA.

FA is developed based on the behavior of fireflies [1] and the light they emit. The easy approach and wide applications in the domain of telecommunication, clustering, damage identification, etc., are drawing attention of several researchers these days. This chapter presents a comprehensive study of FA and its modified versions. We discuss in detail each one of them. Section 6.2 introduces the behavior of firefly, its motivation to be used as an algorithm, and finally standard FA. The later part of this section covers famous modified FA algorithms developed till date. Section 6.3 outlines some interesting applications of FA in various fields. It also discusses why this bio-inspired algorithm forms an instrumental basis for many optimization problems. Results of the performance comparison of algorithms discussed are analyzed in Section 6.4. We eventually end the chapter by a discussion and conclusion leaving the reader with an insight into if you can solve your current problem using the FA algorithm.

6.2   Firefly Algorithm

6.2.1   Firefly Behavior

Several species of fireflies produce continuous, short, and rhythmic flashes which is a beautiful sight to watch in summers in some tropical regions. There exists a unique flash pattern for each species which is said to be produced by a process of bioluminescence. Such varying flash patterns majorly accomplish two tasks: to attract mating partners and to attract potential prey. Additionally, flashing can also function as a protecting warning mechanism to inform potential predators of the bitter taste of fireflies.

The throbbing flash, the speed of flashing, and also the quantity of time between the flashes form a part of the signal system that brings each sex along. Females reply to a male's distinctive pattern of flashing within the same species, whereas in another species, feminine fireflies will snoop on and even mimic the pairing flashing pattern of alternative species in order to lure and eat the male fireflies who could be fooled by the flashes and assume these female fireflies as a possible appropriate mate. Some tropical fireflies form a biological self-organized behavior by even synchronizing their flashes.

We know that the intensity of light at a particular distance say "r" from the source of light obeys the inverse-square law [8]. To mention mathematically, as distance r increases, the light intensity I decreases as given in the equation below:

$$I \propto \frac{1}{r^2}$$

Furthermore, light is absorbed by air too which makes the intensity of light weaker and weaker as the distance grows. These factors combined limit the visibility of fireflies upto several hundred meters at night. This distance is supposedly enough for fireflies to communicate among themselves.

The flashing of light can be formulated as an objective function for optimization, making it a possible new optimization algorithm: Firefly Algorithm (FA) [9].

6.2.2   Standard Firefly Algorithm

We make use of flashing behavior characteristics to develop the novel FA (Figure 6.2). To describe the algorithm in detail, we first explain the three main rules followed:

a) All fireflies are unisex [10]. Thus, each firefly can be attracted to all other fireflies present irrespective of sex.
b) Attractiveness toward a firefly is proportional to its brightness. Therefore, given two fireflies, the one having lesser brightness will move toward to brighter one. As brightness decreases with an increase in distance. If there is no brighter one than a specific firefly, it will move randomly.
c) The brightness of light emitted by a firefly is determined or affected by the landscape of objective function f(x).

Firefly Algorithm

Objective function $f(x)$, $x = (x_1, ..., x_d)^T$.
Generate an initial population of n fireflies x_i ($i = 1, 2, ..., n$).
Light intensity I_i at x_i is determined by $f(x_i)$.
Define light absorption coefficient γ.
while (t <MaxGeneration),
for $i = 1 : n$ (all n fireflies)
    for $j = 1 : n$ (all n fireflies) (inner loop)
    if ($I_i < I_j$)
        Move firefly i towards j.
    end if
        Vary attractiveness with distance r via $\exp[-\gamma r^2]$.
        Evaluate new solutions and update light intensity.
    end for j
end for i
Rank the fireflies and find the current global best g_*.
end while
Postprocess results and visualization.

Figure 6.2 The pseudocode for Firefly Algorithm [8].

For a maximization problem, the brightness of light can be proportional to the value of the objective function. Based on the three rules mentioned, the pseudo code for FA can be defined as follows.

For simplicity, the flowchart (Figure 6.3) can be referred to defining all the steps followed in the FA. Initially, the population is defined with light intensity and location of each firefly. Relative distance and attractiveness is calculated among each pair of firefly in the population, keeping in mind the three rules defined for a FA. Based on attractiveness, the lower intensity firefly moves toward the one having higher intensity and its location is updated along with attractiveness. These updates of the location of fireflies continue with iteration until the termination criterion is met. The termination criterion can be the maximum number of iterations, a tolerance from the optimum value if it is known or no improvement is achieved in consecutive iterations.

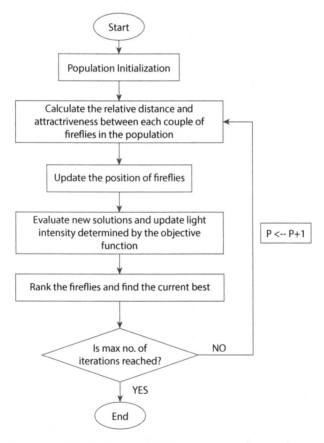

Figure 6.3 Flowchart of Firefly Algorithm [13].

6.2.3 Variations in Light Intensity and Attractiveness

There are two main issues to be looked into in FA: first being the variation in the intensity of light and second is the formulation of attractiveness [8]. As discussed above, we know that attractiveness among fireflies is determined by their brightness, which, in turn, can be associated with the objective function encoded for the problem of optimization. In a simple case of a maximum optimization problem, the brightness of firefly (I) at a particular location, say x, can be said to be a function of x as follows:

$$I(x) \propto f(x)$$

However, the term attractiveness β is relative. It is defined by other fireflies; some may think one as a potential mate while others may not. It varies with distance r_ij, between fireflies i and j. Additionally, attractiveness varies with the degree of absorption too as light intensity varies with distance and gets absorbed by travel medium (say air). According to inverse square law, the light intensity at distance r can be defined as follows:

$$I(r) = \frac{I(s)}{r^2}$$

where I(s) refers to the intensity at source of light. In a given medium having fixed light absorption coefficient y, the intensity of light varies with distance (r). To avoid singularity at r = 0 in the expression $I(r) = I(s)/r^2$, the combined effect of both the inverse-square law and absorption can be approximated as the following Gaussian form:

$$I(r) = I_0 e^{-\gamma r^2}$$

where I_0 refers to light intensity of source at distance = 0 (Gaussian form).

As attractiveness of a firefly is proportional to the intensity of light as seen by adjacent fireflies, we can now define the attractiveness β of a firefly by

$$\beta(r) = \beta_0 e^{-\gamma r^2}$$

where β_0 refers to attractiveness at distance = 0. To ease the calculation, the above equation can also be approximated as follows:

$$\beta(r) = \beta_0(1 + \gamma r^2)$$

6.2.4   Distance and Movement

The distance between two (Figure 6.4) fireflies i and j, at locations x_i and x_j, respectively, can be computed using Cartesian distance formula

$$r_{ij} = \|x_i - x_j\| = \sqrt{\sum_{k=1}^{d}(x_{i,k} - x_{j,k})^2}$$

where xi,k is the kth component of the spatial coordinate x_i of ith firefly. In a 2D case, we have

$$r_{ij} = \sqrt{(x_i - x_j)^2 + (y_i - y_j)^2}$$

The movement of firefly i toward a brighter firefly j is determined by

$$x_i = x_i + \beta_0 e^{-\gamma r_{ij}^2}(x_j - x_i) + \alpha\left(rand - \frac{1}{2}\right)$$

where the second term represents the attraction. The third term is randomization, with α being the randomization, where rand is a random number generator uniformly distributed in [0,1]. For most of our implementation, we can take $\beta_0 = 1$ and $\alpha \in [0, 1]$.

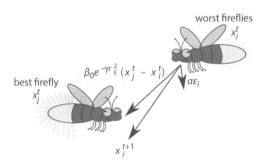

Figure 6.4 Decision of movement of firefly [44].

Table 6.1 Parameters and notations of Firefly Algorithm [12].

S. no.	Notation	
	Parameter	**Notation in algorithm**
1	Brightness	Objective function
2	Beta (β)	Attractiveness
3	Alpha (α)	Randomization parameter
4	Gamma (γ)	Absorption coefficient
5	No. of generations (g)	Iteration
6	No. of fireflies (n)	Population
7	Problem dimension (D)	Dimension

Table 6.1 gives detail of all the parameters and notations in the equations used to describe FA including its objective function, attractiveness, randomization parameter, the absorption coefficient of travel media, firefly population size, and the dimension of the problem (whether 2D or 3D).

6.2.5 Implementation of FA

A demo version of implementation of FA without Lévy flights can be found at https://www.mathworks.com/matlabcentral/fileexchange/29693-firefly-algorithm, the Mathworks file exchange Website. In the MATLAB code, the values of the parameters are set as follows:

$\alpha 0 = 0.5$,
$\gamma = 1$ and
$\beta 0 = 1$.

The parameters mentioned can be adjusted to solve various problems of varying scale. In order to demonstrate how the FA works, a simple example of the four-peak function is used [8]. The function is defined as follows:

$$f(x,y) = e^{-(x-4)^2 - (y-4)^2} + e^{-(x+4)^2 - (y-4)^2} + 2\left[e^{-x^2 - y^2} + e^{-x^2 - (y+4)^2} \right],$$

where $(x, y) \in [-5,5] \times [-5,5]$. As shown in Figure 6.5, the function reaches four peaks with

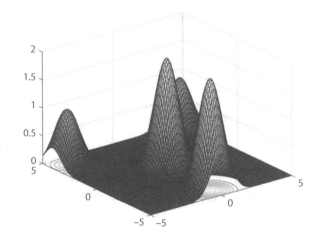

Figure 6.5 Landscape of a function with two equal global maxima.

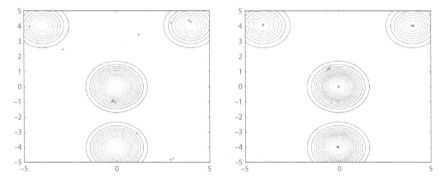

Figure 6.6 The initial locations of 25 fireflies (left) and their final locations after 20 iterations.

two local peaks with f = 1 at (−4,4) and (4,4);
two global peaks with f_{max} = 2 at (0,0) and (0, −4).

In Figure 6.6, we can observe that all four of these optima can be found using 25 fireflies in about 20 generations. So, the total number of function evaluations is about 500. This is much more efficient than most existing meta-heuristic algorithms.

6.2.6   Special Cases of Firefly Algorithm

To gain a better understanding, we now analyze the FA system more cautiously. In equation,

$$x_i = x_i + \beta_0 e^{-\gamma r_{ij}^2}(x_j - x_i) + \alpha\left(rand - \frac{1}{2}\right),$$

we observe that γ acts as an important scaling parameter [33].

Case A: $\gamma = 0$
At one of the extreme, we can set $\gamma = 0$, to represent that there is no exponential decay, and thus, the visibility of firefly is very high. In this case, all fireflies are visible and they can see each other in the whole domain being considered and we have the equation as (putting $\gamma = 0$)

$$x_i^{t+1} = x_i^t + \beta_0\left(x_j^t - x_i^t\right) + \alpha\left(rand - \frac{1}{2}\right)\wedge t$$

- FA becomes a variant of differential evolution (DE) without crossover when $\gamma = 0$, $\alpha = 0$, and $\beta 0$ is fixed. In this case, if x_j is replaced by the best solution in the group g^*, then this reduced FA obtained is equivalent to a special case of accelerated particle swarm optimization [20] (APSO).
- If $\beta_0 = 0$, FA becomes equivalent to the basic simulated annealing (SA) having α as the cooling schedule.

Thus, it is clear that DE, APSO, and SA are all special cases of the standard FA. In other words, in a nonlinear system, FA can be regarded as a combination of APSO, SA, and DE enhanced in a nonlinear system. This can be a reason for FA to outperform these algorithms for many applications.

Case B: $\gamma \gg 1$
Considering another special extreme case when $\gamma \gg 1$ [33], would mean that the visibility range is very short. In this case, the fireflies are unable see each other clearly. With respect to this, each firefly flies randomly and independently. In fact, if $\gamma_{ij}^{r^2} = 1$, then the exponential term $\exp\left[\gamma_{ij}^{r^2}\right]$ will decrease. Now, the range of influence (R) can be defined by

$$R = \frac{1}{\sqrt{\gamma}}$$

Therefore, in order to make sure that fireflies fly within a range such that they a visible to each other, a good value of γ should be linked to the limits of the design variables. In case of lack of prior knowledge about its possible scale/limit of the value to be considered, we start with $\gamma = 1$ for majority of the problems and then change it when required. In theory, $\gamma \in [0, \infty)$, but in practice, we can use $\gamma = O(1)$, which means that we can use $\gamma = 0.001$ to 1,000 for most of the problems.

6.2.7   Variants of FA

The standard FA is very efficient, but there is still room for improvement. In the last 5 years, researchers have tried various ways to enhance the performance and speed up the convergence of the FA. As a result, quite a few variants have been developed [19, 37, 42]. However, because the literature is expanding rapidly and more variations are appearing, it is not possible to list all these variants here. This section briefly summarizes some of these variants:

- Discrete FA (DFA): FA was initially developed to solve problems of continuous domain. Sayadi *et al.* [19] extended the FA to deal with discrete variables which made the FA algorithm more powerful to be used in various applications. Many researchers have been using this modification to solve NP-hard scheduling problems like hybrid flow shop scheduling problems [28, 29] (https://arxiv.org/pdf/1806.01632. pdf). Extracting information from images is now easier with the development of an FA-based method for image segmentation, developed by Hassanzadeh *et al.* [18], which has been proven to be more efficient than the standard Otsu's and recursive Otsu method. On the other hand, Jati and Suyanto discretized the FA and showed its effectiveness in solving the NP-hard traveling salesman problem. For the purpose of assemble sequence planning, discrete double population was used by Zhang *et al.* [14] (https://arxiv.org/pdf/1806.01632. pdf).
- Adaptive FA: Few researchers thought the fixed parameters to be modified in the standard FA. They developed methods such that an algorithm can itself adapt to the problem and vary parameter value as per the requirement. This innovation helped Baykasoglu and Ozsoydan to solve mechanical design problems [2], and Gálvex and Iglesias [6] developed a

memetic self-adaptive FA for shape fitting (https://arxiv.org/pdf/1806.01632.pdf).

- Modified/Enhanced FA: There has been on-going research to generate algorithms on top of the standard FA. Researchers tend to combine algorithms to solve a problem of interest. Also, modifications in attraction parameters, light intensity, random movement, or a combination of these have become popular. These variations led to significant enhancement in performance of FA. For example, for controller design Gupta used modified FA [5]. Wang e al. utilized light intensity differences [15] in one of their work and also developed an FA with neighborhood interaction [17].

- Chaotic FA (CFA): Coelho *et al.* in 2011 proposed that introduction of chaos in FA can lead to increased global search mobility of FA for achieve a robust global optimal solution. This variation of FA known as CFA outperformed other algorithms. The intrinsic chaotic characteristic of FA was studied by Yang. It was observed that under different parameter ranges enhanced performance can be achieved by tuning β and γ [46]. Meanwhile, Gandomi *et al.* studied carried out extensive performance comparisons and concluded that this chaos introduction gives a performance boost to standard FA [45].

- Multi-objective FA (MOFA): Sometimes, an algorithm is required to achieve multiple objectives in a single run. This can get complex. Nature-inspired FA is used for single-objective optimization only. But Yang also extended the standard to multi-objective optimization [11] of continuous design problems [47].

- Multi-objective discrete FA (MDFA). The multi-objective FA was further modified by Apostolopoulos and Vlacho. They developed a discrete version for MOFA to be used in the economic emission load dispatch problem. This variant of FA proved to be efficient enough compared to single objective and continuous FA. In the same time, a group of authors proposed another variant of MOFA for an optimal workload management tool for minimizing energy consumption in grid computing [48]. Production scheduling systems require multiple decisions to be made at a time. Li and Ye used MOFA to solve this problem [50].

- Hybrid FAs (HFA): FA and DE each have their own advantages. Combining the two give rise to a new algorithm paradigm called HFA. Both algorithms when combined promote information sharing among the population and, in turn, increase the search efficiency for the optimal solution. Not only DE, but other nature-inspired algorithms when combined with FA make a HFA. Giannakouris *et al.* [49] obtained good results on combining FA with ant colony optimization. There have been several works showing that hybrid algorithms can be a powerful tool for many applications.
- Parallel FA with predation (pFAP): Prey-predator algorithm (PPA) and FA are both meta-heuristic algorithms which have their own differences and similarities. For various optimization problems like graph coloring, traveling salesperson problems FA with predation have proved to yield a superior performance.

6.3   Applications of Firefly Algorithm

FAs have drawn attention of several researchers since the introduction of concept was published by Yang in 2008. It is due to the critical features of algorithm that makes it applicable to a plethora of problems in day to day life. Many researchers take inspiration from these nature-inspired algorithms and achieve optimal solutions. From a pool of applications available [18, 19, 21, 22, 30, 38, 41], we present and focus on a few that can be of interest of variety of readers.

6.3.1   Job Shop Scheduling

Scheduling means arranging an event at a particular time, in order to achieve a goal. We can observe scheduling in various domains like schools, offices, transportation, etc. A key application of it is associated with factory floor management involving production of machines, parts, and tools. The end product is often a culmination of various smaller parts called Jobs which need to be machined individually before they can be finally put together. In such scenario, it is often critical to manage the resources efficiently in order to achieve a continuous production line. This means that each point, where a subtask in the production system has to be performed, should receive the required components as fast as possible (ideally without any delay). So, scheduling the processes and part availability at each level of production at the right time becomes critical.

The job shop scheduling (JSP) problem consists of a set m machines {M1, M2, ..., Mn}, and a collection of n jobs {J1, J2, ..., Jn} to be scheduled, where each job must pass through each machine once only. Each job has its own processing order and it has no relation to the processing order of the other job. JSP problems are non-polynomial–hard problem, so its complexity is more [35]. Since such a process requires complex combinatorial optimization under various constraints, it is often difficult to solve.

Use of the FA showed promising results in solving such problem more efficiently as compared to other algorithms previously considered [35].

6.3.2 Image Segmentation

Recent advancements in the field of computer vision have seen various applications being introduced. One of the most used applications of such sort is face recognition which is available to use in almost every smartphone these days. One might be curious to know how the computer is able to differentiate a face from the other components in an image. The answer is: image segmentation. It is a process by which an algorithm is able to differentiate between various key objects within the scene of a camera. This information is then fed to a classifier algorithm which, using machine learning, is able to identify the object under different categories. An example is presented in Figure 6.7, wherein the algorithm is able to differentiate between regions. This is done primarily by identifying the borders separating the two regions consisting of different colors.

Figure 6.7 Image segmentation example [51].

While there are many ways to determine this boundary between two regions, one such way is to calculate the histogram of color changes over the complete image. This provides the information about image sections with the maximum changes in the color and is thus marked as potential segment boundary. FA in conjunction with different search algorithms have shown to produce good image segmentation results with faster implementation time [27]. FA was also shown to perform better than existing algorithms like K-means clustering in scenarios where the images are noisy, i.e., images of some sort of distortion [36].

6.3.3   Stroke Patient Rehabilitation

Brain computer interface (BCI) is a system which detects the signals in brain to use as a stimulus in other systems. The applications include navigation, military, gaming, and robotics. In healthcare, it is being used for rehabilitation of motor actions in stroke patients suffering from damaged nerves. For helping these patients, computer scientists are working to study data obtained from patients' electroencephalography (EEG) report. The idea is to extract features from this data which can signify intent for specific motor actions. However, EEG data is not easy to perform signal processing on, since it has high dimensions of these features. Only by eliminating the redundant features can the BCI optimize the space complexity [23] of such applications and also reduce classification inaccuracy.

The FA has shown to successfully reduce the EEG data to obtain the best subset of features and improve classification accuracy. The algorithm was further enhanced with the help of learning automata algorithm to capture features specific to motor imagery. This combination proved significantly better than other existing algorithms like Genetic Algorithm [7] and Adaptive Weight Particle Swarm Optimization Algorithm [39].

6.3.4   Economic Emission Load Dispatch

Thermal power generation needs to be efficient and reliable in order to match both electric demands from the consumer as well as profitability, while taking care of the environmental impact of their operations. This creates an interesting problem of optimizing the power output of a generation station taking all different boundary conditions into account. The Economic Emissions Load Dispatch is an online process of allocating generation among the available generating units to minimize the total generation cost and satisfy the equality and inequality constraints like minimum production of toxic gases [22].

Therefore, in this case, the objective function should maximize the power output of the plant, while at the same time trying to minimize the emissions. In various studies, it was shown that FA proved to be an efficient and effective solution for such optimization problem. It was also shown to be better than stochastic nature-inspired algorithms [22].

6.3.5 Structural Design

In civil engineering, people often have to deal with development of truss structures (Figure 6.8). When several beams are arranged together to form a rigid structure capable of functioning as one unit, then it forms a Truss structure. One might have often come across such structures in their daily life like in bridges, building construction machines, and stadiums.

In these cases, it is often important to optimize the structure in order to have maximum rigidity while at the same time minimizing the overall weight of the structure. Another challenge arrives when having to use minimum number of beams for reliable operation, thus trying to optimize the underlying profitability of the structure. The FA is used in such problems to optimize both geometry and sizing of the structure [31].

Other than those described above, FA [24] has been used in various other domains as well. FA helped in solving the traveling salesman problem efficiently [37]. Traveling salesman problem involves finding an optimal path for the salesman to travel such that he covers all the houses in an area without having to cover any street twice in one iteration. In the case of antenna design, FA can be used for optimization and was shown to outperform algorithms like ABC [34]. In the field of image processing, FA has also proved to be an

Figure 6.8 Truss structure in bridges [52].

efficient solution for digital image compression. It has been shown to use the least computation time for the task [30]. FA was also shown to be helpful in solving nonconvex economic dispatch problems [25] along with valve loading effect [40]. In software testing, FA helped in achieving superior performance by generating independent test sequences [32].

6.4   Why Firefly Algorithm is Efficient

In the previous sections of this chapter, we have discussed about the main steps involved in FA and how it works and have shown a working implementation of the same in MATLAB software. In this section, we would elaborate as to why this algorithm performs so well in practice. Based on swarm-intelligence, there are three main features that give this algorithm an extra edge. Firstly, it has the capability of automatic subdivision; secondly, it possesses the ability to deal with multimodal data which is the need of the hour in many optimization problems existing today; and lastly, it provides high ergodicity and diversity in the solutions [33] Figure 6.9.

- Based on the concept of attractiveness, FA allows the entire population to subdivide itself into numerous subgroups. Each subgroup swarm around each local optima of mode as depicted in the Figure 6.5 of the implementation section. The global optimal solution can be found out of all these possible modes.
- This multi-swarm nature of FA to find multiple optimal solutions simultaneously makes it naturally suitable to handle nonlinear, multimodal optimization problems easily. The technique of subdivision enables fireflies to find all optima simultaneously if the population size is sufficiently higher than the number of modes. Mathematically, average distance of a group of fireflies seen by the adjacent groups is controlled by $1/\sqrt{\gamma}$. In the extreme case, when $\gamma = 0$, the whole population will not subdivide.
- We have discussed that FA is a good combination of APSO, SA, and DE. Therefore, it seems to work better than these algorithms.
- Last but not the least, parameters of FA as discussed in Table 6.1 [12] can be tuned to control the randomness with each proceeding iteration. This aids for speed up convergence of optimization problem. This feature of FA makes it more

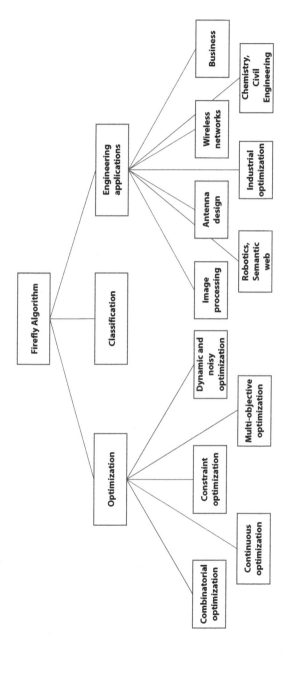

Figure 6.9 Taxonomy of firefly applications [43].

attractive to deal with continuous problems, clustering and classifications, and combinatorial optimization as well.

6.4.1 FA is Not PSO

FA and Particle Swarm Optimization (PSO) are both algorithms based on swarm intelligence. Thus, it is obvious that they have few things in common. But, they possess significant differences too along with the fact they both are based on different inspiration from the nature [33]. Main differences include the following:

- Due to the nonlinear interaction among the fireflies with respect to the attraction term $\beta_0 e^{-\gamma r_{ij}^2}$, FA can lead to richer characteristics in population properties as compared to PSO which is linear in terms of x_i and v_i.
- This nonlinearity enables FA with the ability of multi-swarming which makes it unique from other algorithms like PSO which lack this property. FA has the capability to find local optimal solutions by automatic subdivision and thus deal with multimodal problem more efficiently.
- The objective function of FA lacks velocity unlike PSO. But, this, in turn, proves to be an advantage as FA does not have to deal with the initialization problems and instability for high velocities of particles.
- FA possess scaling control (with the of factor γ), while PSO has no scaling control. This scaling parameter provides FA with more flexibility. All these differences enable FA to search the design spaces more effectively for multimodal objective landscapes.

6.5 Discussion and Conclusion

In this chapter, we studied in detail about the firefly behavior and how they use it to attract their mate and potential preys. It is intriguing to see how, based on this natural behavior of an organism, researchers have been able to develop a novel algorithm to solve complex continuous and discrete optimization problems. We describe the standard algorithm in detail with the help of flowchart and also introduce the variants of this meta-heuristic algorithm [3] which have been developed in recent years.

The FA algorithm is very efficient in itself to achieve optima. But, we see in the chapter that there has been continuous trial of improving the basic FA. The combinations of FA with various other optimization techniques have been tried. Also, the changes in parameters of the objective function have proved to bring significant improvement in the outcome with faster convergence of the standard FA. Furthermore, with these hybrid combinations [16] and modifications, FA is able to turn into a multi-objective optimization problem from a single-objective optimization which is the need of the hour.

This easy algorithm has found its way to solve various kinds of problems in numerous fields of science including, but not limited to, image processing, telecommunication, structural and antenna design, feature selection and fault detection, job scheduling, and other dynamic problems. We also discuss technically why this algorithm works so well as compared to other optimization problems and found that it exhibits automatic division of groups into subgroups to find local optimal solution which can be later combined to find the global optimal solution. This is the same with fireflies who in order to find potential mate a prey move toward each other and form groups. We tried to implement this behavior using MATLAB software. This implementation can be used to generate modified algorithms discussed in the chapter.

References

1. Erdal, F., A firefly algorithm for optimum design of new-generation beams. *Eng. Optim.*, 49, 6, 915–931, 2017.
2. Baykasoglu, A. and Ozsoydan, F.B., Adaptive firefly algorithm with chaos for mechanical design optimization problems. *Appl. Soft Comput.*, 36, 152–164, 2015.
3. Carbas, S., Design optimization of steel frames using an enhanced firefly algorithm. *Eng. Optim.*, 48, 12, 2007–2025, 2016.
4. Gope, S., Goswami, A.K., Tiwari, P.K., Deb, S., Rescheduling of real power for congestion management with integration of pumped storage hydro unit using firefly algorithm. *Int. J. Electr. Power Energy Syst.*, 83, 434–442, 2016.
5. Gupta, A. and Padhy, P.K., Modified Firefly Algorithm based controller design for integrating and unstable delay processes. *Eng. Sci. Technol. an Int. J.*, 19, 1, 548–558, 2016.
6. Gálvez, A. and Iglesias, A., New memetic self-adaptive firefly algorithm for continuous optimisation. *Int. J. Bio-Inspired Comput.*, 8, 5, 300–317, 2016.
7. Ghorbani, M.A., Shamshirband, S., Haghi, D.Z., Azani, A., Bonakdari, H., Ebtehaj, I., Application of firefly algorithm-based support vector machines for prediction of field capacity and permanent wilting point. *Soil Tillage Res.*, 172, 32–38, 2017.

8. Yang, X.S., Firefly algorithms for multimodal optimization. *Lect. Notes Comput. Sci. (including Subser. Lect. Notes Artif. Intell. Lect. Notes Bioinformatics)*, vol. 5792 LNCS, p. 169–178, 2009.

9. Yang, X.-S., Firefly Algorithms, in: *Nature-Inspired Optim. Algorithms*, p. 111–127, 2014.

10. Akhoondzadeh, M., Firefly algorithm in detection of TEC seismo-ionospheric anomalies. *Adv. Space Res.*, 56, 1, 10–18, 2015.

11. Bahadormanesh, N., Rahat, S., Yarali, M., Constrained multi-objective optimization of radial expanders in organic Rankine cycles by firefly algorithm. *Energy Convers. Manage.*, 148, 1179–1193, 2017.

12. Umbarkar, A.J., Balande, U.T., Seth, P.D., Performance evaluation of firefly algorithm with variation in sorting for non-linear benchmark problems. *AIP Conf. Proc.*, pp. 1–9, 1836, June, 2017. https://aip.scitation.org/doi/abs/10.1063/1.4981972

13. Casciati, S. and Elia, L., The Potential of the Firefly Algorithm for Damage Localization and Stiffness Identification, in: *Studies in Computational Intelligence*, vol. 585, p. 163–178, 2015.

14. Zhang, Z., Yuan, B., Zhang, Z., A new discrete double-population firefly algorithm for assembly sequence planning. *Proc. Inst. Mech. Eng. Part B J. Eng. Manuf.*, 230, 12, 2229–2238, 2016.

15. Wang, B., Li, D.-X., Jiang, J.-P., Liao, Y.-H., A modified firefly algorithm based on light intensity difference. *J. Comb. Optim.*, 31, 3, 1045–1060, 2016.

16. Ghorbani, H., Moghadasi, J., Wood, D.A., Prediction of gas flow rates from gas condensate reservoirs through wellhead chokes using a firefly optimization algorithm. *J. Nat. Gas Sci. Eng.*, 45, 256–271, 2017.

17. Wang, H. *et al.*, Firefly algorithm with neighborhood attraction. *Inf. Sci. (Ny)*, 382, 374–387, 2017.

18. Hassanzadeh, T., Vojodi, H., Moghadam, A.M.E., An image segmentation approach based on maximum variance intra-cluster method and firefly algorithm, in: *2011 Seventh International Conference on Natural Computation*, vol. 3, p. 1817–1821, 2011.

19. Sayadi, M., Ramezanian, R., Ghaffari-Nasab, N., A discrete firefly metaheuristic with local search for makespan minimization in permutation flow shop scheduling problems. *Int. J. Ind. Eng. Comput.*, 1, 1, 1–10, 2010.

20. Singh, N. and Kumar, Y., Multiobjective economic load dispatch problem solved by new PSO. *Adv. Electr. Eng.*, 2015, 1–7, 2015.

21. Kougianos, E. and Mohanty, S.P., A nature-inspired firefly algorithm based approach for nanoscale leakage optimal RTL structure. *Integr. VLSI J.*, 51, 46–60, 2015.

22. Apostolopoulos, T. and Vlachos, A., Application of the firefly algorithm for solving the economic emissions load dispatch problem. *Int. J. Comb.*, 2011, 1–27, 2010.

23. Maher, B., Albrecht, A.A., Loomes, M., Yang, X.-S., Steinhöfel, K., A firefly-inspired method for protein structure prediction in lattice models. *Biomolecules*, 4, 1, 56–75, 2014.

24. Poursalehi, N., Zolfaghari, A., Minuchehr, A., A novel optimization method, Effective Discrete Firefly Algorithm, for fuel reload design of nuclear reactors. *Ann. Nucl. Energy*, 81, 263–275, 2015.

25. Kanimozhi, T. and Latha, K., An integrated approach to region based image retrieval using firefly algorithm and support vector machine. *Neurocomputing*, 151, 1099–1111, 2015.

26. Hung, H.-L., Application firefly algorithm for peak-to-average power ratio reduction in OFDM systems. *Telecommun. Syst.*, 65, 1, 1–8, 2017.

27. Rajinikanth, V. and Couceiro, M.S., RGB histogram based color image segmentation using firefly algorithm. *Proc. Comput. Sci.*, 46, 1449–1457, 2015.

28. Marichelvam, M.K., Prabaharan, T., Yang, X.S., A discrete firefly algorithm for the multi-objective hybrid flowshop scheduling problems. *IEEE Trans. Evol. Comput.*, 18, 2, 301–305, 2013.

29. Marichelvam, M.K. and Geetha, M., A hybrid discrete firefly algorithm to solve flow shop scheduling problems to minimise total flow time. *Int. J. Bio-Inspired Comput.*, 8, 318–325, 2016.

30. Horng, M.-H., Vector quantization using the firefly algorithm for image compression. *Expert Syst. Appl.*, 39, 1, 1078–1091, 2012.

31. Kazemzadeh Azad, S., Optimum design of structures using an improved firefly algorithm. دانشگاه علم و صنعت ایران, 1, 2, 327–340, 2011.

32. Srivatsava, P.R., Mallikarjun, B., Yang, X.-S., Optimal test sequence generation using firefly algorithm. *Swarm Evol. Comput.*, 8, 44–53, 2013.

33. Yang, X.S. and He, X.S., Why the firefly algorithm works? *Stud. Comput. Intell.*, 744, 245–259, 2018.

34. Chandrasekaran, K. and Simon, S.P., Network and reliability constrained unit commitment problem using binary real coded firefly algorithm. *Int. J. Electr. Power Energy Syst.*, 43, 1, 921–932, 2012.

35. Udaiyakumar, K.C. and Chandrasekaran, M., Application of firefly algorithm in job shop scheduling problem for minimization of makespan. *Proc. Eng.*, 97, 1798–1807, 2014.

36. Vishwakarma, B. and Yerpude, A., A New Method for Noisy Image Segmentation using Firefly Algorithm. *Int. J. Sci. Res.*, 3, 5, 1721–1725, 2014.

37. Palit, S., Sinha, S.N., Molla, M.A., Khanra, A., Kule, M., A cryptanalytic attack on the knapsack cryptosystem using binary firefly algorithm, in: *2011 2nd International conference on compfiuter and communication technology (ICCCT-2011)*, p. 428–432, 2011.

38. Yang, X.S., Firefly Algorithm, stochastic test functions and design optimisation. *Int. J. Bioinspired Comput.*, 2, 2, 78–84, 2010.

39. Liu, A., Chen, K., Liu, Q., Ai, Q., Xie, Y., Chen, A., Feature selection for motor imagery EEG classification based on firefly algorithm and learning automata. *Sensors*, 17, 11, 2576, 2017.

40. Yang, X.-S., Hosseini, S.S.S., Gandomi, A.H., Firefly algorithm for solving non-convex economic dispatch problems with valve loading effect. *Appl. Soft Comput.*, 12, 3, 1180–1186, 2012.

41. Horng, M.-H., Lee, Y.-X., Lee, M.-C., Liou, R.-J., Firefly metaheuristic algorithm for training the radial basis function network for data classification and disease diagnosis, in: *Theory new Appl. swarm Intell.*, vol. 4, p. 115–132, 2012.

42. Dhal, K.G., Quraishi, M.I., Das, S., Development of firefly algorithm via chaotic sequence and population diversity to enhance the image contrast. *Nat. Comput.*, 15, 2, 307–318, 2016.

43. Fister, I., Fister Jr., I., Yang, X.S., Brest, J., A comprehensive review of firefly algorithms. *Swarm Evol. Comput.*, 13, 34–46, 2013.

44. Yoshimoto, E. and Heckler, M.V., Optimization of Planar Antenna Arrays Using the Firefly Algorithm. *J. Microw. Optoelectron. Electromagn. Appl.*, 18, 1, 126–140, 2019.

45. Grewal, N.S., Rattan, M., Patterh, M.S., A linear antenna array failure correction using firefly algorithm. *Prog. Electromagn. Res.*, 27, 241–254, 2012.

46. Yang, X.S. and He, X., Firefly Algorithm: Recent advances and applications. *Int. J. Swarm Intell.*, 1, 1, 36–50, 2013.

47. Yang, X.S., Multiobjective firefly algorithm for continuous optimization. *Eng. Comput.*, 29, 2, 175–184, 2013.

48. Arsuaga-Rios, M. and Vega-Rodriguez, M.A., Multi-objective firefly algorithm for energy optimization in grid environments, in: *International Conference on Swarm Intelligence*, 2012, September, Springer, Berlin, Heidelberg, p. 350–351.

49. Giannakouris, G., Vassiliadis, V., Dounias, G., Experimental study on a hybrid nature-inspired algorithm for financial portfolio optimization, in: *Hellenic Conference on Artificial Intelligence*, 2010, May, Springer, Berlin, Heidelberg, p. 101–111.

50. Li, H. and Ye, C., Firefly algorithm on multi-objective optimization of production scheduling system. *Adv. Mech. Eng. Appl.*, 3, 1, 258–262, 2012.

51. Tanner, G., FastAI Image Segmentation, 2019, March, [Online]. https://towardsdatascience.com/fastai-image-segmentation-eacad8543f6f.

52. Wikipedia, [Online]. https://en.wikipedia.org/wiki/Truss.

7

The Comprehensive Review for Biobased FPA Algorithm

Meenakshi Rana

Department of Chemistry, Ashoka University, Sonepat (Haryana), India

Abstract

In the era of technology and advancement, a human always tries to sophisticate the lives of humans and nature is a rich source of inspiration, which give fantastic ideas to researchers to solve many problems of daily life. A few years back we never touched on the idea of how to implement the idea of using the class of nature of bats or ants, genes that can be used to develop optimization algorithms. Nature always helps mankind with the solutions. For a long time, researchers working on optimization techniques which are inherited by nature and can be utilized as optimization tools for many engineering problems. A flower pollination algorithm (FPA) which is based on characteristics of flowering plants caught the attention of researchers for optimization problems. FPA is a computational metaheuristic approach that takes its metaphor from flowering plants. A problem of optimization is approached through Evolutionary Computation Techniques (ECTs). The basic idea behind this approach is randomness and some deterministic rules which are developed to mimic the behavior of natural entities. The difficulty to search the existence of several global and local optima is tackled finely through ECT approach. This works well for locating single optimum but fail to provide multiple solutions. FPA is characterized by a small number of parameters which make it promising in solving optimization problems and multi-objective complex ones also [1]. It is embedded with mechanism of local and global exploration feature which is complementary and helps the algorithm to work efficiently.

Keywords: Optimization, algorithms, meta-heuristic, computational, parameters, optimum, randomness, deterministic

Email: meenakshi.rana_phd21@ashoka.edu.in

S. Balamurugan, Anupriya Jain, Sachin Sharma, Dinesh Goyal, Sonia Duggal and Seema Sharma (eds.) *Nature-Inspired Algorithms Applications*, (181–208) © 2022 Scrivener Publishing LLC

7.1 Introduction

Optimization is the phenomenon of determining a certain value for particular parameters which are subject to constraints, so that some measure of optimality is satisfied. In past few years, the optimization subject has received enormous importance primarily because of the rapid emerging science and technology in computing, communication, environment, and society. Optimization can be found everywhere in every activity related to mathematics or basic sciences in which a numerical information is being processed. So, the widespread applicability of optimization and its requirements make researchers to find the various methods and tools for its easy usage. Nature-inspired optimization algorithm is usually attempt to find a good approximation to the solution of those complex problems.

Several researchers have been focused on optimization algorithms, those seek to behave as natural systems. Genetic algorithm (GA) developed by Professor Holland [2, 43] and his group of students in early 1970's firstly imitates some of the processes observed in natural evolution. This is most widely used and popular algorithms for optimization problems. This algorithm is key to many modern nature-inspired algorithms since the population of the individual is used to search for an optimal solution. Mostly, the nature-inspired algorithms are population based algorithms. In the primary step of the search, population of individuals use the search space, but later, final step is more focused toward the exploitation [48].

If the algorithm is more tilted toward the exploitation, then it will converges more speedily but stuck somewhere in a local optimum. Whereas, convergence speed will be slower down if an algorithm sustains more exploitation features. Optimization is form of mathematical procedure for getting an optimal allocation of scare resources. Different types of optimization problem exist. All optimization problems have an objective function, constraints, and variables which lead to further improvement. One can observe that there is no such optimization algorithm which will give superior results to all the problems. One cannot predict variable operators and selection mechanism that will always give you desired outcomes. That is why there is need to develop new algorithms to solve different types of problems as one technique will not always work the best.

Three categories of optimization techniques are stochastic optimization, robust optimization, and dynamic optimization. The main interest behind this study on the nature-inspired computational approach is to identify among the connectivity, social consumption, and rise. The work done here is needed in the scientific society to utilize the use of computing to demonstrate the living phenomenon and to investigate and upgrade our lives by use of computers. This study will substantially contribute in bringing the inspiration of computer-based solutions through a wide range of natural process.

7.1.1 Stochastic Optimization

Stochastic optimization (SO) process is related to randomness in the minimization or maximization of a function. It contains uncertainty and imprecision. The forms in which randomness is presents are noise in measurements or Monte Carlo randomness in search procedure, or both. Some of the common techniques are direct search methods, stochastic approximation, stochastic programming, simulated annealing genetic algorithm etc. Some applications of SO in real life are new drug design network in traffic control designing missile. Theoretically, it has proven the quality of the solutions generated. Practically, it is limited and based on data and modeling of complex problems.

7.1.2 Robust Optimization

Robust optimization (RO) deals with data uncertainty. There are two motivational factors of RO. Firstly, the uncertainty model is alternatively determined and set based. This motivational concept is the most basic and appropriate parameter of uncertainty in many applications. Second motivational factor is the computational feasibility and tractability. For a given optimization problem, the application of RO depends on the structure of uncertainty set and where the computational feasibility plays important role. Further, classification models for RO contains local vs. global and probabilistic vs. non-probabilistic. This optimization technique is also called as min-max or worst case approach due to its nature of problem. It is also helpful for the parameters which include estimation process and contain estimation errors. RO technique is applicable to every genetic optimization problem as it is strong and healthy in which numerical data can be distinguished from the structure of the problem. The main challenge of RO is that it gives the same weight and values to all the uncertain parameters. RO technique is quite impressive as it contains cost effectiveness increment of stability qualitative and quantative robustness. Also, it does not significantly increase the complexity of the considered optimization problems.

7.1.3   Dynamic Optimization

Dynamic optimization (DO) is referred as dynamic programming which includes the process of finding the optimal solution for one or more control parameters of a system. There are several approaches of DO which are based on calculus variations deals with optimization discrete time and extend the static optimization. It is used to provide the possible number of solution for a given problem. The flow chart of DO implementation works as system controller a performance criteria and an algorithm to execute the control. The important attribute of DO are optimal substructure and overlapping sub-problems. The steps involve in development of DO algorithm are as follows:

a) Characterization of the structure for an optimal solution.
b) Recursively define the value of an optimal solution.
c) Computation of value of an optimal solution in a bottom up fashion.
d) Construction of an optimal solution from computed information.

Practical application of the concept of DO is universal and flexible which can be applied to the execution of any problem. The main benefit of this technique is that it performs within itself by dividing the problems into a set of simpler sub-problems. Each sub-problem is solved only once using either top down or bottom up approach. Based on memorization technique it is applied where the solutions of sub problems are based on its parameter's values. Solving computational time at the expense of modest expenditure in storage memory.

7.1.4   Alogrithm

Artificial intelligence (AI) has been outmost regulation to be viewed in field of computer technology. The development and examination of framework which is logical based. Nature inspired computation; meta heuristics and computational intelligence are common examples of algorithm from AI. One can be highly inspired and astonished by computation utilization on bio-inspired process to mimic the living marvels. Outcome based on computational intelligence can be broadly divided into five major fields: swarm intelligence, evolutionary computation [46], artificial neural network, artificial immune system, and fuzzy systems.

7.1.5   Swarm Intelligence

Swarm intelligence (SI) is a process of adaptive strategy which ignores individual respond on centralized control structure; it takes collective intelligence as a noticed behavior. It is a simple self-organizing co evolution and widely applied in the domains of optimization searching methods research DNA computing improvement heating system planning etc. Swarm Intelligence includes bird flocking, cuckoo, search animal herding. It contains two sub fields ant colony optimization which originated by trail of the ant behavior and particle swarm optimization which is inspired by flocking and swarming property.

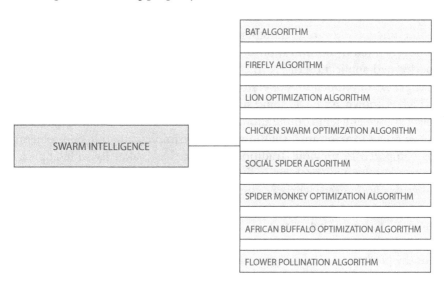

7.2   Related Work to FPA

For problems based on nonlinear and multi-objective bat algorithm (BA) [4] can work with simply and flexibly. Researchers get inspired by the phenomenon of bats special high level capability of bio-sonar which is used by them to get their prey, obstacles roosting crevices, detection, and distinguish between different types of insects which is known as echolocation. The performance of BA [4] depends on automatic zooming and frequency tuning. Automatic zooming is the capability based on the automatic switch from exploration direction to the local insensitive exploitation. Frequency tuning is the variation of frequency is performed on the echolocation.

The echolocation feature of micro bats is used to frame model BA. There are SO-based important implementations of BA like stochastic resonance for MIR images enhancement, neuron model that is based on multi-objective optimization property of bat algorithm [3]. Adaptions of two operational features to increase the performance of BA are iterative local search and stochastic inertial weight. In terms of accuracy, speed and convergence stability they contribute to BA efficiency. It fails to provide stable optimization results due to low global exploration ability. This weakness is overcome by researchers such as BA that has better ability to get out of local optima. Firefly algorithm (FA) inspired by capability of fireflies having short and rhythmic blazing light which give luminous sight in the sky. The flash light is used to model the warning signals. Bioluminescence is the phenomenon of generating the flash light. Different light intensity is represented as optimization problem [5]. Kwiecien and Filipowicz [6] performed application of FA in cost optimization of queuing system. Kai Zenger [7] developed FPA operator by adding crossovers and mutation GA which is known as FPA-GA and successfully operated on CEC2005. FA has been shown efficient computational procedure for simultaneously produce alternatives to an optimal solution. Its simple implementation on problems as compared to previous traditional approaches makes its wide applications. To solve a SO problem in linear phase, finite impulse response (FIR) filter design is used, whereas differential evolution (DE) is known as the best performer for such type of problems. On treatment of FIR designing filters, FA showed better results than other relevant algorithms (PSO and GA). The improvement is shown not only for convergence speed but also for the performance of designed filter.

In the past few years, many natures inspired processes are appointed for developing artificial intelligence meta heuristic algorithms to reduce the stochastic of optimization problems. Simulation of nature evolution phenomenon of living organisms to get their present optimized state. Exploration or diversification makes the algorithm to explore search space efficiently by randomization factor. While exploitation or intensification tends to search nearby the current best solution. To find the high-quality solution there must be a balance between diversification and intensification. In this section the other algorithms are described with ideas inspired from nature inspired activities.

GA [43] defined the biological evolution process of chromosomes via selection, crossover, and mutation process. Each candidate solution in the search space is taken as a chromosome that results according to their fitness value. Parents selected for breeding for generating new solutions by using exploitation of high fitness solutions in the current generation.

Swapping of two selected chromosomes is takes place in crossover phase. For mutation process, there is random change in some parts of chromosomes in order to hide from local optima and exploring search space.

Eberhard and Kennedy [8] developed evolution computing possibilities with swarm intelligence in 1995 as present Particle Swarm Optimization (PSO). In PSO, exploration and exploitation are mainly controlled by inertia weight factor which determines the effect of the previous velocity on the current velocity of a particle. In the previous iterations, the value of inertial weight is large to increase velocity for more exploration. It is observed that the value of inertial weight is decreased to slow velocity reaching to zero which shows more exploitation. The brood parasitism of cuckoo bird is mimicked as cuckoo search (CS) introduced by Yang and Deb [9]. The bird search for nest to replace her eggs with their new ones was taken as idea of exploration and solutions are new born ones. If the dropped egg is identified by the host bird, then it will be replaced by a new one and exploitation is done.

Lion optimization (LO) is an algorithm based on population and inspired by lion's social system. The uniqueness of lion's social behavior and their collaboration characteristic described as "pride" makes them strongest mammal in animal kingdom. Two unique behaviors of lion are taken to frame the model: one is territorial defense and second is territorial takeover. LO can work on huge search space to solve continuous, single variable and multi-variable optimization problem. LO can be used for data clustering SO problem.

Chicken swarm optimization (CSO) [49] algorithm inspired by the social behavior of chickens. Roosters, hens, and chicks are fitness values of chickens. Hierarchal order is the main characteristic of CSO algorithm. CSO is used to solve the design of speed reducer. A virtual machine consolidation problem based on dead lock free algorithm has been utilized by researchers on CSO modeling. This implementation helps CSO to achieve higher convergence rate as compare to other deadlock free migration algorithm. The application to identify the maximum power point tracking control of a photovoltaic system is also an example of an improved version of CSO.

7.2.1   Flower Pollination Algorithm

Every living organism exists on earth has a goal of producing offspring for the next generation. Flowers make the world beautiful. You have seen many different varieties of flowers around you. They are not only to make them look beautiful but also, a vital part of a plant life cycle. A flower contains seeds, which get spread away from the parents and grow into new plants in other places, termed as Pollination. Darwin theory of "Survival of the fittest" plays leading role in understanding of process of optimized pollination. Angiosperms of flowering plants survived for more than 100 million years by process of pollination. Pollination studied by Frankel and Galun [10] described as a phenomenon of reproduction in flowering plants. When a male gamete (pollen) is transferred to the female stigma for fertilization. For uni sexual type flowers species that contains reproductive organs male stamens and female (carpels) in different flowers. In bisexual species both reproductive organs are contained in the same flower. The beauty (color of petals and fragrance) of flower makes pollinators like birds, insects, and bees to attract them which preserve the flower constancy. Some flowers and insects have an incredibly special type of flower pollinator partnership. Some flowers only attract a particular species of birds and insects for effective pollination. This relationship helps pollinators to ensure nectar supply with less exploring. Pollination classification is divided into two types: Cross pollination process (Figure 7.1) in which process of transferring pollen grains takes place between two different flowers of different plants. In Self-pollination process (Figure 7.2) the transfer of pollen grains is take place between two flowers of same plants. Due to pollination transfer of pollen grains from the male part to the female part take place. After this, pollen releases a male gamete that fertilizes a female gamete in the ovule and mixes their genetic material. After the fertilization, ovule grows to form a seed.

Pollination can be of two forms: abiotic and biotic. Biotic pollination in which transfer of pollen requires a pollinator's service for fertilization process by visiting a flower or sipping nectar. Abiotic pollination can be done by wind diffusion in water or gravity which has very few chances of occurrence.

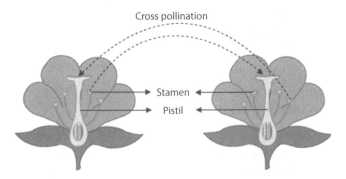

Figure 7.1 Flowers showing cross-pollination. Picture source: https://vivadifferences. com/self-pollination-vs-cross-pollination-differences-you-must-know/.

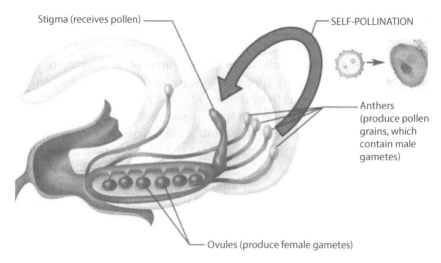

Stigma (receives pollen)

SELF-POLLINATION

Anthers
(produce pollen
grains, which
contain male
gametes)

Ovules (produce female gametes)

Figure 7.2 Flower showing self-pollination process. Picture source: https://
vivadifferences.com/self-pollination-vs-cross-pollination-differences-you-must-know/.

Keeping alive the fittest flowering species is key idea behind the flower pollination algorithm (FPA) through reproduction process. Initially, flower or pollen is a candidate solution with an assumption that one flower in each plant and each flower produce one pollen. Further optimization is processed and diffusion through search space is done. The process is studied by biotic and cross-pollination where movement of pollen grain is represented by Levy flight. Levy flight is random step size.

In the picture, a butterfly is a pollinator sipping nectar form the marigold flower and performed the process of pollination.

7.2.2   Versions of FPA

FPA consist of two types of version: 1) binary version and 2) multi-objective version. Since multi-objective optimization problems are typically complex to solve. The approach to solve multi-objective problem is different from single-objective problems. In single-objective optimization problem, the optimal solution can be a single point in the solution space, while for bi-objective, there is curve and tri-objective consists of surface. The conclusion is drawn from this, more the complex type of problem hyper surface we get. This make very challenging to solve high dimensional problems including design problems in engineering which require producing many points for good approximation. The proposed MOFPA is very efficient for multi-objective problems when tested on 11 test functions. The binary FPA version is implemented for feature selection. BFPA uses Boolean search space to compose the final set when applied to some public and private data sets.

7.2.3   Methods and Description

The main of idea of this process of pollination is survival of the fittest and the optimal reproduction of plants in terms of numbers as well as fittest (Figure 7.3). This is referred as optimization process of plant species. Optimization can be understood as process of searching to locate the best solution to a problem. This searching can be done by using some external tools basically mathematical models. Hence, we can solve these problems by using optimization algorithm to find the best solution. Since, there is no assurance that best solution always be reachable. The search for optimal solution can be processed by taking some assumptions. Likewise, each flower only produces one pollen gamete. The time complexity of FPA is shorter for its easy implementation. An observation has been seen while studying the cost of optimization of tabular column under compressive load using FPA against cuckoo search algorithm fuzzy rules and engineering optimization techniques. It is concluded that FPA showed the best efficient results and it is very effective method and convergence of the algorithm is very much efficient one. This algorithm is applicable on continuous single-objective and multi-objective problems. Biotic and cross-pollination are linked to global pollination process as it may occur over long distances. While self-pollination is local pollination process. Biotic pollinators such as bats, bees, birds, and insects fly or jump randomly which is refer as step length obeys Levy distribution. The Levy distribution (Figure 7.4) is example of stable

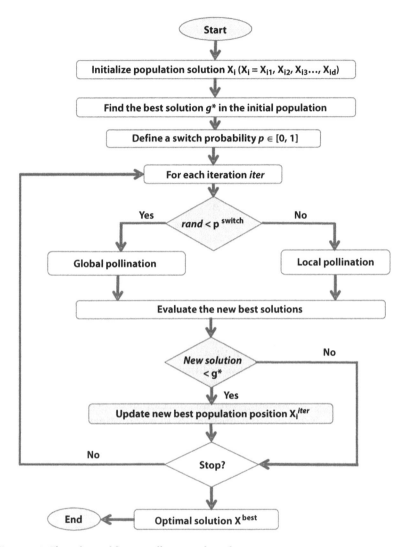

Figure 7.3 Flow chart of flower pollination algorithm.

distribution for the study of Brownian motion. Levy distribution for probability density function f, a random variable X in range of {0,∞}.

$$f(x) = \frac{1}{\sqrt{2\pi}} \frac{1}{x^{\frac{3}{2}}} \exp\left(-\frac{1}{2x}\right), x \in (0, \infty)$$

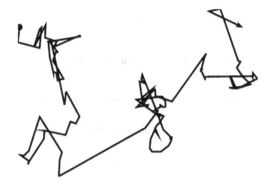

Figure 7.4 Fifty steps of Levy flights. Picture source: https://www.researchgate.net/figure/Levy-flights-in-consecutive-50-steps-starting-at-the-origin-0-0-marked-with_fig1_235979455.

In 2012, Yang [12, 14] formulated the characteristics of (Table 7.1) FPA in flowering plants. He developed the algorithm by considering the four rules which are:

RULE 1: The global pollination process takes place via biotic and cross-pollination through movement of pollinators in the form of Levy flights.
RULE 2: Abiotic and self-pollination is known as local pollination process.
RULE 3: The flower constancy which is developed by pollinators like bees is equivalent to a reproduction probability that is proportional to the similarity of two flowers involved.

Table 7.1 Characteristics of FPA.

General algorithm	Flower pollination algorithm
Decision variable	Pollen gametes or flowers
Solution	Pollen gametes or flowers
Old solution	Old flower/old pollen gametes
New solution	New flower/new pollen gamete
Best solution	Current best solution
Fitness function	Not defined
Initial solution selection	Random selection
Process of generation new solution	Flying or local random walk

RULE 4: Switching between local and global pollinations is controlled by probability p € [0, 1] with a simple assumption toward local pollination for reasons relating to the approximation of the algorithm to the real case.

The application of these rules is based on a basic assumption that each plant has only one flower and each flower produces only one pollen gamete.

7.2.3.1   Reproduction Factor

A reproduction factor (R-factor) is a parameter to check the fittest sequence of jobs for execution. To find the fittest sequence job depends on having minimum overall execution time. Further R-factor is also used to determine local best (L-best) and global best (G-best) among all possible sequences.

7.2.3.2   Levy Flights

They are used to calculate the length of the step to improve the quality of solution. One can drive the step size from Levy flights. Levy flights are in the range (0, 1) which is helpful to determine the small steps, large steps and number of steps. A number of different sequences are generated with permutation process by using Levy flights. They also increase the speed of algorithm by deciding about the position of job and length of jobs to swap in sequence.

The four rules are mathematically formulated with three main features.

1. Global Search

As it is assumed that each plant contains only one flower and each flower produces one pollen gamete. The x_i represents to a flower or a pollen gamete. Pollinator's job is to find the location of optimum point in the whole search space. The benefit of considering biotic and cross-pollinators is that they can travel a long distance obeying Levy flights. The variance of Levy flight is more than the Brownian motion makes the Levy flight more efficient one. The transition of rule into mathematical formulation is carried out by Yang [11, 12]. The global pollination process and flower constancy which lessen the cost of exploring can be represented by equation:

$$x_i^{t+1} = x_i^t + \gamma L(\lambda)\left(g^* - x_i^t\right)$$

where x_i^t = pollen ith or the solution vector x_i at "t" iteration
$\quad x_i^{t+1}$ = generated solution vector at t+1 iteration.
$\quad\quad g_*$ = current best solution
$\quad\quad\quad \gamma$ = scaling factor used to control step size.
$\quad L(\lambda)$ = Levy flights based step size.

Levy distribution is valid for large steps s > 0. $L(\lambda)$ corresponds strength of the pollination. Mantegna [16] (Bazant [17]) studied the best value for lambda is between [0.75, 1.95] and one should take positive value to control the scale factor. Yang [3, 13] used the scale factor 0.01 for FPA to prevent pollen from flying away.

$$L \sim \frac{\lambda \Gamma(\lambda)\sin\left(\dfrac{\pi\lambda}{2}\right)1}{\pi s^{1+\lambda}}\ (s \gg s_0 > 0)$$

Here, $\Gamma(\lambda)$ is standard gamma function, distribution is valid for large steps s > 0.

2. Local Search
Local pollinators can better exploit the area at the optimum value location. For this time to reduce the exploitation time, the flower constancy will be in small neighborhood. On combining Rule 2 and Rule 3, the flower constancy can be written mathematically as follows:

$$x_i^{t+1} = x_i^t + \epsilon\left(x_j^t - x_k^t\right)$$

where x_j^t and x_k^t represent pollen gametes of different flowers of the same plant species.
$\left(x_j^t - x_k^t\right)$ represents the flower constancy in a limited neighborhood and parameter ϵ is chosen arbitrary in [0,1] to approximate this selection to a local random walk Yang [14, 12] in 2012.

3. Switch Probability
Switch probability works to control between local and global search in FPA. Pollination can be processed either at the local scale or global scale. It determines diversity percentage and intensification during research. Probability of those flowers to get pollinate by local neighboring is more rather than far away. The mean of switch probability or proximity probability "p" is

used for switching between common global pollination to intensive local pollination. Initially, the proposed value is p = 0.5 but later for most of applications p = 0.8 works better. Yang [11, 12] performed FPA on 10 test functions and one design optimization problem, and the results obtained are better than basic GA and basic particle swarm optimization.

7.2.3.3 User-Defined Parameters

To get optimal parameters for FPA, we need to run the algorithm many times, which is time-consuming and also optimal parameters are different for every other problem. The size of the population (n), the scale factor (γ), the Levy distribution L(λ), and switch probability are roughly estimation user-defined parameters which are observed by Yang [11, 12].

Size of the population of solution (n)	Determined according to the problem, for satisfactory results one should limit the size due to complexity of (n)
Switch probability (p)	p = 0.8 (Yang [14]) p = 0.2 (Draa [15])
Levy distribution index (λ)	1.5 (Yang [14]) [0.75, 1.95] (Mantegna [16], Bazant [17])
Scale factor (γ)	Any positive size, γ = 0.01

7.2.3.4 Psuedo Code for FPA

Begin

Objective function:minimize or maximize F(x), x=($x_1,x_2,x_3,....x_d$)
Initialize a population of n flowering species using random solutions
Find the best solution g^* in the initial population
Select a number in [0, 1] with switch probability P
While *(t < maximum iteration number)*
    For m = 1;n
        If *random > p then*
            Create a d-dimensional step vector L with the Levy flight distribution
            Do global pollination with $x_i^{t+1} = x_i^t + \gamma L(\lambda) x \left(g^* - x_j^t \right)$

Else

> *Create from a uniform distribution in [0,1]*
> *Select x_j^t and x_k^t from population randomly*
> *Do local pollination with $x_i^{t+1} = x_i^t + \left(x_i^t - x_k^t \right)$*

End if

> *Calculate the objective function for new solutions*
> *If the objective function corresponding to new solutions are*
> *better, update new solutions*

End for

> *Obtain current best solution g**

End while

end

7.2.3.5   Comparative Studies for FPA

Yang [18] proposed a mathematical analysis of FPA via using Markov chain theory. He proved that FPA can converge to optimal solution as the experiment was made on well-known benchmarks in order to exhibit the convergence ability of FPA practically.

On comparison with other met heuristics models on solving different optimization problems. With comparison to BA, Sakib [4] studied that FPA outperforms in terms of convergence, solution quality and consistency on continuous optimization problems. Pandya [18] compared BA, FPA and PSO with optimal power flow (OPF) problem of highly stressed modified IEEE300 bus test system, BA offers more efficient results rather than DPA and PSO. Hegazy [20] studied the comparison between MCS, ABC and previous algorithm on least square support vector machine optimization problem (LS-SVM) the best results are showed by FPA-LS-SVM method. HS performs better than FPA in many cases for software testing observed by Nasser [21]. FPA performances well with small numbers rather than larger ones of thresholds. Rathasamuth and Nootyaskool [22] compared between FPA, PSO and GA on discrete search space which shows FPA has better convergence rate than others. Ismail and El-Henawy [23] compare

FPA with PSO for solving integer programming problems with branch and bound method.

7.2.3.6   Working Environment

Yang [14] done basic implementation of FPA by using MATLAB language. MATLAB is a programming language used for development of algorithm, data analysis visualization and numerical computational analysis. It consists of matrix-based computation designed for scientific and engineering use.it is widely used for solving algebraic and differential equation and numerical integration image processing parallel computing signal processing optimization and many more [47]. The performance of FPA depends on factors like make span, speed up and efficiency. Make span is the total length of the scheduled when all the simulation job are finished their execution. Speed up is the ration of the time taken by old algorithm with time taken by new algorithm. Efficiency is defined as the ration of speed up to the number of processors to number of processors. For more approaches, many contributions were introduced for implementing FPA in different languages. C++ and java languages were used for FPA by Yang and Widihananta [24]. Bhatia [25] developed FPA toolkit in LabVIEW™. Putra and Anggorowati [26] introduced FPA by R language. R language is a well-developed simple to use for statistical computing and graphics.

7.2.3.7   Improved Versions of FPA

To magnify the efficiency of FPA, there are several improvements were made to overcome some issues related to premature convergence for a number of given problems as studied. These refinements are made in global search and local search parameters. They are discussed briefly here.

7.2.3.7.1   Modified FPA (MFPA)

Dasgupta *et al.* [27] introduced a new constant scaling factor to control the local pollination instead of a random number to increase the convergence factor for FPA. Also, to adjust the best solution, an additional exploitation step was added further. The results showed that the proposed algorithm is working efficiently for solving small and medium scale instances while larger ones still need enhancement. MFPA is applicative in solving economic dispatch problems of electrical power systems.

7.2.3.7.2   Improved FPA With Chaos (IFPCH)

Abdel-Raouf [28] introduced the chaotic maps (logistic map, chebyshev map, tent map, etc.) which are evolution functions that generate a determinant bounded sequence of bound numbers based on the initial condition with different time domain instead of basic random numbers. The selection was made due to random like, non-period, and non-converging properties for parameter adaptation. The switch probability Levy step and local pollination random number are defined according to the selected chaotic map in IFPCH. On application to calculate the numerical value of definite integrals, the proposed algorithm shows effective results.

1. FPA with dimension by dimension improvement (DDIFPA) [28]. Wang and Zhou [36] modified FPA through implementing three features:

   (a) Local neighborhood search strategy (LNSS)
   (b) Dimension by dimension evaluation and improvement strategy (DDEIS)
   (c) Dynamic switching probability strategy (DSPS)

LNSS increases local pollination where only the best neighbor solutions with a pre-defined topology are used to update solution instead of whole population. DDEIS deals with multi-dimensional problems by modifying dimension by dimension. DSPS is responsible for modifying the switching probability with respect to the present iteration and the total number of iterations. Twelve benchmarks were tested for DDIFPA and results show DDIFPA exploitation more efficiently the search space for unimodal and had more accurate solutions.

2. FPA with complex valued encoding (CFPA)
   The CFPA was inspired from amphipod where each chromosome consists of two alleles. This complex valued encoding scheme was developed by Zhao and Zhou [39]. It consists of two vectors: one is real parts and other is imaginary parts which updated in parallel to increase the population randomness and the performance of FPA. CFPA and FPA both tested on 10 well-known benchmarks which show CFPA faster and more robustness than FPA.

3. Elite opposition-based FPA (EOFPA)
   Zhou [40] proposed three subsidiary enhancements in EOFPA.

(a) Global elite opposition based learning strategy (GEOLS)
(b) Local self-adaptive greedy strategy (LSGS)
(c) Dynamic switching probability strategy (DSPS)

GEOLS applied for getting better solutions by increasing the exploration phase via evaluating the candidate solutions and their opposite solutions simultaneously. In LSGS, a greedy solution is calculated and highly tuned in early iterations to escape from local optima afterward the adjustment of the greedy solution become smaller at the end of iterations. DSPS adjust the switching probability value dynamically with respect to iterations. Eighteen benchmark functions and two engineering problems were tested by EOFPA which exposed the more accurate and stable results than FPA.

7.2.3.7.3   Application of FPA

The frequent research work on ECT has been approached for locating the global optimum. However, in the accomplishment for multiple desired solutions in field of engineering, the best solution may not always be apt due to several realistic constraints. The challenge of locating all the optima in a single run is more complex than global optimization. Some techniques have been applied to original ETC in order to generate their multimodal extensions. The inspiration taken for the development of several evolutionary computation algorithms with multimodal capacities was biological systems which at certain level performed the multimodal optimization process [50]. This also helps to understand the biological systems, for examples, Clonal Selection Algorithm and the Multimodal Gravitational Search Algorithm (MGSA).

For the development of nature-inspired algorithm Yang [1] proposed Single-Objective Flower Pollination Algorithm (SFPA). It was a benchmark as implemented on functions as results shows that the efficiency of SFPA with respect to GA and PSO. SFPA was used in Wireless Sensor Network (WSN) to overcome low energy adaptive clustering hierarchy (LEACH). Experimental simulations results show better results for SFPA. The optimization was performed in two stages: (1) search for the optimal vessel of the retina. (2) By using local search cluster center is obtained. SPFA convergence toward the optimal solution is very fast as if SFPA was robust with some multimodal, low- and high-dimensional continuous functions. Some of the experiments with treatment of SFPA were able to obtain the pressures and molar fractions of the liquid phase. The performance of SFPA was appreciable fast to that of BA on the basis of comparative simulations results for continuous optimization problems.

Further Yang [1] extended SFPA to MFPA multimodal flower pollination algorithm to approach the multi-objective problems. MFPA was processed on specific functions and structural design. In comparison to many algorithms like multi objective differential evolution (MODE), differential evolution for multi objective optimization (DEMO), GA and PSO. Since the development of FPA, there is a numerous range of diverse applications published in many research papers. The multimodal adaptation performed with three operators proposed by Cuevas and Reyna-Orta [41]. The process of finding potential local and global optima is based on memory utilization. Secondly, a new selection process instead of elitist selection to ensure solution diversity. In multi-modal system both global and local optima describe two important characteristic a good fitness value and representation of the best fitness in a certain neighborhood. The past and new solution in overall evolutionary process is being implemented into memory mechanism. This is done in two divergent phases of initialization and capture. The memory mechanism allows multiple approaches of individuals in a single execution. Previously the set size of final solution is same as size of initial population while taking multiple solution registration.

One of very interesting application of FPA is in the field of power systems. The search for the optimal solution with multiple fuel sources like oil, natural gas, coal involves the minimization of fuel cost. This refers as Economic load Dispatch (ELD) problem. The unit constraints consider being optimization problem in power system operation. Non-linear, non-convex, and non-smooth optimization problem is the main characteristics of ELD. Application of various optimization techniques on ELD problem like PSO because it is simple and effective to apply and GA to resolve its non-smooth and complexity of ELD not show promising results. But a significant feature of FPA makes the algorithm easier to implement and faster to reach optimum solution. The switch probability parameter makes possible to escape from local minimum solution by transferring between local and global pollination. FPA helps to find the global solution for ELD problems in power system. The results are compared with other algorithms and obtained ones show promising aspects of FPA. The performance of FPA shows better convergence characteristics computational efficiency and less CPU time when compared to PSO and GA.

There is a hybrid FPA which is combination of FPA with other metaheuristic algorithms like PSO and GA. The limitation of FPA having shortest period of time to converge the optimal solution is reduced by hybridization. Abdel-Raouf [28] developed a hybrid of Single FPA and chaotic harmony search (FPCHS) to enhance the search accuracy. On treatment to Sudoku puzzles, results of hybrid of SFPA and FPCHS converge faster to the optimal solution than FPCHS. The hybrid of PSO and SFPA improved performance on application to solve constrained global optimization problem. To maintain the balance between exploitation and exploration to improve efficiency of the algorithm, Yang [3] combined eagle technique with SFPA, known as ESSFPA which only use 10% of the computational time compared to PSO. Some features are introduced by Wang and Zhou [36] like neighborhood searching strategy, dynamic switching probability strategy, and dimension-by-dimension update and improvement strategy to increase convergence speed and quality of solution. Kanagasabai and Ravindhranath Reddy [35] introduced SFPA and PSO jointly named as (SFPAPSO). There are different order in which hybridized algorithm is being executed like parallel sequential or interleaved. One of best parts of hybridized algorithms is that it compromises the Levy flight–based exploration capabilities of FPA. Nabil and Von Zuben [34] combined local pollination with the theoretical principles of immunology.

FA is combined with FPA by Kalra and Arora [5] which work according to basic FA included search for local optimum and finding the best solution. Then, switching function directs the search process either to FA global search or FPA local search. The advantage of using hybridized algorithms is lower computational time and faster convergence which are important aspects for optimization problems. Many people tried their hands on the hybridization formulation, for example, Chakraborty [33] evolved FPA with DE and new dynamic adaptive weight is taken over switching probability. Further Tsai [38] merged FPA with DE in a parallel manner during the search process the best fit are stored and interchanged between both algorithms via communication strategy. Salgotra and Singh [37] do the same procedure by taking Bat algorithm.

The final solution of PSO was improved in Abdel-Raouf [28] and Abdel-Baset [29] proposed FPA. The hybridization of ant colony system (ACS) and FPA proposed two combinations presented by Ku-Mahamud [30] and Gambardella [31]. Only FPA global pollination is being considered for increasing the exploration capabilities of ACS in first combination while the second considers FPA for adjusting the final solution of ACS. Artificial bee colony (ABC) is combined with FPA and simplex method which work as follows: first, FPA is applied by replacing the global search by elite-based mutation process designed by Ram [32]. It works after the resultant solution is found and the current best solution is updated. But if the replacement of current best solution is failed, then a counter is increased. When the limit of counter is reached, simplex method is used to enhance the solution.

7.3   Limitations

The binary version of FPA is not much detailed in literature. FPA cannot be able to solve binary problems and produce binary solutions. The binary meta-heuristic algorithms like binary CS, binary PSO, and binary GA. The solution is typically comprised of a set of binary numbers or bits.

7.4   Future Research

The adaptations of FPA in numerous domains are review to offer researchers a glance of the applications of FPA [45]. This inspires researchers to propose novel applications and identify the areas which require improvement. FPA is divided in two major classifications of SFPA and MFPA depending on the nature of optimization problem. Areas where FPA applications are studied are energy structural design function optimization games images and WSN. FPA is builded with few parameter settings which increase its effectiveness and make its performance better than other nature-inspired algorithms. Further extension of FPA or binary FPA can be done in future. Since the algorithm is new and presently under explorations by the research community. FPA can further explored in other research domains like carbon dioxide emission quantum computations. The more exploration to more fields improve the performance of FPA; one can look for what are optimum parameters values required for execution of FPA and do further comparative studies to distinguish which biologically inspired algorithm can best be hybridized with FPA. Application of FPA on fuzzy logic is studied further. Applying FPA to solve geographical information system application will also be curious to observe. Applications to machine learning problems, analyzing the effect of hybrid FPA with other methods, will be interesting to learn. He *et al.* proved that the mathematical study of global convergence on various optimization problems which guaranteed the global convergence but the mathematically study of rate of convergence has not been proved yet. In future, studies can focus on the theoretical analysis of convergence rate stability and robustness of FPA. To overcome the tuning control and variations of parameters can also be interest of research in future. FPA has shown good results for some combinatorial optimization problems but, for large scales, it is still problematic. The population-based algorithms including FPA use simple structure for updating variants of population; one can go for investigation for the possibility of updating them in non-synchronized unstructured way. It will

Table 7.2 Various types of applications of FPA [19].

Field	Application area
Computer science	Cloud computing [44], data clustering, optical wavelength division multiplexing (WDM) system, wireless senor network (WSNs), graph coloring problem.
Bioinformatics	Neural network training, feature selection.
Operational research	Integer programming problem, economic load dispatch problem, fractional programming problem, distributed generation (DG) optimal locations, assembly sequence optimization, vehicle path planning problem, congestion management problem (CM).
Food industry	Liquid-liquid equilibrium modeling, shrinkage of triaxial porcelain containing palm oil fuel ash, generating healthy nutritional meals for older adults.
Imaging science	Fractional image compression, medical image segmentation, visual tracking system, atomic potential matching [51].
Meteorology	Wind speed forecasting.
Medicine	Feta head segmentation, retinal vessel segmentation.
Engineering	Multi pass turning parameters, control of multi-area power systems, optimal power flow problem (OPF), optimal reactive power dispatch (ORPD) problem, load frequency control, antenna positioning problem, optimal capacitor locations, inverse kinematic problem (PUMA Robot), hydrocarbon combustion problem, and double azeotrope calculation problem, vertical tubular columns optimization, weight optimization of cantilever beams, mass dampers tuning, multi-machine system optimal control, Optimal relay coordination, manufacturing cell design, solar photovoltaic (PV) systems parameter estimation.
Education	Selection of university academic results

be interesting to see if they work for mixed parallel series population with random mixing.

7.5   Conclusion

FPA is a potentially powerful and effective tool for solving different optimization problem in a wide range of applications (Table 7.2). New modifications and advancements can enhance its performance even further [42]. Biologically inspired algorithm has been one of the effective methods to solve the optimization problems; in 2012, the FPA has been implemented in many fields proposed by Xin-She Yang [14]. FPA is a powerful tool in solving engineering computer science operational research problems. It is one of the more commonly used algorithms until now. The selection of suitable metaheuristic for given optimization problem is more specific problem. Some of FPA parameters need to be adjusted and basic FPA need amendments to enhance the performance and algorithm disposal from premature convergence and time consuming task. The overview of FPA main structure previous studies variants and applications are studied. FPA is current state of interest in optimization techniques despite the abundance of nature inspired algorithms already in the solution basket.

References

1. Yang, X.S., Karamanoglu, M., He, X., Flower pollination algorithm: a novel approach for multiobjective optimization. *Eng. Optim.*, 46, 9, 1222–1237, 2014.
2. Goldberg, D.E. and Holland, J.H., Genetic algorithms and machine learning, 1988, https://deepblue.lib.umich.edu/bitstream/handle/2027.42/46947/10994_2005_Article_422926.pdf.
3. Fister, I., Yang, X.S., Fong, S., Zhuang, Y., Bat algorithm: Recent advances. In *2014 IEEE 15th International symposium on computational intelligence and informatics (CINTI)*, IEEE, pp. 163–167, 2014.
4. Sakib, N. *et al.*, A comparative study of flower pollination algorithm and bat algorithm on continuous optimization problems. *Int. J. Soft Comput. Eng.*, 4, 3, 13–19, 2014.
5. Kalra, S. and Arora, S., Firefly algorithm hybridized with flower pollination algorithm for multimodal functions. In *Proceedings of the international congress on information and communication technology,*

pp. 207–219, Springer, Singapore, 2016, https://link.springer.com/chapter/10.1007/978-981-10-0767-5_23.

6. Lim, S.M. and Leong, K.Y., A Brief Survey on Intelligent Swarm-Based Algorithms for Solving Optimization Problems, in: *Nature-inspired Methods for Stochastic, Robust and Dynamic Optimization*, J. Del Ser and E. Osaba (Eds.), IntechOpen, 2018, 10.5772/intechopen.76979, https://www.intechopen.com/books/nature-inspired-methods-for-stochastic-robust-and-dynamic-optimization/a-brief-survey-on-intelligent-swarm-based-algorithms-for-solving-optimization-problems.

7. Fouad, A., Zenger, K., Gao, X.Z., A Novel Flower Pollination Algorithm based on Genetic Algorithm Operators. In *Proceedings of The 9th EUROSIM Congress on Modelling and Simulation, EUROSIM 2016, The 57th SIMS Conference on Simulation and Modelling SIMS 2016*, vol. 142, pp. 1060–1066, Linköping University Electronic Press, 2018.

8. Kennedy, J. and Eberhart, R., Particle swarm optimization. In *Proceedings of ICNN'95-International Conference on Neural Networks*, vol. 4, pp. 1942–1948, IEEE, 1995.

9. Yang, X. and Deb, S., Cuckoo Search via Lévy flights, in: *2009 World Congress on Nature & Biologically Inspired Computing (NaBIC)*, pp. 210–214, Coimbatore, India, 2009.

10. Frankel, R. and Galun, E., Pollination mechanisms, reproduction and plant breeding, in: *Monographs on Theoretical and Applied Genetics*, Germany, FR, 1977.

11. Yang, X.S., *Nature-inspired metaheuristic algorithms*, Luniver press, 2010.

12. Alyasseri, Z.A.A., Khader, A.T., Al-Betar, M.A., Awadallah, M.A., Yang, X.S., Variants of the flower pollination algorithm: a review. In *Nature-Inspired Algorithms and Applied Optimization*, pp. 91–118, Springer, Cham, 2018, https://doi.org/10.1007/978-3-319-67669-2_5.

13. Yang, X.-S., Firefly algorithms for multimodal optimization, in: *International symposium on stochastic algorithms*, Springer, Berlin, Heidelberg, 2009, https://doi.org/10.1007/978-3-642-04944-6_14.

14. Yang, X.S., Flower Pollination Algorithm for Global Optimization. In *Unconventional Computation and Natural Computation. UCNC 2012. Lecture Notes in Computer Science*, J. Durand-Lose and N. Jonoska (Eds.), vol. 7445, Springer, Berlin, Heidelberg, 2012, https://doi.org/10.1007/978-3-642-32894-7_27.

15. Draa, A., On the performances of the flower pollination algorithm–Qualitative and quantitative analyses. *Appl. Soft Comput.*, 34, 349–371, 2015, https://doi.org/10.1016/j.asoc.2015.05.015.

16. Mantegna, R.N. and Stanley, H.E., Stochastic process with ultraslow convergence to a Gaussian: The truncated L??vy flight. *Phys. Rev. Lett.*, 73, 2946–2949, 1994, 10.1103/PhysRevLett.73.2946.

17. Abdel-Basset, M. and Shawky, L.A., Flower pollination algorithm: a comprehensive review. *Artif. Intell. Rev.*, 52, 4, 2533–2557, 2019, https://doi.org/10.1007/s10462-018-9624-4.

18. He, X. *et al.*, Global convergence analysis of the flower pollination algorithm: a discrete-time Markov chain approach. *Proc. Comput. Sci.*, 108, 1354–1363, 2017, https://doi.org/10.1016/j.procs.2017.05.020.

19. Pandya, K.S., Dabhi, D.A., Joshi, S.K., Comparative study of bat & flower pollination optimization algorithms in highly stressed large power system, in: *2015 Clemson University Power Systems Conference (PSC)*, pp. 1–5, Clemson, SC, USA, 2015.

20. Hegazy, O., Soliman, O.S., Salam, M.A., Comparative study between FPA, BA, MCS, ABC, and PSO algorithms in training and optimizing of LS-SVM for stock market prediction. *Int. J. Adv. Comput. Res.*, 5, 18, 35–45, 2015, Retrieved from https://search.proquest.com/scholarly-journals/comparative-study-between-fpa-ba-mcs-abc-pso/docview/1718579109/se-2?accountid=179891.

21. Nasser, A.B., Zamli, K.Z., Ahmed, B.S., Dynamic Solution Probability Acceptance within the Flower Pollination Algorithm for t-way Test Suite Generation. *arXiv preprint arXiv*:1902.11160, 2019, https://arxiv.org/ftp/arxiv/papers/1902/1902.11160.pdf.

22. Rathasamuth, W. and Nootyaskool, S., Comparison solving discrete space on flower pollination algorithm, PSO and GA, in: *2016 8th International Conference on Knowledge and Smart Technology (KST)*, pp. 18–21, Chiang Mai, Thailand, 2016.

23. El-henawy, I. and Ismail, M., An improved chaotic flower pollination algorithm for solving large integer programming problems. *Int. J. Digital Content Technol. Appl.*, 8, 3, 72, 2014.

24. Bansal, S., Flower Pollination Algorithm: Basic Concepts, Variants, and Applications, in: *Applications of Flower Pollination Algorithm and its Variants*, p. 1. https://www.springer.com/gp/book/9789813361034.

25. Bhatia, N.K., Kumar, V., Rana, K.P.S., Gupta, P., Mishra, P., Development of a flower pollination algorithm toolkit in LabVIEW™, in: *2016 3rd International Conference on Computing for Sustainable Global Development (INDIACom)*, pp. 309–314, IEEE, 2016, March, https://ieeexplore.ieee.org/abstract/document/7724277.

26. Putra, A.P. and Anggorowati, M.A., MetaheuristicFPA: an implementation of flower pollination algorithm in R, 2016, https://CRAN.R-project.org/package=MetaheuristicFPA.

27. Dasgupta, D. and Michalewicz, Z. (Eds.), *Evolutionary algorithms in engineering applications*, Springer Science & Business Media, 2013.

28. Abdel-Rauf, O., El-Henawy, I., Abdel-Baset, M., A novel hybrid flower pollination algorithm with chaotic harmony search for solving sudoku puzzles. *Int. J. Mod. Educ. Comput. Sci.*, 6, 3, 38, 2014.

29.   Hezam, I.M., Abdel-Baset, M., Hassan, B.M., A hybrid flower pollination algorithm with tabu search for unconstrained optimization problems. *Oper. Res.*, 1, 5, 2016, https://digitalcommons.aaru.edu.jo/isl/vol5/iss1/4.

30.   Ku-Mahamud, K.R., Hybrid ant colony system and flower pollination algorithms for global optimization, in: *2015 9th International Conference on IT in Asia (CITA)*, IEEE, 2015.

31.   Versino, C. and Gambardella, L.M., *Artificial Neural Networks — ICANN 96*, vol. 1112, p. 221, 1996.

32.   Pant, S., Kumar, A., Ram, M., Flower pollination algorithm development: a state of art review. *Int. J. Syst. Assur. Eng. Manage.*, 8, 2, 1858–1866, 2017.

33.   Chakraborty, D., Saha, S., Dutta, O., DE-FPA: a hybrid differential evolution-flower pollination algorithm for function minimization. In *2014 international conference on high performance computing and applications (ICHPCA)*, pp. 1–6, IEEE, 2014, 10.1109/ICHPCA.2014.7045350.

34.   Nabil, E., Badr, A., Frag, I., Khozium, M.O., A Proposed Artificial Immune Genetic Algorithm, 2016, http://dspace.must.edu.eg/handle/123456789/630.

35.   Kanagasabai, L. and RavindhranathReddy, B., Reduction of real power loss by using Fusion of Flower Pollination Algorithm with Particle Swarm Optimization. *J. Inst. Ind. Appl. Eng.*, 2, 3, 97, 2014, https://doi.org/10.12792/jiiae.2.97.

36.   Wang, R. and Zhou, Y., Flower pollination algorithm with dimension-by-dimension improvement. *Math. Probl. Eng.*, 2014, https://doi.org/10.1155/2014/481791.

37.   Singh, M., Verma, A., Sharma, N., Bat optimization-based neuron model of stochastic resonance for the enhancement of MR images. *Biocybern. Biomed. Eng.*, 37, 1, 124–134, 2017, https://doi.org/10.1016/j.bbe.2016.10.006.

38.   Tsai, P.W., Pan, J.S., Dao, T.K., Zheng, W.M., A parallel optimization algorithm based on communication strategy of pollens and agents. In *Advances in Intelligent Information Hiding and Multimedia Signal Processing*, pp. 315–324, Springer, Cham, 2017, https://doi.org/10.1007/978-3-319-50212-0_38.

39.   Zhao, C. and Zhou, Y., A Complex Encoding Flower Pollination Algorithm for Global Numerical Optimization. In *Intelligent Computing Theories and Application. ICIC 2016. Lecture Notes in Computer Science*, D.S. Huang, V. Bevilacqua, P. Premaratne (Eds.), vol. 9771, Springer, Cham, 2016, https://doi.org/10.1007/978-3-319-42291-6_67.

40.   Zhou, Y., Wang, R., Luo, Q., Elite opposition-based flower pollination algorithm. *Neurocomputing*, 188, 294–3105, 2016, https://doi.org/10.1016/j.neucom.2015.01.110.

41.   Cuevas, E., Reyna-Orta, A., Díaz-Cortes, M.A., A Multimodal Optimization Algorithm Inspired by the States of Matter. *Neural Process. Lett.*, 48, 517–556, 2018, https://doi.org/10.1007/s11063-017-9750-z.

42. Diab, N. and El-Sharkawy, E., Recent advances in flower pollination algorithm. *Int. J. Comput. Appl. Technol. Res.*, 5, 6, 2016.

43. Goldberg, D.E. and Holland, J.H., *Genetic algorithms and machine learning*, 1988, https://deepblue.lib.umich.edu/bitstream/handle/2027.42/46947/10994_2005_Article_422926.pdf.

44. Babu, M. and Jaisiva, S., Optimal reactive power flow by flower pollination algorithm. *Asian J. Appl. Sci. Technol.*, 3, 137–141, 2017, https://link.springer.com/article/10.1007/s42235-019-0030-7.

45. Haruna, C., Shuib, L., Abdullahi Muaz, S., Abubakar, A., Baballe Ila, L., Zubairu Maitama, J., A review of the applications of bio-inspired flower pollination algorithm, 2015, https://doi.org/10.1016/j.procs.2015.08.438.

46. Wang, R., Zhou, Y., Zhou, Y., Bao, Z., Local greedy flower pollination algorithm for solving planar graph coloring problem. *J. Comput. Theor. Nanosci.*, 12, 11, 4087–4096, 2015, https://doi.org/10.1166/jctn.2015.4322.

47. Kaur, R. and Kachroo, P., Evaluation and comparison of make span time in bnp scheduling algorithm. *Int. J. Futuristic Sci. Eng. Technol.*, 1, 6, 2013, 10.7753/IJCATR0506.1003.

48. Diaz-Gomez, P.A. and Hougen, D.F., Initial population for genetic algorithms: A metric approach. *In Gem*, pp. 43–49, June 2007, https://www.semanticscholar.org/paper/Initial-Population-for-Genetic-Algorithms%3A-A-Metric-Diaz-Gomez-Hougen/9f3851cc8f617b2052f3db30e4c0017d5673cc29.

49. Wu, Z., Yu, D., Kang, X., Application of improved chicken swarm optimization for MPPT in photovoltaic system. *Optim. Control Appl. Methods*, 39, 2, 1029–1042, 2018, https://doi.org/10.1002/oca.2394.

50. Liang, J.J., Qu, B.Y., Suganthan, P.N., Hernández-Díaz, A.G., Problem definitions and evaluation criteria for the CEC 2013 special session on real-parameter optimization, in: *Computational Intelligence Laboratory, Zhengzhou University, Zhengzhou, China and Nanyang Technological University, Singapore, Technical Report*, 201212, 34, 281–295, 2013.

51. Zhou, Y., Zhang, S., Luo, Q., Wen, C., Using flower pollination algorithm and atomic potential function for shape matching. *Neural Comput. Appl.*, 29, 6, 21–40, 2018, https://doi.org/10.1007/s00521-016-2524-0.

Nature-Inspired Computation in Data Mining

Aditi Sharma

Biofuel Group, International Centre for Genetic Engineering and Biotechnology (ICGEB), New Delhi, India

Abstract

Nature-inspired computation and data mining are two areas that attempt to develop novel computing techniques inspired by nature and applying them to complex real-world data, thus discovering relevant information from the big data. All the computation techniques that come under nature-inspired computing have been briefly discussed in the book chapter with respect to data mining. The major focus of the chapter is application of nature-inspired computation in data mining with benefits and challenges. Mostly used optimization techniques have been covered in detail to develop better understanding of the readers. This chapter will assist the readers as a guide to deepen the information gain and correlate with the real-world complications.

Keywords: Nature-inspired computation, data mining, algorithm, swarm intelligence, evolutionary computation, evolution strategies, molecular biology, artificial immune system

8.1 Introduction

In the recent times, both nature-inspired computation and data mining are two hot research topics of the scenario and has acquired great popularity. Nature-inspired computation is an emerging field imitating natural phenomenon from nature [1]. Nature intrinsically is the best instance which has helped time and again to solve the real-world problem and proved to be the most efficient and effective solution. Today, nature-inspired algorithms are

Email: aditi17142@iiitd.ac.in

successfully employed in combinatorial optimization, image processing, and neural networks [1]. Data mining is a process of extraction of relevant information from big data with the help of machine learning algorithms, statistics, and database management system [2]. Data mining process is accomplished by several steps such as selection of the data, pre-processing of the collected data, transformation, data mining for extracting relevant pattern, and, lately, transformation and evaluation of the results [3]. The flow chart in Figure 8.1 reveals the convergence of two approaches data mining and nature-inspired computation to obtain better results for real-world problems. Several applications have been proved to be the boon to complex problems. For instance, cluster analysis in data mining has been used in different aspects such as image pattern recognition, business, market, and security [1, 2]. Additionally, the applications are not limited to engineering domain but also extended to different domains. For example, in robotics and automation, human behavior is mimicked. This is adding ease to the humans as the technology is advancing [11, 38].

Introducing the concept of soft computing, nature-inspired computation has become even more efficient in solving real problems. Soft computing is designed to provide solutions by creating intelligent computation. The nature-inspired techniques are artificial neural network, swarm intelligence, and evolutionary algorithms [4]. Soft computing is an amalgamation of artificial immune system and swarm intelligence-based approaches inclusive of evolutionary computation and artificial neural computation

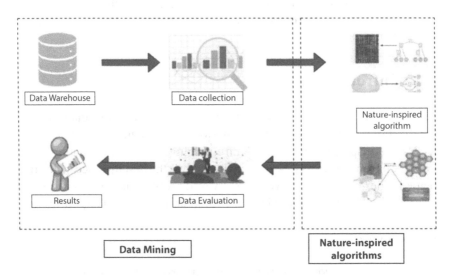

Figure 8.1 The flow chart of amalgamation of data mining with nature-inspired computation. Each image courtesy: Internet.

and firefly algorithm [4]. Evolutionary algorithms were also used in the neural networks for instance, evolutionary feed-forward neural networks, and evolutionary deep neural networks which were used for development. Evolutionary algorithm was used where the single objective was in nature. Evolutionary algorithms are used to edify multi-layer preceptor in order to get minimum error possible.

For health care approaches, productive periodic frequent pattern was used to detect problems. In case of determining patient's diagnosis, prophesy data mining was making into use. Data mining points to build a model that is either descriptive or predictive and set about big band of data and assist in discovering knowledge and hidden trends in the data [26].

8.2 Classification of NIC

1. Swarm intelligence
2. Natural evolution
3. Biological neural network
4. Molecular biology
5. Immune system
6. Biological cells

8.2.1 Swarm Intelligence for Data Mining

Swarm intelligence implies to collective behavior of natural agents with limited cognitive performance but works efficiently when unified. Data mining is the most popular field explored for years now, while swarm intelligence comparably is an emerging sub-domain of artificial intelligence providing efficient and competent brilliance of natural agents of nature, for instance, social behavior of flock of birds, ant colonies, and beehives wherein the agents of nature work together to solve the complex natural problems. The efficiency and popularity of swarm intelligence has led to the expansion of several data mining algorithms. Moreover, in recent years, the swarm intelligence has acquired importance in research area especially in ant colony optimization (ACO) and particle swarm optimization (PSO). Cuckoo search (CS), biogeography-based optimization (BBO), and artificial bee colony are inclusive of the optimization techniques under swarm intelligence. Few new concepts have been raised by swarm intelligence; these include quality principle, proximity principle, principle of diversity, and stability [4]. PSO is considered to solve the concrete optimization problems [1].

8.2.1.1   Swarm Intelligence Algorithm

1) The strength value of each spot is assessing. Strength values are liaised among particles as per certain topology.
2) Then, every particle reconditioned its personal and community finest information. The loop resumes till ending conditioned. Ants liaise with each other in the case of typical ACO by aroma updating.
3) Each ant needs to make a workable path before it can check the strength. The path construction step might be little different from particle swarm intelligence (PSO) and SIAs for real parameter optimization.
4) Path construction is theoretical modernize mechanism. Ants make the new solution via pheromone as they do not have private memory. Most important is the path which is once build then the calculation of the strength value will not be important. Figure 8.2 reveals the different living beings creating their own shortest paths.
5) For combining increasing problems, the strength value is evaluated as the same time as the path is unfinished. In this case, both the strength evaluation phase and swarm modernize phase are appeared out to be single phase [5, 11, 35, 38].

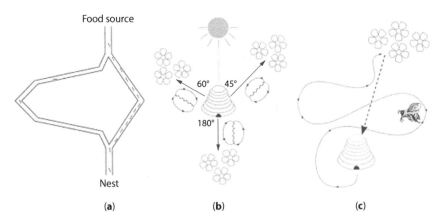

Figure 8.2 Swarm intelligence: (a) ants discovering two paths, selected the shortest path; (b) honeybee wiggle dance conveying a Pi vector (c) showcasing Levy flight and path combination [11].

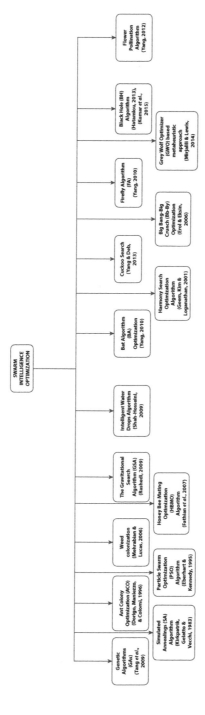

Figure 8.3 The flow chart of swarm intelligence-based algorithms [35].

The swarm intelligence is categorized in two broad classifications: Effective search and data organizing. See Figure 8.3 suggests the flow chart of swarm intelligence-based algorithms.

Effective Search: This refers to a technique where individuals of a swarm of search space but in slightly different manner. In the ACO approach, search space is discrete, and thus, the solution is interpreted by path employed by an ant. In the PSO approach, the search space is continuous, and locations of search space are defined and updated clearly [38].

Data Organizing: This refers to second category, an approach where group of swarms move data instances that are kept on two-dimensional feature space. This helps in suitable clustering of the data. Ant-based sorting and prey models fall under this category [38].

8.2.1.2   Applications of Swarm Intelligence in Data Mining

1. The vogue swarm intelligence has set in motion the evolution of various data of data mining algorithms. There are two techniques based on swarm intelligence of which the first one is effective search in which a single swarm go through a sample space and search for solutions for the data mining. Another is data organizing in which swarm move data examples that are two-dimensional feature spaces in order to get an acceptable sampling solution of data.
2. Both techniques start in defining the domain in which swarm individuals will work by call up problem framework. All the swarm intelligence subjected techniques first call up the search space framework. After which the single swarm begins their charge of generating data mining solutions.

8.2.1.3   Swarm-Based Intelligence Techniques

1. Ant colony optimization
2. Particle swarm optimization
3. Cuckoo search
4. Biogeography-based optimization
5. Cat swarm optimization

8.2.1.3.1   Ant Colony Optimization

ACO principles were the first time adopted by ant system. It is metaheuristic algorithm which is directly adopted and implemented from real ants [4]. The model is employed for solving hard combinatorial optimization problems.

Four typical and notable ant behaviors are witnessed such as forging, division of labor, collective transport, and cluster formation [4]. In ACO algorithm, ants build and apply candidate solutions, thereby making choices based on bias system. The bias system is that numerical statistics which is further based on false pheromone trails and the available heuristic data [4]. The key highlight here is that each time pheromone traits are reformed while algorithm execution takes place in order to make ants search bias [4].

Also, because ant system performance was not comparable to traditional methods, several ACO-based algorithms could create efficient and superior functioning for many applications. The foremost improvement in ACO algorithm is the steadiness between exploration of solution space and better manipulation of the best solution, thereby efficiently avoiding inactivity [1]. The most important contribution by ACO is the conventional swarm intelligence algorithm.

8.2.1.3.1.1 ANT COLONY OPTIMIZATION ALGORITHM

1. Characterize the solution space with a construction graph.
2. Calibrate ACO parameters; initialize pheromone trails.
3. Initiate recreation of ant solutions with each simulation agent walk on the construction graph facilitated by pheromone trails. Refer to Figure 8.4 depicting the ant colony optimization algorithm processes.

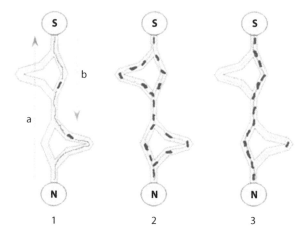

Figure 8.4 Ant colony optimization algorithm processes. N and S depict nest and source with a as ongoing direction while b is returning direction. Figure 8.4.1 depicts a starting process where ants started finding a path between nest and source and lay pheromone. Figure 8.4.2 depicts intermediate process where ants are roaming throughout the path. Figure 8.4.3 depicts almost all the ants chose path with highest pheromone [11].

4. Upgrade pheromone intensities.
5. Go to step 3. Repeat the procedure till the conditions: convergence and termination meet [11].

8.2.1.3.1.2   Application of ACO in Data Mining

1. ACO primarily was employed in data mining for the purpose of supervised machine learning.
2. Specifically, ACO has been used for clustering as well as in Bayesian network, weight optimization in artificial neural network.
3. Real-world problems such as routing, classification, protein folding, tele-communications.
4. Traveling salesman is solved using ant-based clustering techniques.
5. ACO algorithm helps in retaining the memory of entire colony instead of previous creation(book).
6. ACO algorithm performs better against genetic and artificial neural network [41].

8.2.1.3.1.3   Challenges in ACO-Based Data Mining

1. The requirement of discretization of all the variables and learning time are the current challenges in ACO-based classification approach.
2. The research in ACO-based algorithm is more of practical than theoretical.
3. Coding complexities are higher due to instant changes in global and local updates [28, 41].

8.2.1.3.2   Particle Swarm Optimization

Particle swarm optimization, a population-founded stochastic algorithm abbreviated to PSO, was discovered to optimize continuous non-linear functions by Eberhart and Kennedy. This originated from the simulation of bird blood during social behavior [5]. The algorithms imitate the behavior of animals that do not possess any leader, work together such as fish schooling or bird flocking [6]. Due to convincing results of the optimization technique, PSO stands promising and beneficial. It has two aspects: firstly, improved performance of the optimization approach with the help of altering parameters, increasing population diversity and fuse with other

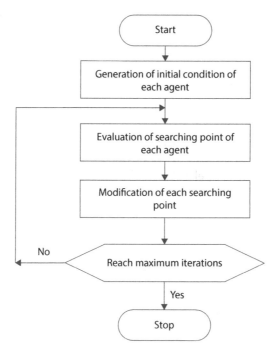

Figure 8.5 The generalized flow chart for particle swarm optimization [11].

optimizing methods [5]; and secondly, applications in several different domains for instance training neural network, data clustering medicine, security systems, etc. [19]. Figure 8.5 shows the generalized flow chart for particle swarm optimization.

8.2.1.3.2.1 PARTICLE SWARM OPTIMIZATION ALGORITHM

1) Opt out an irregular subgroup of M particles.
2) Find the best impartial function among the previously best and the worldwide best impartial function.
3) For **U1, U2** uniformly distributed random vectors [0,1], modernize the velocity
$$V = W{*}V + T1{*}U1{*}(p - x) + T2{*}U2. {*}(g - x).$$
where V is the velocity, W is inertia weight, T1 and T2 is the constant parameters, P is the previously best position, g is the global best position, whereas x is the current position.
4) Modernize the location $x = x + V$.

5) Apply the bounds. If any accent of x is outside the bound, then make it equal to that bound. The components which were set to bound, if the velocity of that component lies outside the bound, set the velocity of that component to zero.
6) Assess the objective function x.
7) If the function x is less than the previous (p), then set p = x, which find out to be that p is the best position particle. Apply it to all the particle of the swarm.
8) In the earlier step. if the value of best function was less. then set flag = true or else flag = false [20, 21].

8.2.1.3.2.2　Applications of PSO in Data Mining

1. Data clustering with the support of PSO is producing better and efficient results in real-world data. Global optimal complications are a big challenge in the field of engineering [22]. But due to PSO influenced by objective function of continuity, complications are transformed to advantages [19, 24].
2. PSO is also applicable in classification problem of instances with respect to databases [7].
3. PSO has been used in electronics domain [5]. Digital circuit evolution has been done using PSO in order to solve the complications of the human designs [5]. As when the complexity of the functions changes, also the input and output change, making it all the more problematic for the human designs created [23].
4. While when PSO applied with genetic algorithm, it reduces the computational intensity and leads to convergence of the approach and resulting in reduced hardware evolution as well [5].
5. Furthermore, it is employed in identification of emergent system [12] and recommender system [11].

8.2.1.3.2.3　Challenges of PSO in Data Mining

1. PSO does not deal with the complications of scattered data.
2. It does not work with non-coordinate system such as energy field and particle rules in the energy field [41].

8.2.1.3.3 Cuckoo Search

Cuckoo search abbreviated as CS is one of the metaheuristic optimization algorithms developed in 2006 [4, 8]. It is a combination of brood parasitism and cuckoos, additionally simulation model of levy flight. CS is based on three principles that are employed for the computation:

i. Each cuckoo bird lays an egg, thereby discards its one egg in an arbitrarily opted nest.
ii. The nest with best or high quality of eggs will be chosen, thus carried to the next generation. The count of existing host nests is fixed.
iii. Also, the eggs laid by cuckoo bird is discovered based on probability of 0 and 1 by the host bird [13, 14].

8.2.1.3.3.1 Cuckoo Search Algorithm

1) Synchronize the starting value of the host nest proportion **m**, and the highest number of repetitions.
2) Place the egg in the **n** nest (**n** is the irregularly selected nest). Cuckoo bird's egg is very alike as of host egg.
3) Compare the strength of cuckoo's egg with the host egg.

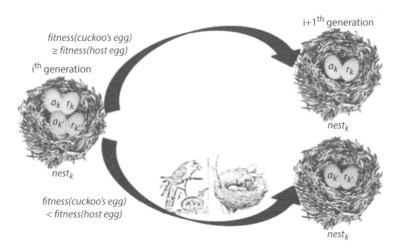

Figure 8.6 The flow chart of cuckoo algorithm.

4) If cuckoo egg is to found better than the host egg, then put back the egg in the nest **n** by cuckoo's egg.

5) If it is found out by the host bird, then the nest is rejected and then the new one is built up. Repeat the steps 2 to 5 until the condition is not satisfied [27]. Figure 8.6 depicts the flow chart of cuckoo algorithm.

8.2.1.3.3.2 CHALLENGES OF CUCKOO SEARCH IN DATA MINING

1. CS is applicable for solve only continuous problems not considering the discrete ones.
2. The capability of the cuckoo algorithm is limited to solve complex problems.
3. The algorithm is with the set of problems regarding adaptability and achieving ideal research output [27, 28].

8.2.1.3.3.3 APPLICATIONS OF CUCKOO SEARCH IN DATA MINING

1. CS has been the major contributor for the breast cancer classification in case of mammogram image [15].
2. It has assisted in automatic detection of the disease diabetes [16].
3. Also, CS has been employed in capacity of the wind power plants [17].
4. CS is employed in wireless sensor networks [18].
5. Clustering is an unconfirmed categorization method of data mining. It splits up the set of data into groups formed on the similitude between the data objects, such that similitude entity falls in the same cluster and different entity fall in different cluster.
6. CS is non-specific and strong for many accession problems and it has also interesting features like implementation and good figuring efficiency.
7. K-means is the most popular algorithm because of its simplicity and algorithm. But there is inconvenience with this algorithm so that is why we approached the CS algorithm because of trapping in the optimal solutions.

8.2.1.3.4 Biogeography-Based Optimization

Biogeography is the study of topographical allocation of biological beings. MacArthur and Wilson were the first one to develop a mathematical model

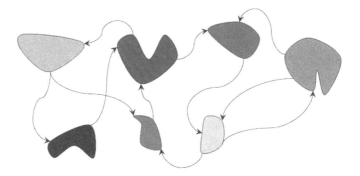

Figure 8.7 Species depicting migration with the help of islands via floating, flying, and swimming.

of biogeography in 1967. This described the migration of species from an island to another, evolution of new species, and regarding their extinction. With this concept of biogeography, Simon designed a BBO algorithm in 2008 [30]. The species depicting migration with the help of islands through floating, flying, and swimming as witness by Figure 8.7.

Standard BBO model

The two steps are involved in the procedure

i. BBO migration
ii. mutation

BBO Migration

BBO migration is probabilistic in nature. For any problem solution, immigration rate is employed to whether to immigrate each of its attributes or not, separately. If this stochastic decision is made in favor of immigration, then a second random decision is taken. Based on emigration rate, emigration solutions are provided [30].

Mutation

Mutation in BBO is probabilistic function that helps in alteration of solution features. The prime focus and aim of mutation are to enhance diversity among the population [30].

8.2.1.3.4.1   BIOGEOGRAPHY-BASED OPTIMIZATION ALGORITHM (PSEUDO)

1. Standard biogeography algorithm.
2. For every solution, set emigration rate, emigration rate is directly proportional fitness.
3. For every solution, nth candidate solution, immigration rate is set.
4. Entire population is reaching to the temporary population.
5. For every solution, nth candidate solution is inversely proportional to population size.
6. For each solution, set feature index.
7. Decide immigration.
8. Select the emigrating solution.
9. End process if next solution feature is available.
10. Decide whether to mutate.
11. Go to next solution [30].

8.2.1.3.4.2   CHALLENGES OF BBO IN DATA MINING

1. BBO is not enough in dealing with complicated complex problems for instance low population diversity and slow convergence rate. Several algorithms are created as enhanced version of BBO [31].
2. Due to several challenges, BBO has been enhanced and upgraded to BBMSO, an improved version of BBO based on multiple sequence alignment [32].

8.2.1.3.4.3   APPLICATIONS OF BBO IN DATA MINING

1. BBO is employed in engineering field with the purpose of power management and the economic analysis of an autonomous hybrid power plant.
2. BBO is a vital algorithm regarding parameter estimation and control.
3. BBO is used in gene expression data to select most relevant genes for the classification and contribute in network problems and data analysis [29, 31].
4. Also, BBO operator is removed to decrease the calculation complication and more systematic random-scaled differential operators are integrated into BBOs. Secondly in order

to maintain equilibrium and exploitation, the BBO's shifting operator is replaced with a dynamic heuristic to increase the local search ability. Lastly, a worst position algorithm is integrated into better algorithm to avoid local optima. WRBBO is also applied in a clustering optimization for better optimization efficiency.

8.2.1.3.5   Cat Swarm Optimization

Optimization is the process of finding the best solution from all the feasible solutions. One key problem of this operation is the vastness of the search because of which it is not possible to check the workable solution in an allotted time. To stop the vastness of the search problem, some theoretical methods can be brought up into use; these methods usually amalgamate some predetermined and uncertainty courses of action together and then repeatedly compare the solution until the adequate one is found. These processes can be classified into trajectory-based classes and population-based classes. In trajectory-based type, only single agent searching in the search space is used to find the most favorable solution. In population-based process, which is also known as swarm intelligence, more than one agent searching in the search space is used to find the most favorable solution. Agents usually move in two stages, utilization and research: in the first stage, they move worldwide to find favorable areas, whereas in the second stage, they search localized to come across better solutions in those favorable areas. Interchange between these two stages in any method is very important influencing toward utilization and research will decrease accomplishment and produce unpleasant results [25].

Cat swarm optimization (CSO) is a process which was discovered by Chu *et al.* in 2006. It is stimulated by the natural conduct of cats; it has a narrative technique in coining utilization and research stages. It has also been applied in the field of science and engineering [25].

8.2.1.3.5.1   CAT SWARM OPTIMIZATION ALGORITHM

CSO is a constant and single objective process. It is incline by recline and detecting conduct of cats because they seem to be inactive and spend most the time recline as depicted by Figure 8.8. During recline, their responsiveness is high and they are conscious of what is going around them, as they observe the things around them, they start moving toward the object quickly. CSO algorithm is basically based on these two conducts of the cats. It is formed by two stages: detecting and seeking stages. Each stage represents different solutions having its own position and strength value [25].

Seeking Mode
(Sleeping and Looking)

Tracing Mode
(Chasing Laser Pointers)

Figure 8.8 Cat swarm optimization mainly inspired by the observations of cat. Ref: Internet.

In order to achieve the favorable solutions, the following steps are needed to be considered:

1) State the higher and lower bound for the answer set.
2) Irregularly generate J cats (answer set) and expand them in the K-dimensional space having erratic velocity of each cat such that their velocity does not exceed the maximum value.
3) Irregularly categorize the cats into detecting and seeking stages according to mixture ratio (MR).
4) MR is selected in the gap of [0,1]. For an example if several cats J is equal to 20 and MR value is set at 0.1, then 18 cats will go through seeking stage and the rest 2 cats will go through detecting stage.
5) Assess the strength value of all cats by the area name strength function. After that, the best cat is chosen and saved in the memory bank.
6) After that, cats move to any of the two stages (detecting or seeking).
7) After that, for the next step, irregularly reorganize the cats into detecting or seeking stage based on MR.
8) Check the conclusion condition; if satisfied; close the program or else repeat the steps from 4 to 6 [25].

8.2.1.3.5.2   Challenges of CSO in Data Mining

The main drawback of the algorithm which can be considered is the early merging also known as local optima.

8.2.1.3.5.3   APPLICATIONS OF CSO IN DATA MINING

It has been categorized into several different groups as follows:

1) **Electrical Engineering:** To cut back the electricity cost for the shoppers, Hwang *et al.* used both CSO and PSO algorithm; as a result, CSO proved to be the foremost structured and faster than PSO to search out the most effective solution worldwide.

   Also, the economic load dispatch (ELC) and unit commitment (UC) played important role in reduction of the fuel cost. Hwang *et al.* used the CSO algorithm on ELD of wind and thermal generators. Faraji *et al.* also recommended binary CSO (BCSO) algorithm on UC and came up with better results.

   Kumar and Kalavathi also used CSO algorithm so on refine the steadiness of the system in UPFC (unified power flow controller). UPFC is a device to regulate both active and reactive power flows. Lenin and Reddy applied ADSCO (auto dealer supply companies) on reactive power dispatch problem so on minimize the ability loss [25].

   Enhancing available transfer capability (ATC) plays important role in engineering. Nireekshana *et al.* also used CSO algorithm to adjust boundary and position of SVC and TCSC with the aim of maximizing power.

2) **Computer Vision:** Identifying human emotion with the assistance of bio metric approach. Lin *et al.* and Wang and Wu combined the CSO algorithm with support vector machine to check the facial feature of the scholars of the category.

   Vivek and Reddy also used CSO-GA-PSOSVM for the identical purpose. Hadi and Sabah used CSO algorithm in block matching for systematic motion estimation. The aim was to extend the performance and to cut back the quantity of repetition without the decay of image quality.

   Kalaiselvan *et al.* and Lavanya and Natarajan used CSO algorithm to recover watermarks alike to original copy. Hadi and Sabah used EHCSO in an object tracking system for the further improvement of efficiency and accuracy. Yan *et al.* used BCSO for hyper spectral images.

   Ansar and Bhattacharya and karakoyun *et al.* suggested CSO algorithm for image segmentation purposes. Zhang *et al.* merged wavelet entropy, ANN, and CSO algorithm to produce alcohol use disorder (AUD) recognition system. Kumar *et al.* merged the CSO algorithm with functional link artificial neural network (FLANN) to clear out of the unpleasant Gaussian noises from the CT images. Yang *et al.* combined CSO with L-BFGS-B technique to listing non-rigid associative images. Cam applied CSO algorithm to calibrate the parameters for the aim of image enhancement [25].

3) **Signal Processing:** Panda *et al.* used CSO algorithm for IIR (infinite impulse response) recognition. IIR has its application in signal processing [25].

4) **System Management and Combinatorial Optimization:** Shojaee *et al.* suggested using CSO algorithm to maximize system accuracy. There are three basic organizing problems: open shop, job shop, and flow shop.

   Bouzidi and Riffi used the BCSO on job scheduling problem (JSSP) and made a relative study between CSO and the other two multi-objective algorithms which were CS and the ant colony optimization.

   Dani *et al.* also used CSO algorithm on JSSP in which they followed the non-traditional approach to represent cat positions [25].

5) **Petroleum Engineering:** CSO algorithm was used as a better positioning optimization. Chen *et al.* Wang *et al.* used CSO algorithm for oil recovery index [25].

8.2.1.3.5.4 APPLICATIONS OF CAT SWARM OPTIMIZATION IN DATA MINING

1. CSO is one the new analytical optimization algorithm which is based on swarm intelligence. It has better results compared to the other algorithms based on previous research. It was tested on four different datasets.

2. Two clustering viewpoints subjected on CSO which are CSO Clustering (CSOC) and K-Harmonic CSO Clustering are suggested. K-Harmonic Means operation working is planned to filter the population and to increase the merging of the clustering algorithm.

8.3   Evolutionary Computation

Evolutionary computation is a metaheuristic-based, generic population-based algorithm. Such algorithms are mainly applied to combinatorial problems. The approach is familiar to natural selection in nature and reveals a fundamental basis such as the fitter will live and survive, unfit will be unable to continue living and die off, simultaneously, existing the gene pool. Natural selection is the phenomenon of a functional advantage where species compete among themselves and the most fit survives [1] as shown in Figure 8.9 the schematic view of evolutionary algorithm.

The different algorithms comprised the following:

1. Genetic algorithm
2. Evolutionary programming
3. Evolution strategies
4. Genetic programming
5. Classifier systems
6. Combinations/hybrids

8.3.1   Genetic Algorithms

Genetic algorithm is the foremost evolutionary algorithm in the history. The algorithm mimics the neo-Darwinian evolution theory remarking survival of the fittest theory. Basically, the genetic algorithm is used to recreate a binary from an entirely random image. The algorithm is formed of four aspects:

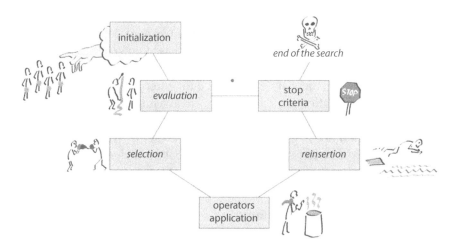

Figure 8.9 The schematic view of evolutionary algorithm. Ref: Internet.

i. Creation of strings of population.

ii. Evaluate each created string.

iii. Select best strings.

iv. Perform genetic modifications to create new population of strings.

8.3.1.1   Applications of Genetic Algorithms in Data Mining

1. The application of genetic algorithm in data mining is a boon to the data mining complex problems. For instance, automatic search in data mining for the purpose of understanding and knowing the relationships between characteristics in databases. The real problem for the effective and efficient data mining is the volume and complication of the target database. While there is ample usage of different machine learning algorithms, but genetic algorithm has its own benefits. For example, employing the genetic algorithm approach with the objective of success in dealing with scale search and the optimization problems. Additionally, the algorithm helps in improving the performance of clustering and classification algorithms in data mining domain [42].

2. The contribution and functionality of genetic algorithm with respect to commerce and management is another decent application. The huge size data in commerce utilizes genetic algorithm in managing the data. Also employ usage of machine learning classification approach.

3. Genetic algorithm has been known as one of the advantages for data mining technique. The usage of data mining approach to the best employee group based on genetic algorithm is another instance. The approach associate's information management system required for enterprise employees. The entire attention and priority are given to managing the information and conveying only the key highlights [43].

4. In data mining, genetic algorithm can be employed to optimize parameters and or determine knowledge by itself [33, 34].

8.3.2   Evolutionary Programming

In the field of artificial intelligence, evolutionary programming is a kind of genetic algorithm. The approach employs neo-Darwinian evolutionary theory to create a population based on quality criteria. The approach finds the solutions by an iterative process including probabilistic selection of the fittest and finest solutions. The variations are done by genetic operators such as crossover and mutation [1].

8.3.2.1 Applications of Evolutionary Programming in Data Mining

1. Data mining is a potential domain applied to the huge data collected from present business environment. In order to improve the managerial decision-making, fresh data mining approach has been introduced which utilizes evolutionary programming. This is done to apply its functionality in Bayesian networks alongside to the marketing data. Also, there have been two network learning problems. One uses dependency analysis, whereas the other employs search for network structure [44].
2. Application of evolutionary programming-based method that operates data mining on the databases represented as graphs. Having said that, huge amount of data is collected and stored nowadays, of which most of the data is structural data. These data are naturally represented as graphs. In such cases, the searching expertise of evolutionary programming is utilized so as to discover certain patterns or graphs that are known to be repeating in the structural data [45].
3. In data mining, the evolutionary programming assists with robustness and its rule generation for its convenient structure.

8.3.3   Genetic Programming

Genetic programming is the subset of genetic algorithms [34]. The approach uses the principles of genetic and natural selection [34]. The algorithm optimizes only one parameter resulting in complex results. In such cases, multi-objective genetic programming is utilized. Figure 8.10 implies to the genetic programming assisting in converting Darwinism into algorithm.

8.3.3.1 Applications of Genetic Programming in Data Mining

A big data is mined and applied optimum genetic programming and obtain results to generate compact and accurate models for complicated nonlinear civil engineering systems [34].

Figure 8.10 Genetic programming assisting in converting Darwinism into algorithm. Ref: Internet.

1. Usage of genetic programming algorithm in case of development of attribute construction. Basically, for a defined data set, the attributes are the relevant part that defines the data space representation. The quality of the data space determines the performance of data mining algorithm. In order to provide solution to this complex problem, genetic programming algorithm is employed. The algorithm helps in construction of new attributes of the data set considered, working as most important step pre-processing of the step leading to best results of a data mining algorithm [46].
2. Additionally, genetic programming is used on medical classification complex problems from a conventional database. The results are acquired with the help of neural networks. Thus, it is concluded that genetic programming algorithm performs comparable in both classification the generalization approach [47].

8.3.4   Evolution Strategies

Evolution strategy is one of the important mechanisms of evolutionary algorithms. This was first proposed by three students: Bienert, Reichenberg, and Schwefel in 1964 in order to mechanically augment an aerodynamic problem. This assists in providing solutions to optimization problems with the help of a concept iterative procedure. Evolution strategy is a global optimization algorithm which is stimulated by nature inclusive of adaption theory and evolution by natural selection. This approach is inspired by species-based process of evolution for instance phenotype, hereditary, and variation sin genetic make over [1].

8.3.4.1   Applications of Evolution Strategies in Data Mining

The foremost vital feature of ES is usage of self-adaptive mechanisms in order to control the process of mutations. It optimizes search progress by considering optimization parameters for mutating the obtained solutions.

1. In data mining, evolution strategies create a series of arbitrary rules to check in contradiction to training dataset. The changes arbitrary rules are selected that closely fit the data and thereby such rules are mutated. Later, the process is iterated till a rule result from it that matches completely with the training data [8].
2. Evolution strategies have been helpful from the use of metamodels in designing an optimal air foil shape under the viscous flow concerns. Most importantly, evolution strategies along with mathematical model can help in demonstrating the gain in computational time.

8.3.5   Differential Evolutions

Differential evolution is another archetype from evolutionary algorithm. The algorithm was first proposed by Stron and Price in 1995 in order to globally optimizing the continuous search space. A population-based stochastic exploration method where the difference from other algorithms lies in the arithmetic groupings of individuals is given by mutation. In case of genetic algorithm, the mutation is the result of small trepidations to the genes of the involved individuals.

8.3.5.1   Applications of Differential Evolution in Data Mining

1. Differential algorithms are relevant to real optimization complications such as NP-hard optimization problems. This is applicable in real-world DNA microarray, neural network,

clustering problems, and single- and multi-objective functions [8].

2. Differential evolution in data mining has been most beneficial, in real-time problems such as antenna synthesis and microwave imaging.

8.4   Biological Neural Network

The most natural intelligent and natural inspiring is the human brain. Nerve cells or neurons are the basic units of the nervous system. The brain controls with the help of simple basic processing units and result in great computational power [1]. The simulation of this real process is achieved by artificial neural network.

8.4.1   Artificial Neural Computation

Artificial neural network is based on statistical signal processing, capable of solving paradigms [1]. The key contributors in the computation are neuron and weights. Neuron is a set of densely interrelated simple processing units. Each element in the unit is connected to neighbors with changeable strengths called a weight [1]. Figure 8.11 reveals the basic structure of artificial neural network.

In data mining, artificial neural network is functioning in weather forecasting, prediction, and analysis, also in case of recognition of speech, text, video, and face expressions.

8.4.1.1   Neural Network Models

1. The perceptron
2. Multilayered feed forward ANN models

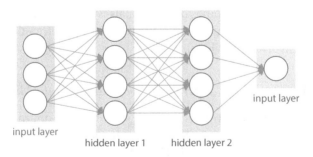

Figure 8.11 The basic structure of artificial neural network.

3. Recurrent ANN models
4. Radial basis function ANN models

8.4.1.2   Challenges of Artificial Neural Network in Data Mining

The foremost challenges we come across is the total absence of the concept of autonomous learning algorithm [25]. At each point, learning rates needs to be set accordingly and readjusted, most importantly need to adjust network so that they can well-versed with the generalized dataset [25].

8.4.1.3   Applications of Artificial Neural Network in Data Mining

1. Artificial neural network is useful when it does not have a priori information and knowledge regarding the data mining dataset. Also, this helps in establishing highly nonlinear and multivariate relationships [25]. It assists in solving stock market problem as well [25].
2. Application of data mining problem in finding fault and prediction in boiler's burner system in power plant by utilizing the potential of artificial neural network. Due to the complexity of burner management systems and its working environment, the fault in the burner systems tends to become high. Finding fault in the burner is quite a complex problem. The approach includes the functionality of data clustering, prediction, and learning process with the help of neural network [48].

8.5   Molecular Biology

The basic unit of living organism is cell. Cell can independently live such organisms are known as unicellular organisms such as bacterial and ciliates, or in a group called as multi-cellular organisms, for example, mammals and human beings. S. Marcus provides an equation for life where life is a combination of DNA software and membrane hardware. Functioning of these cells can be discovered with the help of membrane computing [13]. Figure 8.12 shows the membrane computing model.

8.5.1   Membrane Computing

Membrane computing is a domain of computer science which aims to abstract computing concepts and generate models originated from

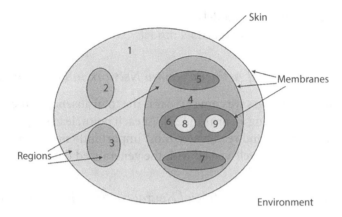

Figure 8.12 Membrane computing model Ref: Internet.

structure and function of living cells. In turn, these living cells are organized in tissues or high order structures [39].

8.5.2 Algorithm Basis

The computing models are called membrane systems or P systems. These systems are parallel, distributed, and processing cell-like compartmental designs.

The three essential features of membrane systems are as follows:

i. An ordered arrangement of membranes knows as tree structure.
ii. Few multisets of the objects.
iii. Determinate sets of rules associated to these regions.

Rules can transmute objects and modify the membrane structures such as creating, dividing, dissolution, and moving of the objects in the compartment architecture [39].

8.5.3 Challenges of Membrane Computing in Data Mining

The major drawback of the algorithm is it cannot mimic the exact living system in in-silico systems.

8.5.4 Applications of Membrane Computing in Data Mining

1. The functioning of membrane computing is established in the field of computer science, life sciences, biology, computer graphics, and various linguistics such as static sorting

and parsing in automata. Finally, most contribution to the NP compete optimization techniques [1]. P models also contribute in biological dynamics, modeling respiration in bacteria, etc. Also, it is used in combination with clustering algorithms.

2. A membrane clustering algorithm is intended to accord with automatic clustering problem. Where the membrane-like system is designed as it is computing context. With this, an enhanced and improved velocity model is created, utilizing a good clustering partitioning for the entire data set [49].

3. Additionally, membrane computing helps in dealing with unsupervised learning problem [50]. The algorithms are amalgamated with fuzzy membrane clustering approach in order to develop modified enhanced differential evolution mechanism. Therefore, achieving a decent fuzzy partitioning is discovered for the entire data set [51].

8.6 Immune System

Nature has constantly proven to be an inspiration for the technology development and biological advancement [3]. One among several, natural system is natural immune system. Soft computing is a recently proposed paradigm comprises of several computational approaches [3] in robust data mining. The computational approaches include neural networks, computational evolutionary techniques, and combinations based on artificial immune system amalgamated with advanced soft computing [3, 40]. Recent advancements in artificial immune system have led to revolutionize scientific community. But artificial immune system itself has been explored and its applications advanced by Forrest *et al.* [9, 10]. Also, it is observed that immune system that of lymphocyte elements functions efficiently than the conventional method of immune system of nerve cells (neurons). But, the practical application of the immune system including lymphocytes elements is still a challenge in the domain of data mining [3].

8.6.1 Artificial Immune System

An artificial immune system is a major class of computer intelligence as shown in Figure 8.13 the multi-layer structure of the immune system. It is a framework for distributed, adaptive system applicable in different fields. The algorithm consists of two threads of research: firstly, usage of mathematical

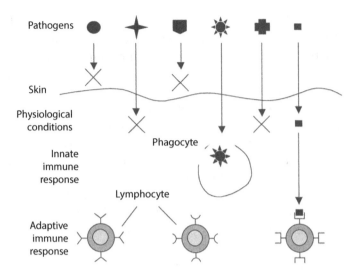

Figure 8.13 The multi-layer structure of the immune system Ref: Internet.

and computational methods in the modeling of immunology; and secondly, integration of immune system in the progress of engineering explanations.

8.6.1.1 Artificial Immune System Algorithm (Enhanced)

1. Set population with cross section input data.
2. Load up antigen population data.
3. Antigen population data is equivalent to remaining training data.
4. Repeat the process.
5. Introduce antigen set to each population in network.
6. Calculate all distance values.
7. Calculate simulation level.
8. Assign B cells to population based on stimulation level.
9. Eliminate weak B cells from population.
10. If not completed, then clone and mutate residual B cells.
11. Assimilate new cells.
12. Repeat until termination condition is fulfilled.
13. Fuse final population.

8.6.1.2 Challenges of Artificial Immune System in Data Mining

1. The biggest challenge is astonishing number of antibodies that contribute to the major immune system as in the

defence cells are noticed to contribute to learned repertoire of defence cells of the immune system. Any transformation in the cell can lead to decrease in this repertoire.

2. The second non-trivial challenge is to be able to sustain the antibodies repertoire, which is said to be taken for granted. In such cases, the population prematurely end up to the small subset of the diverse repertoire that basically is learned [12, 36].

8.6.1.3   *Applications of Artificial Immune System in Data Mining*

1. Artificial immune system model is employed in the computer security systems. This further depends on data files, preserving the reliability of those data files, detected the unauthorized and unauthenticated users along with prevention form virus intake and its spread.

2. In case of UNIX process monitoring, the algorithm detects intervention in the computer systems and protect the system from malicious attackers [36].

3. Additionally, classification rule discovery design incorporated with artificial immune system and the fuzzy systems is employed. The major constituents of these two algorithms are a sequential covering method and a rule evolution method [51].

8.7   Applications of NIC in Data Mining

1. Data mining techniques and nature-inspired algorithms are employed for query expansion. Query expansion information retrieval is a research domain that emphases on storing, organizing in a structured manner, and access to the information. The prime objective of information retrieval is to satisfy users' requirements to find useful information in the large volume data.

2. In the field of bioinformatics, data mining is used in the form of machine learning problems, classification, regression, and clustering the biological data [37].

3. Query expansion has been time and again applied to email services, news services, microblogs, and social media.

4. It has also served the domains such as health and medical services [2].

8.8   Conclusion

The entire book chapter reveals the overview of nature-inspired computation in data mining and its applications in solving the real-life problems. The diversity of real-world challenges makes it difficult, but a hybrid of different computation techniques makes it easier to understand and implement solutions. Moreover, data mining approach and nature-inspired computation is providing ease in reaching out to solutions. While in cases, where data is limited or incomplete, such algorithms can be difficult to implement, thereby leading to undesirable results or irrelevant information. For instance, looking at the present scenario, COVID-19 has taken toll over the world, with limitations such as incomplete information of the patients and their history, thus making it even more complicated to provide best and most efficient solution.

References

1. Martens, D., Baesens, B., Fawcett, T., Editorial survey: Swarm intelligence for data mining. *Mach. Learn.*, 82, 1, 1–42, 2011.
2. Khennak, I. and Drias, H., Data mining techniques and nature-inspired algorithms for query expansion. *ACM Int. Conf. Proceeding Ser.*, 2018.
3. Nasraoui, O., Dasgupta, D., Gonzalez, F.A., A novel artificial system approach to robust data mining. In GECCO Late Breaking Papers (pp. 356–363), July 2002.
4. Bindu, H., Padmavati, S., Visvavidyalayam, M., Nature-inspired computation techniques and its applications in soft computing: Survey. *Int. J. Res. Appl. Sci. Eng. Technol.*, 5, VII, 1906–1916, 2017.
5. Song, M.P. and Gu, G.C., Research on particle swarm optimization: A review. *Proc. 2004 Int. Conf. Mach. Learn. Cybern.*, August 2004, vol. 4, pp. 2236–2241.
6. Rini, D.P. and Shamsuddin, S.M., Particle swarm optimization: Technique, system and challenges. *Int. J. Appl. Inf. Syst.*, 1, 1, 33–45, 2011.
7. De Falco, I., Della Cioppa, A., Tarantino, E., Facing classification problems with Particle Swarm Optimization. *Appl. Soft Comput. J.*, 7, 3, 652–658, 2007.
8. Yang, X.S. and Deb, S., Engineering optimisation by cuckoo search. *Int. J. Math. Model. Numer. Optim.*, 1, 4, 330–343, 2010.
9. Forrest, S., Perelson, A.S., Allen, L., Cherukuri, R., Self-nonself discrimination in a computer. *Proceedings of 1994 IEEE Computer Society Symposium on Research in Security.*
10. Timmis, J., Knight, T., de Castro, L.N., Hart, E., An overview of artificial immune systems. *Computation in Cells and Tissues*, pp. 51–91, 2004.

11. Ranjbar-Sahraei, B., Tuyls, K., Caliskanelli, I., Broeker, B., Claes, D., Alers, S., Weiss, G., Bio-inspired multi-robot systems, in: *Biomimetic Technologies*, pp. 273–299, Woodhead Publishing, Cambridge, UK, 2015.

12. Nayak, J., Naik, B., Behera, H.S., A novel nature-inspired firefly algorithm with higher order neural network: performance analysis. *Eng. Sci. Technol. Int. J.*, 19, 1, 197–211, 2016.

13. Hemeida, A.M., Alkhalaf, S., Mady, A., Mahmoud, E.A., Hussein, M.E., Eldin, A.M.B., Implementation of nature-inspired optimization algorithms in some data mining tasks. *Ain Shams Eng. J.*, 11, 2, 309–318, 2019.

14. Wang, Z., Gao, S., Wang, J., Yang, H., & Todo, Y. (2020). A Dendritic Neuron Model with Adaptive Synapses Trained by Differential Evolution Algorithm. *Comput. Intell. Neurosci.*, 2020, 2020.

15. Kajela, D. and Manshahia, M.S., Nature-inspired computational intelligence: A survey. *Int. J. Eng. Sci. Math.*, 6, 7, 374–416, 2017.

16. Cagnoni, S. and Castelli, M., Special issue on computational intelligence and nature-inspired algorithms for real-world data analytics and pattern recognition. *Algorithms*, 11, 25, 2018.

17. Song, M.P. and Gu, G.C., Research on particle swarm optimization: A review, in: *Proceedings of 2004 International Conference on Machine Learning and Cybernetics (IEEE Cat. No. 04EX826)*, 2004, August, vol. 4, IEEE, pp. 2236–2241.

18. Zhang, Y., Wang, S., Ji, G., A comprehensive survey on particle swarm optimization algorithm and its applications. *Math. Probl. Eng.*, 2015, 2015.

19. De Falco, I., Della Cioppa, A., Tarantino, E., Facing classification problems with particle swarm optimization. *Appl. Soft Comput.*, 7, 3, 652–658, 2007.

20. Rini, D.P., Shamsuddin, S.M., Yuhaniz, S.S., Particle swarm optimization: Technique, system and challenges. *Int. J. Comput. Appl.*, 14, 1, 19–26, 2011.

21. de Almeida, B.S.G. and Leite, V.C., Particle Swarm Optimization: A Powerful Technique for Solving Engineering Problems, in: *Swarm Intelligence-Recent Advances, New Perspectives and Applications*, IntechOpen, London, UK, 2019.

22. Van der Merwe, D.W. and Engelbrecht, A.P., Data clustering using particle swarm optimization, in: *The 2003 Congress on Evolutionary Computation, 2003. CEC'03*, 2003, December, vol. 1, IEEE, pp. 215–220.

23. Nezamabadi-pour, H., Rostami-Shahrbabaki, M., Maghfoori-Farsangi, M., Binary particle swarm optimization: Challenges and new solutions. *CSI J. Comput. Sci. Eng.*, 6, 1, 21–32, 2008.

24. Chuang, L.Y., Hsiao, C.J., Yang, C.H., Chaotic particle swarm optimization for data clustering. *Expert Syst. Appl.*, 38, 12, 14555–14563, 2011.

25. Ahmed, A.M., Rashid, T.A., Saeed, S.A.M., Cat swarm optimization algorithm: A survey and performance evaluation. *Comput. Intell. Neurosci.*, 2020, 2020.

26. Mirza, S., Mittal, S., Zaman, M., A review of data mining literature. *Int. J. Comput. Sci. Inf. Secur. (IJCSIS)*, 14, 11, 2016.

27. Yang, X.-S. and Deb, S., Engineering optimisation by cuckoo search. *Int. J. Math. Model. Numer. Optim.*, 1, 4, 330–343, 2010.

28. Wang, G., A comparative study of cuckoo algorithm and ant colony algorithm in optimal path problems, in: *MATEC Web of Conferences*, vol. 232, EDP Sciences, p. 03003, 2018.

29. Simon, D., Biogeography-based optimization. *IEEE Trans. Evol. Comput.*, 12, 6, 702–713, 2008.

30. Ma, H., Simon, D., Siarry, P., Yang, Z., Fei, M., Biogeography-based optimization: A 10-year review. *IEEE Trans. Emerging Top. Comput. Intell.*, 1, 5, 391–407, 2017.

31. Zhang, X., Wang, D., Chen, H., Improved biogeography-based optimization algorithm and its application to clustering optimization and medical image segmentation. *IEEE Access*, 7, 28810–28825, 2019.

32. Yadav, R.K. and Banka, H., IBBOMSA: An improved biogeography-based approach for multiple sequence alignment. *Evol. Bioinf.*, 12, EBO-S40457, 2016.

33. Sudholt, D., The benefits of population diversity in evolutionary algorithms: a survey of rigorous runtime analyses, in: *Theory of Evolutionary Computation*, pp. 359–404, Springer, Cham, 2020.

34. Gandomi, A.H., Sajedi, S., Kiani, B., Huang, Q., Genetic programming for experimental big data mining: A case study on concrete creep formulation. *Autom. Constr.*, 70, 89–97, 2016.

35. Chakraborty, A. and Kar, A.K., Swarm intelligence: A review of algorithms, in: *Nature-Inspired Computing and Optimization*, pp. 475–494, Springer, Cham, 2017.

36. Andonie, R. and Kovalerchuk, B., Neural networks for data mining: Constrain and open problems, in: *ESANN*, 2004, April, pp. 449–458.

37. Vaishali, P.K. and Vinayababu, A., Application of data mining and soft computing in bioinformatics. *Int. J. Eng. Res. Appl. (IJERA)*, 1, 3, 758–771.

38. Gupta, S., Bhardwaj, S., Bhatia, P.K., A reminiscent study of nature-inspired computation. *Int. J. Adv. Eng. Technol.*, 1, 2, 117, 2011.

39. Păun, G. and Pérez-Jiménez, M.J., Membrane computing: Brief introduction, recent results and applications. *Biosystems*, 85, 1, 11–22, 2006.

40. Sharaf, A.M. and Elgammal, A.A., Novel AI-based soft computing applications in motor drives, in: *Power Electronics Handbook*, pp. 1261–1302, Butterworth-Heinemann, Oxford, UK, 2018.

41. Management Association, I, *Nature-Inspired Computing: Concepts, Methodologies, Tools, and Applications*, 3 Volumes, pp. 1–1780, IGI Global, Hershey, PA, 2017.

42. Marmelstein, R.E., Application of genetic algorithms to data mining, in: *Proceedings of 8th Midwest Artificial Intelligence and Cognitive Science Conference (MAICS-97)*, E. Santos Jr. (Ed.), AAAI Press, pp. 58–65, 1997.

43. Jun-Shan, T., Wei, H., Yan, Q., Application of genetic algorithm in data mining, in: *2009 First International Workshop on Education Technology and Computer Science*, 2009, March, vol. 2, IEEE, pp. 353–356.
44. Wong, M.L., Lee, S.Y., Leung, K.S., A hybrid data mining approach to discover Bayesian networks using evolutionary programming, in: *GECCO*, 2002, July, vol. 2, pp. 214–222.
45. Bandyopadhyay, S., Maulik, U., Cook, D.J., Holder, L.B., Ajmerwala, Y., Enhancing structure discovery for data mining in graphical databases using evolutionary programming, in: *FLAIRS Conference*, 2002, May, pp. 232–236.
46. Otero, F.E., Silva, M.M., Freitas, A.A., Nievola, J.C., Genetic programming for attribute construction in data mining, in: *European Conference on Genetic Programming*, 2003, April, Springer, Berlin, Heidelberg, pp. 384–393.
47. Brameier, M. and Banzhaf, W., A comparison of linear genetic programming and neural networks in medical data mining. *IEEE Trans. Evol. Comput.*, 5, 1, 17–26, 2001.
48. Rakhshani, E., Sariri, I., Rouzbehi, K., Application of data mining on fault detection and prediction in boiler of power plant using artificial neural network, in: *International Conference on Power Engineering, Energy and Electrical Drives*, 2009, March, IEEE, pp. 473–478.
49. Peng, H., Wang, J., Shi, P., Riscos-Núñez, A., Pérez-Jiménez, M.J., An automatic clustering algorithm inspired by membrane computing. *Pattern Recognit. Lett.*, 68, 34–40, 2015.
50. Peng, H., Wang, J., Pérez-Jiménez, M.J., Riscos-Núñez, A., An unsupervised learning algorithm for membrane computing. *Inf. Sci.*, 304, 80–91, 2015.
51. Alves, R.T., Delgado, M.R., Lopes, H.S., Freitas, A.A., An artificial immune system for fuzzy-rule induction in data mining. In *International Conference on Parallel Problem Solving from Nature*, 2004, September, Springer, Berlin, Heidelberg, pp. 1011–1020.

Optimization Techniques for Removing Noise in Digital Medical Images

D. Devasena*, M. Jagadeeswari, B. Sharmila and K. Srinivasan

Department of EIE & ECE, Sri Ramakrishna Engineering College, Coimbatore, India

Abstract

Nowadays, image processing algorithms use optimization to find the best solution in some criteria. Optimization is one, which is used to optimize a required solution with minimum error. The evolutionary computation methods are based on derivative free methods. Which uses the objective function to find the best solution. There are different types of evolutionary algorithm which includes Particle Swarm Optimization (PSO), Bat (BA) method, Fire Fly (FF) method, Social Spider Optimization (SSO), Collective Animal (CA) behavior, Differential Evolution (DE), Genetic Algorithms (GA), and Bacterial Forging Algorithm (BFA). Thus, these evolutionary algorithms addresses the real-time image processing problems.

The removal of noise in medical and satellite images must be very accurate, because during noise removal, details in a medical image embedded with diagnostic information should not be destroyed. The visual quality of the medical image is reduced, and it results in complicate diagnosis and treatment. In satellite images, the analysis and classification becomes harder when its noise is treated. By using optimization techniques the visual perception of the images are improved.

Keywords: Image denoising, evolutionary algorithms, medical imaging, particle swarm optimization, filtering, wiener filter

Corresponding author: devasena.mohan@srec.ac.in

S. Balamurugan, Anupriya Jain, Sachin Sharma, Dinesh Goyal, Sonia Duggal and Seema Sharma (eds.)
Nature-Inspired Algorithms Applications, (243–266) © 2022 Scrivener Publishing LLC

9.1   Introduction

Optimization has an important role in image denoising to find the noisy pixels and forming it as a noise cluster, in optimizing the filter coefficients and threshold value of the wavelet coefficients to efficiently remove the noises present in images. It gives improved performance and it is also used to optimize the parameters of the nonlinear filters. PSO is also used to find the best value for the parameters.

Initially, input images are decomposed using curvelet transform with ridgelet analysis. Curvelet transform (frequency domain) decomposes the image into subband, smooth partitioning, analysis of the component, and renormalizations. The ridgelet analysis is applied to the decomposed images, and the denoising coefficients are optimized using optimization algorithms. This identifies the pixels with speckle noise and initiates the filter. Then, the Hybrid Wiener filter (HWF) (spatial domain) is used to denoise the noisy pixels.

The optimization algorithms used in the thesis are PSO which is populationbased optimization technique whose populations are swarms and a new optimisation algorithm is also proposed in this thesis which is called Dragon Fly Optimization algorithm (DFOA). These PSO with curvelet transform and HWF (PSO-HWF) and DFOA with curvelet transform and HWF (DFOA-HWF) denoising methods tested over standard SAR images, US images, MRI images, and real-time medical images and performance metrics are measured.

Image denoising is a preprocessing step in image enhancement which suppresses the noise present in it. Depends upon the noise, the performance of the denoising algorithm differs. In medical images and satellite images, due to low light conditions and imaging techniques, the noise may occur which degrades the specimen images, which leads to loss of precise and accurate information. Thus, noise creates an artifact which leads to false diagnosis. For precise and accurate diagnosis of medical images, the image should be sharp, clear, and free from noise. Nowadays, due to advances in medical imaging techniques, the quality of the image is preserved with high resolution but it ends up with more number of pixels per unit area. This finally leads to occurrence of noises in images. These noises blur the quality of the images, and also it leads to false diagnosis of images.

Hence, denoising is an important task for precise and timely diagnosis of images. There are different types of imaging techniques and these techniques introduce different types of noises in images. Depending upon the basic mathematical formulation of noises, the denoising algorithm can be decided. Based on the noise model, image denoising algorithm and optimization techniques were used.

9.2 Medical Imaging Techniques

There are different types of imaging techniques used in medical field for localizing the various abnormalities in the different organs present in the body. The significance of various types of imaging techniques along with the noises is presented. The medical practitioners use the images from medical imaging techniques to analyze and examine the diseases. The imaging techniques used are different from natural photographic images and they are used to reflect the anatomy of internal organs of the body and also find applications in clinical assessment of various organs.

9.2.1 X-Ray Images

It is used to spot the broken bones. It is based on that the tissues can absorb photons from an X ray beam. Mostly, bones can absorb more photons than the tissues. The number of photons entering the target body is detected using image detectors which convert it to a digital image. It also used in Chest X ray in order to detect pneumonia and mammograms. With the image detector, the average number of photons detected in a pixel is 100, but statistically, every pixel does not detect 100 photons. Some pixels may appear darker and some may be lighter depends upon the photons. These darker and lighter are random in nature and the distribution of photons in X ray imaging is random in nature and the noise appeared here is called as quantum noise which reduces the visual perception of the image is reduced.

9.2.2 Computer Tomography Imaging

It is used to capture the subtle changes present in the tissue of the body and it involves measuring of X-ray transmission through the patient from large number of views by using many detectors. The mammography used to detect breast cancer using Computer Tomography (CT) imaging modality. CT scans are used to identify tumors, lesions, location, depth, and spread of tumors. They are used in many applications and it provides high spatial resolution and it shows small contrast variations in tissues. But, noise in CT images reduces the prime objective of CT imaging technique, i.e., visibility of low contrast objects. Gaussian noise occurs in CT images.

9.2.3 Magnetic Resonance Images

The abnormalities which are not visualized using X-ray and CT images are analyzed by using Magnetic Resonance Imaging (MRI) technique. It works using the magnetic properties and MRI sensors detect the protons released. A physician is able to detect the difference between the tissues by using the magnetic properties. It is used to produce detailed anatomical images without damaging the tissues. It creates detailed clear picture when compared to X-ray and CT images and regions like brain, spinal cord, nerves, and ligaments. The noises like Rician noise, Gaussian noise, and Rayleigh noise occur in the images due to MRI. The main sources of noises in MRI images are due to electronic interference in receiver and due to radio emissions of ions in the patient body. These noises cause random fluctuations which reduce the contrast of the images and disturb the qualitative and quantitative evaluation as well as disturb the features of the images.

9.2.4 Positron Emission Tomography

A nuclear medicine–based radio technology is Positron Emission Tomography (PET). It is the primary imaging modality used for the detection and spread of cancer. The PET imaging is a scanning device which detects the photons emitted from the tissues or organs by the radionuclide. This technique is based on the detection of radioactive rays when a small amount of radioactive rays is applied to the patient's vein. It is also used to measure rate of consumption of glucose by the body parts. It is also used to distinguish benign and malignant tumors. The PET images are characterized by high level of noise when compared to the CT images and MRI images. The noises in the image occur due to inherent variations in the electronic recorder and detector systems.

9.2.5 Ultrasound Imaging Techniques

It is used to facilitate the visualization of the real-time images in the body. It is also used to visualize the internal body structure like ovaries, joints, muscles, and important in obstetrics. It does not require any ionizing radiations, and the sound waves are transmitted and returning echoes are detected and it is used to moving structures in real image. Returning sound waves induces noise in the captured image. The major noise which affects the ultrasound images are speckle noise. When ultrasound waves are passed into the medium, the echoes are transmitted back from the medium, which creates error in the images captured.

9.3   Image Denoising

The above said imaging methods used to capture the images which introduce various types of noises in medical images. Gaussian, Poisson, Quantum, Rician, and Speckle are types of noise distribution. These noises reduce the visual capability of the images and reduce visual perception of the images. It corrupts the image information and it becomes unsuitable for the future analysis. Image denoising plays a vital role in removing noises in images, but before proposing the denoising algorithm, the characteristics of the noise should be studied. Image denoising is most important pre-processing step used to minimize the noise in digital images. Image denoising algorithms are classified based on the type of noise that should be removed and based on spatial and frequency domain approaches. The noise model varies for different types of noise. Based on the noise data, the performance of the denoising algorithm varies. The impulse noise degrades image quality that occurs due to image transmission and sensor temperature.

In spatial domain, all the filters directly work on the input image; it means that it works directly on the pixels. The linear filters uses mean concept which is a classical method of image denoising. The disadvantage is its blurs the image. The nonlinear filter uses median concept which preserve the image edges. The transform domain techniques are classified based on the analysis function as spatial and wavelet domain filtering. They are time consuming and produce artefacts in the processed image. It is identified that the nonlinear filters lead to development of many low complexity algorithms, which provide satisfactory results when compared to the other methods. The low complexity nonlinear filters are developed because of its simplicity and easy implementation.

9.3.1   Impulse Noise and Speckle Noise Denoising

These are the classical methods of denoising algorithms for reducing impulse and speckle noise.

Median filters are more suitable to remove impulse noises. In this, a two-dimensional mask is applied to the pixels of input image and it produces distortion when the window size is enormous. Standard Median (SM) filter substitutes the existing pixel value with median value of its neighbors within the processing image. Applying the SM filter uniformly for the whole image would modify intensities of the uncontaminated pixels [2].

But various approaches of median filter have been developed like Weighed Median Filter (WMF) [1]. Here, the non-negative integer weight is assigned to the filter window of the image. The filtering procedure is used to sort the samples in the processing window and replace the sorted samples with the corresponding weight, and a median value is calculated for the formed new sequence.

Then, Center Weighted Median Filter (CWMF) was proposed in which the filter gives more weight to the center pixel, which was presented in [7]. Compared to WM filter, the CWM performance is better and results in less computational time. Adaptive Weighted Median Filter (AWMF) is the modification of WM filter which eliminates the problems faced with the SM filter. Adaptive Median Filter (AMF) is the enhanced SM filter, in which the variation depends upon the median value of the surrounding pixel. If the median value is impulsive, then the size of the window will vary. ROAM is superior to the nonlinear mean filter where it fails to remove the negative impulses present.

In the above denoising algorithms, the filter itself acts as a detector of impulses present in the images. In Switching Median Filter (SMF), the switching scheme is introduced, where impulse detection algorithms [6, 12] are employed before the filtering process. Based on the detection results, the pixels values are modified. However, when the images are highly corrupted, it is difficult to detect and hence the error will propagate within the neighborhood regions. A Progressive Switching Median (PSM) filter [15] has been developed which gives a better resolution high noise density corrupted images.

From the extension of SMF, an Alpha Trimmed filter was proposed [11], which uses impulse detection algorithm. A Decision Tree filter [3] was proposed for the removal of RVIN. It is a binary tree with three modules, which decides the position of the current pixel. The three modules completely detect the noises present in the smooth region and in an edge region. To reconstruct the noisy pixel, an edge preserving filter is used. It chooses the edges and calculates the edge distance of the pixels, in which pixel with small difference has close relationship. Then, the value is reconstructed. This method performs well when compared to the conventional median filters.

Adaptive Filter is proposed by [8], which is best for removing RVIN. A Rank Ordered Absolute Differences (ROAD) statistics was proposed to remove RVIN [9], and ROAD is used to detect the noise pixel by considering four smallest absolute differences in the processing window. Then, a trilateral filter is adopted to filter out the impulses. In RVIN, the pixel values of the noisy region may be closer to the neighboring values, the ROAD values are not enough to identify the corrupted values, and Rank Ordered Logarithmic absolute Differences (ROLD) [14] was proposed which use a logarithmic function on the absolute differences. With the ROLD noise detector, Edge Preserving Regularization (EPR) is used to filter out the impulses. An Non-local Switching Median (ASM) filter was proposed [13] which overcomes the performance of Adaptive Switching Weighted Median (ASWM) filter, and its second phase, EPR is used to replace the noisy pixels. EPR is excellent to modify the corrupted pixels. Triangular-Based Linear Interpolation (TBLI) was used as a detector [10] which used to identify the pixels corrupted by RVIN. The Measures of Dispersion (MOD) identifies the noisy pixel by measuring MOD values.

The speckle denoising algorithm follows Homomorphic filtering which reduces noise in images. For the removal of additional noises, there are different methods like least mean squares, averaging filter, wiener filtering, and wavelet-based denoising methods are adopted. Speckle reduction filters are differentiated as scalar filters and adaptive filters. Scalar filters are based on local statistics which removes the speckle in homogenous layer and preserves the details. The mean filter and median filter are classified as scalar filters. Lee, Forst, and Kuan proposed a variety of adaptation techniques used in adaptive filters.

The disadvantage of Lee filter is that it cannot effectively remove the speckles. An enhanced Lee filter was proposed in which the pixel value is changed by the average value weighted average value. The edge enhanced Lee filter was proposed which is based on ratio-based edge detection used along with modified Lee filter which removes the speckles effectively at both low and high variance.

9.4   Optimization in Image Denoising

The removal of noise in medical and satellite images must be very accurate, because during noise removal, details in a medical image embedded with diagnostic information should not be destroyed. Visual quality of medical image is reduced where diagnosis become difficult. In satellite images, the analysis and classification becomes harder when its noise is treated. To improve the performance of the filter, optimization techniques are used. There are many nature-inspired optimization algorithm related to SI proposed for survey of optimizing the image denoising algorithms. The evolutionary computation algorithm presents co-evolutionary algorithm in which the social organisms that are ecologically intimate which leads to inspiration of co-evolutionary algorithms. SI is an innovative optimization technique which uses the collective behavior of animal societies. Several optimization algorithms are proposed based on the swarming behavior. They are PSO, ACO, HS, BFA, BA, etc.

9.4.1   Particle Swarm Optimization

PSO swarm accelerates itself to find the best solution. Based on the best solution, all other swarm particles accelerate according to vectors of velocity and position.

In the PSO algorithm, it generates initial population with particles and finds fitness function for each particle and deploys the particles randomly in the search space. The pbest and gbest values based on the fitness function, the velocity, and position values are updated till stop condition is met. It optimizes the parameters in the PSO algorithm, and during the iteration, the particles accelerates it to find the best solution.

There are two operations performed for determining best solutions. One is updating the velocity of the particles which is defined as the direction and distance followed by the particle. It is based on the attraction of the particle based on the success of the neighbor particles. Next is updating the position of the particles by updating the coordinates. Then, each particle updates the best position on every iteration.

9.4.2   Adaptive Center Pixel Weighted Median Exponential Filter

The proposed filter uses logarithmic transformation and the conversion of multiplicative to additive noise that is called as homomorphic filtering. The Adaptive Center Pixel Weighted Median Exponential Filter (ACPWMEF) uses the concept of homomorphic filtering. Thus, the multiplicative noise model is converted into the additive noise model. Before performing the logarithmic transformation, the image normalization is done. Normalization is the process used to change the range of pixel intensity [4, 5]. Normalized image has zero mean and one variance. It is used to bring the range of intensity values to a normal distribution. The normalization for an n-dimensional gray scale can be performed.

Using the noise variance, the center pixel of the kernel is tuned for noisy image. In the AMF, the noisy pixel is determined by comparing the pixels in the processing window with its neighboring pixels. The pixel which had major difference with the neighborhood values is considered as a noise. It is repeated by varying the neighborhood values and the threshold values. Then, these noise pixels are replaced by the weighted median value of the neighboring points that passed the noise identification test.

The output of the logarithmic transformation image is convoluted with the kernel filter. It uses an averaging filter for denoising. A kernel or a convolution filter called as filter mask is used which is directly imposed on the original image.

The values of the pixel are multiplied with the corresponding values in the mask. Then, add the multiplied values and use the sum to replace the window's center pixel. For every pixel in the image, the steps are repeated. The mean sum cost is computed by using the max and min gray scale values. The proposed filter uses local median value to replace the central pixel value. The size of the moving window is adaptive and it is increased until the condition is met. The minimum and maximum value of the processed window is compared with the center pixel and it changes according to it. If the pixel lies between the minimum and maximum value, then it stays same; otherwise, the pixel is replaced by the windows median value.

In summary, the steps for determining the noise is

- When the middle pixel's gray scale value is equal to the gray scale value's minimum or maximum value then it is called a noisy pixel. So, the noise pixel is numbered as 1 and the noiseless pixel is numbered as 0.
- The modified median filter will be added to the center pixel where the initial center pixel will be replaced by the value equal to the moving window median.
- Kernel or convolution filtering is applied and exponential is taken.
- The despeckling algorithm is assessed using performance metrics.

9.4.3   Hybrid Wiener Filter

Wiener filter is a one which is able to handle both the degradation function and noise as well. It is very efficient in removing the additional noises in the images. This operates in spatial domain as well as in the frequency domain. The output is denoted in the Equation (9.1)

$$y(i,j) = y(i,j) \sum_{m=-N}^{N} \sum_{n=-N}^{M} w(m,n)x(i+m,j+n) \qquad (9.1)$$

and desired output which is given by Equation (9.2)

$$e = E(\{d(i.j) - y(i,j)\}2) \qquad (9.2)$$

and the solution is obtained in Equation (9.3)

$$W = A - 1R \qquad (9.3)$$

These equations are called as Wiener-Hopf equation. The A(m,n) represents the autocorrelation of x(i,j) and R(m,n) represents the cross correlation between d(i,j) and x(i,j).

The autocorrelation and cross-correlation of the function are obtained by using the formula shown in the Equation (9.4) and (9.5)

$$A(m,n) = \frac{1}{M^2} \sum_{j=0}^{M-1} \sum_{j=0}^{M-1} \{(x(i,j)) - (x(i-m, j-n))\} \quad (9.4)$$

$$R(m,n) = \frac{1}{M^2} \sum_{i=0}^{M-1} \sum_{j=0}^{M-1} \{(d(i,j)) - (x(i-m, j-n))\} \quad (9.5)$$

The addition of Wiener filter reduces error.

9.4.4   Removal of Noise in Medical Images Using Particle Swarm Optimization

The optimization technique is implemented to optimize the denoising coefficient which effectively detects the pixels affected from speckle noise and then it initializes the filter to remove the noise. Then, finally, inverse curvelet transform is applied to get minimized mean square error. The flow diagram for the algorithm is shown in Figure 9.1.

9.4.4.1   Curvelet Transform

The idea of transforming the curvelet is to reassemble the image into subbands. A window function is used for smooth partitioning. After multiplying it by a window function, the image now becomes smooth. Partitioning is then done which is used for the analysis of images. The renormalization results in forming a unit square.

The ridgelet transform is used for finding global lines of the size of the image. The algorithm for the curvelet transform is as follows:

> Apply a trous algorithm for scales J = 4
> set $B_1 = B_{min}$ where B_{min} selected is equal to 16

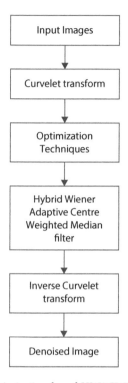

Figure 9.1 Flow diagram of optimization-based HWACWMF.

➢ for j = 1 to 4 do partition and if j modulo2 = 1, then B_{j+1} = 2*B_j else B_{j+1} = B_j

9.4.4.2 PSO With Curvelet Transform and Hybrid Wiener Filter

The PSO is the technique based on the social cooperation and competition in the population based on the social behavior of birds flocking.

PSO is initialized, and the particle is modified for the best solution in each iteration. The solution is called the function of fitness and is called the pbest. The best value is considered the best (gbest) globally. Particle location modified according to pbest and gbest. Each individual particle has its own functions of velocity and position. In a dimension search space D, there is swarm composed of particles where each particle is represented by "i" in a vector of and the particle bet solution p_{best}. Then, the best solution of the subset swarm is given by $g_{best.}$

The velocity updates are given by Equation (9.6)

$$v_{id}(n+1) = W(it) * v_{id}^n + C_1 * rand * (pid - xid^n) + C_2 * rand * (pgd - xid^n)$$

$$(9.6)$$

where $V_{id} = V_{max}$ and "it" represents the number of iterations from 1 to iteration max which is equal to 10. The "rand" represents the value ranging from 0 to 1. The C_1 and C_2 denote the acceleration constant usually a non-negative number; here, it is given as C_1 and $C_2 = 1.05$. By using Equation (9.7), the position of the particles is updated.

$$x_{id}^{n+1} = x_{id}^n + v_{id}^{n+1} \qquad (9.7)$$

From the fitness or goal f is obtained from each swarm and the best solution is found from the each iteration, then if $f(x_i) < f(p_{best})$ and $f(g_{best})$, then p_{best} and $g_{best} = x_i$.

The best score is obtained in order to optimize the coefficients of curvelet transform. In the curvelet transform, the number of sub-bands in the curvelet is selected as 4. It uses a vector containing number of scales for ridgelet transform whose minimum and maximum are optimized to obtain the best score.

After optimizing the parameters of curvelet transform, the HWACWMF is done to filter the noisy pixels and then the image is reconstructed. The algorithm for the PSO-based HWACWMF is given below.

Step1: Load the input noisy image (speckle noise)

Step 2: Apply curvelet transform for the image for J = 4 with no of scales L = [3 4 4 5]

Step 3: To optimize the parameters of the curvelet transform, the PSO method is used.

Step 4: For optimization

- Select the swarm size and maximum number of iterations used is 10.
- Initiate the acceleration constant values C_1 and C_2 which are equal to 1.05.
- The inertia weight parameters are initiated and the option parameters are generated. For the swarm size, the initial particle is determined. By using the minimum and maximum scale of the ridgelet transform, the current pbest and gbest is obtained.
- For each iteration, the values of the particle are changed by using the Equations (9.6) and (9.7).

- The best solution is obtained which is used to optimize the curvelet coefficients.
- Then, apply the HWF to remove the noise.
- To reconstruct the image inverse curvelet transform is used.
- Calculate the performance metrics.

9.4.5 DFOA-Based Curvelet Transform and Hybrid Wiener Filter

The DFOA is a novel SI optimization technique which originates from the swarming behavior of dragon flies. The curvelet coefficients are optimized using DFOA technique. Then, it is filtered using HWACWMF.

9.4.5.1 Dragon Fly Optimization Algorithm

DFOA originates from swarming behaviors of the dragon flies. PSO algorithm is also used to frame DFOA algorithm. Dragon flies swarm for two purposes: one is for hunting and another one for migration. Hunting is termed as static behavior and migration is called as dynamic behavior. The exploration and exploitation are two phase of this optimization technique. In the exploration phase, i.e., in the static behavior, dragons form a small swarm and fly over different areas. In the exploitation phase, i.e., in the dynamic behavior, the dragon flies form a bigger group and move in one direction.

The three primitive principles are considered to analyze the behavior of the flies. Separation (S_i) represents the static collision avoidance of the individuals. Alignment (A_i) indicates the velocity matching of the individuals. Cohesion (C_i) is the attraction of the individuals toward the center. Here, the step vector (velocity updation) is done with the help of these three parameters. These values are optimized for maximum iterations, which is equal to 10.

For updating the position, use Equations (9.8) to (9.14).

The separation is calculated as

$$S_i = \sum_{k=1}^{N} X - X_k \qquad (9.8)$$

The alignment is calculated as

$$A_i = \frac{\sum_{k=1}^{N} v_k}{N} \qquad (9.9)$$

where V_k gives the velocity of the kth neighbor individual.

The cohesion is calculated as

$$C_i = \frac{\sum_{k=1}^{N} x_k}{N} - X \tag{9.10}$$

Based on the three parameters, the attraction and distraction of the individual is calculated from Equations (9.11) and (9.12).

The attraction of the individual is given by

$$F_i = X^+ - X \tag{9.11}$$

where X is the position of the current individual and X^+ is the position of food source.

In the search space to update the positions of the particle, these five parameters are considered. In search space, two vectors are to be updated, step and position. The direction is obtained using Equation (9.13)

$$DeltaX_{(t+1)} = (a * A_i + s * S_i + c * C_i + f * F_i + e * E_i) + w * DeltaX_{(t)} \tag{9.12}$$

the position vectors are calculated as in the Equation (9.14)

$$X_{t+1} = X_t + DeltaX_{(t+1)} \tag{9.13}$$

where t is the current iteration.

9.4.5.2   DFOA-Based HWACWMF

In DFOA-based HWACWMF, the denoised image is first given to curvelet transform in which the image is decomposed into sub-bands and each band smoothly windowed into squares and then it is renormalized. Then, each square is analyzed via ridgelet transform. By using the DFOA technique, the coefficients of the curvelet transform are optimized. Then, HWACWMF algorithm is used to filter the noisy pixels, and finally, a denoised image is obtained.

9.5   Results and Discussions

The PSO-based HWACWMF is tested over the standard SAR images, US images, and MRI images and the performance metrics are compared with the HWACWMF. Initially, the HWACWMF is compared with PSO with curvelet transform (PSO-CVT) algorithm which is an existing method. Then, the performance has been improved by combining PSO-CVT with HWACWMF. The parameters like PSNR, RMSE, and SSIM values are obtained and shown in the Tables 9.1 to 9.3.

The algorithm is tested over the standard test images like SAR images, US images, and MRI images. The images are obtained from online medical images from Thammasat University Hospital. The images taken are (i) Case 189U1/Cyst (US image 1), (ii) Case 190U1/Cyst (US image 2), and (iii) Case 192U1/Cyst (US image 2).

The three sample MRI brain images have been taken for analysis: (i) case bt 17 (MRI image 1), (ii) case bt 34 (MRI image 2), and (iii) case D.ser6. img20 (MRI image 3) and two sample satellite images. This algorithm has been implemented in MATLAB R2013a and the simulation results are obtained. Figure 9.2 shows the sample images used for analysis.

9.5.1   Simulation Results

The algorithm is tested over the standard test images like SAR images, US images, and MRI images. This algorithm has been implemented in MATLAB R2013a and the simulation results are obtained. Noise is introduced for the selected images at various noise densities. Figures 9.3 and 9.4 show the simulation results of the algorithms for noise density varying for 40% and 60%.

9.5.2   Performance Metric Analysis

The quality of the image can be analyzed by both subjective and objective manner. Objective picture analysis plays a vital role in applications for image processing.

The deviation between the input image and denoised image is measured by using RMSE. The effectiveness of the algorithm present in minimized RMSE value. If the original image, then corrupted image and denoised image are represented by I(i,j), J(i,j), and O(i,j). The RMSE is given by Equation (9.14).

Table 9.1 Observation of PSNR values for various filtering algorithms for different sample images.

Sample images	Noise density (40%)				Noise density (60%)			
	ACPWMEF	HWACWMF	PSO HWACWMF	DOAF HWACWMF	ACPWMEF	HWACWMF	PSO HWACWMF	DOAF HWACWMF
US image 1	50.28	51.22	55.08	56.29	44.21	48.19	51.3	52.33
US image 2	52.95	54.64	57.2	58.65	46.76	51.36	54.46	55.69
US image 3	48.08	49.21	51	54.31	41.83	45.06	50.75	53.75
MRI image 1	48.48	49.98	52.3	53.65	42.34	46.94	50.9	51.9
MRI image 2	49.28	49.98	54.36	53.99	46.45	48.42	53.45	54.23
MRI image 3	56.67	57.08	58.17	62.4	55.7	56.80	57.97	59.4
SAR image 1	47.03	47.06	50.3	51.16	41.11	42.96	48.6	49.3
SAR image 2	48.62	48.50	50.4	51.22	41.46	42.04	48.6	49.5

Table 9.2 Observation of RMSE for various filtering algorithms for different sample images.

Sample images	Noise density (40%)				Noise density (60%)			
	ACPWMEF	HWACWMF	PSO HWACWMF	DOAF HWACWMF	ACPWMEF	HWACWMF	PSO HWACWMF	DOAF HWACWMF
US image 1	0.75	0.68	0.433	0.377	1.50	0.958	0.669	0.594
US image 2	0.54	0.46	0.339	0.287	1.13	0.67	0.465	0.404
US image 3	0.97	0.85	0.693	0.473	1.99	1.37	0.713	0.505
MRI image 1	0.926	0.77	0.596	0.511	1.89	1.10	0.701	0.625
MRI image 2	0.84	0.77	0.470	0.491	1.17	0.94	0.522	0.478
MRI image 3	0.36	0.344	0.303	0.186	0.40	0.355	0.310	0.263
SAR image 1	1.09	1.091	0.751	0.680	2.16	1.74	0.914	0.843
SAR image 2	0.911	0.92	0.742	0.676	2.07	1.95	0.914	0.824

Table 9.3 Observation of SSIM for various filtering algorithms for different sample images.

Sample images	Noise density (40%)				Noise density (60%)			
	ACPWMEF	HWACWMF	PSO HWACWMF	DOAF HWACWMF	ACPWMEF	HWACWMF	PSO HWACWMF	DOAF HWACWMF
US image 1	0.922	0.942	0.971	0.974	0.899	0.933	0.945	0.955
US image 2	0.925	0.933	0.977	0.98	0.911	0.925	0.955	0.959
US image 3	0.899	0.925	0.947	0.956	0.842	0.911	0.946	0.952
MRI image 1	0.911	0.925	0.929	0.953	0.888	0.902	0.911	0.922
MRI image 2	0.899	0.927	0.933	0.978	0.893	0.911	0.922	0.931
MRI image 3	0.964	0.966	0.972	0.985	0.95	0.96	0.97	0.981
SAR image 1	0.924	0.935	0.94	0.95	0.888	0.912	0.922	0.920
SAR image 2	0.899	0.931	0.94	0.95	0.838	0.911	0.922	0.920

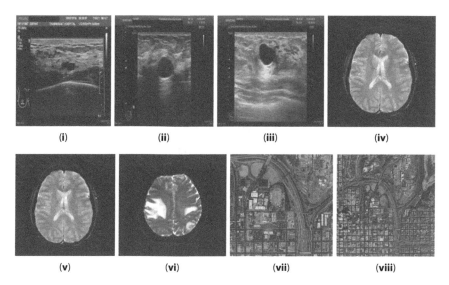

Figure 9.2 Sample standard test images. (i) Case 189U1/Cyst (US image 1); (ii) Case 190U1/Cyst (US image 2); (iii) Case 192U1/Cyst (US image 3); (iv) Case bt 17 (MRI image 1); (v) Case bt 34 (MRI image 2); (vi) Case D.ser6.img20 (MRI image 3); (vii) SAR image 1; and (viii) SAR image 2.

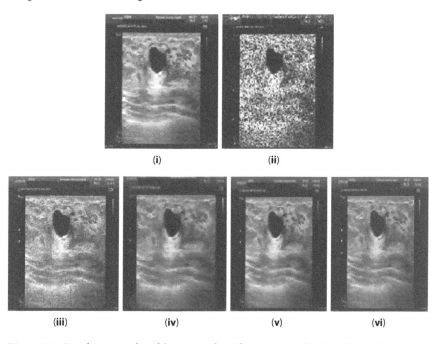

Figure 9.3 Simulation results of denoising algorithms at noise density 40% in US image. (i) Input image; (ii) Noisy image; (iii) ACPWEMF; (iv) HWACWMF; (v) PSO HWACWMF; and (vi) DOAF HWACWMF.

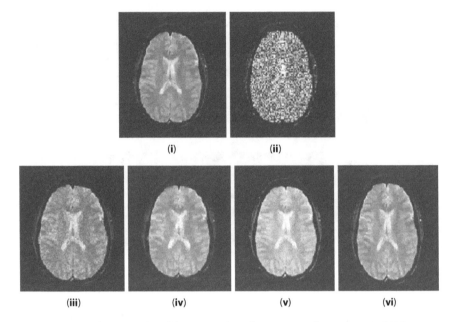

Figure 9.4 Simulation results of denoising algorithms at noise density 40% in MRI image. (i) Input image; (ii) Noisy image; (iii) ACPWEMF; (iv) HWACWMF; (v) PSO HWACWMF; and (vi) DOAF HWACWMF.

$$RMSE = \sqrt{MSE} \tag{9.14}$$

where the MSE value is given by

$$MSE = \frac{1}{MN} \sum\nolimits_{x=1}^{M} \sum\nolimits_{y=1}^{M} (I(i,j) - O(i,j))^2 \tag{9.15}$$

where

I(i,j) is the original image
O(i,j) is the denoised image

PSNR is calculated by using Equation (9.16). PSNR gives noise to signal ratio of the input and processed image.

$$PSNR = 20log_{10}\left(F_{max}/\sqrt{MSE}\right) \tag{9.16}$$

Table 9.4 Difference in average PSNR between HWACWMF and optimization-based algorithms.

Noise density	Difference in average PSNR between HWACWMF and PSO HWACWMF (dB)	Difference in average PSNR between HWACWMF and DOAF HWACWMF (dB)
Low noise density (10%–30%)	1.36	3.18
Medium noise density (40%–60%)	3.46	4.83
High noise density (80%–100%)	1.12	3.14

The SSIM is a good approximation for the perceived image quality. SSI is calculated by using the luminance component of the denoised image from the original image and represented in Equation (9.17).

$$SSIM = \frac{(2\mu_i, \mu_j + C_1)(2\sigma ij + C_2)}{\left(\mu_i^2 + \mu j^2 + C_1\right)(\sigma i^2 + \sigma j^2 + C_2)} \tag{9.17}$$

- The performance metrics for the different images using optimization algorithms are compared for standard deviation varying from 20% to 80%.
- From the results, it is concluded that the DFOA-based filter possesses high PSNR value when compared to PSO-based filters. Table 9.4 shows the average difference in PSNR value between optimization-based algorithm and non-optimized algorithm.
- The DFOA technique is best for reduction of noise in medical images and it provides high PSNR for all noise densities.

9.5.3 Summary

- ACPWMEF and HWACWMF
  - ➢ Gives better value for all the sample images, but in terms of subjective analysis, the image quality is blurred.

- Optimization-based denoising method
  - ➢ PSO HWACWMF gives better result when noise density is medium when compared to low and high noise density and visual perception is also increased.
- DOAF HWACWMF
  - ➢ Improves deviation in average PSNR in low, medium and high noise density.

9.6   Conclusion and Future Scope

In medical diagnostic technology, there are various types of imaging systems used for visualizing the internal tissues and organs for diagnose purpose. Depending upon the imaging systems, different types of noise like impulse noise, Gaussian noise, Rican noise, and speckle noise corrupt the images from visual interpretation. Due to imaging techniques, multiplicative noise called speckle noise is introduced in images.

The proposed algorithm ACPWMEF is tested with standard sample SAR images, US images, and MRI images. The parameters like PSNR, RMSE, and SSIM are measured for all the sample images at different noise density. The parameters provide good results when compared to the existing filters, but it shows deviations in some sample images when compared to the existing. So, the hybrid HWACWMF is proposed which is a combination of ACWMF with Wiener filter that improves the performance in terms of all the parameters like but it blurs the images. So, the visual perception of the denoised image is decreased. To improve the drawbacks and to provide high visual reception for diagnosing the medical images and analyzing the SAR images, optimization techniques are used.

The PSO-HWACWMF and DOAF-HWACWMF are proposed which use optimizing techniques along with the HWACWMF. The algorithm PSO-HWACWMF is compared with the HWACWMF and existing PSO CVT method. The proposed method overcomes the performance of HWACWMF in terms of both subjective and objective analysis. The visual perception of the image is increased in PSO HWACWMF and it also preserves the edges. It performs well in terms of all the parameters and it shows good deviation in average PSNR when compared to HWACWMF which is 3.46 dB in medium noise density. To improve the performance better in all range of noise density, DFOA technique along with HWACWMF is identified. The DFOA HWACWMF is compared with HWACWMF which shows improved deviation in average PSNR between them at low, medium, and high noise density. The DFOA technique is best for reduction of noise in medical images and it provides high PSNR value when compared to all other conventional methods.

The work has been extended in terms of the following:

- The despeckling algorithms can be extended with modifications for the removal of speckle noise in real-time satellite images and medical images.
- Further, all the proposed algorithms can be implemented in an FPGA platform and designed as a portable device for medical diagnosis.

References

1. Roy, A., Singha, J., Manam, L., Laskar, R.H., Combination of adaptive vector median filter and weighted mean filter for removal of high density impulse noise from colour images. *IET Image Proc.*, 11, 6, 352–361, 2017.

2. Abdalla, A.M., Osman, M.S., AlShawabkah, H., Rumman, O., Mherat, M., A Review of Nonlinear Image-Denoising Techniques. *Proceedings of Second World Conference on Smart Trends in Systems, Security and Sustainability (WorldS4)*, pp. 96–100, 2018.

3. Lien, C.-Y., Huang, C.-C., Chen, P.-Y., Lin, Y.-F., An Efficient Denoising Architecture for Removal of Impulse Noise in Images. *IEEE Trans. Comput.*, 62, 4, 631–643, 2013.

4. Devasena, D. and Jagadeeswari, M., FPGA Implementation of Speckle noise removal in Real Time Medical Images. *J. Med. Imaging Health Inf.*, 7, 6, 1263–1270, 2017.

5. Devasena, D., Jagadeeswari, M., Srinivasan, K., Radhika, V., Hybrid Filter for Removal of Speckle noise in Digital Images. *Int. J. Recent Technol. Eng.*, 7, 6, 1561–1564, 2019.

6. Jezebel Priestley, J., Nandhini, V., Elamaran, V., A Decision based Switching Median Filter for Restoration of Images corrupted by high density Impulse Noise. *Proceedings of International conference on robotics, Automation, control and Embedded Systems*, pp. 1–5, 2015.

7. Ko, S.J. and Lee, Y.H., Center weighted median filters and their applications to image enhancement. *IEEE Trans. Circuits Syst.*, 38, 9, 984–993, 1991.

8. Chan, R.H., Ho, C.-W., Nikolova, M., Salt-and-Pepper Noise Removal by Median-Type Noise Detectors and Detail-Preserving Regularization. *IEEE Trans. Image Process.*, 14, 10, 1479–1485, 2005.

9. Garnett, R., Huegerich, T., Chui, C., A Universal Noise Removal Algorithm With an Impulse Detector. *IEEE Trans. Image Process.*, 14, 11, 1747–1754, 2005.

10. Civicioglu, P., Removal of Random-Valued Impulsive Noise from Corrupted Images. *IEEE Trans. Consum. Electron.*, 55, 4, 2097–2104, 2009.

11. Saravana Kumar, S., Ebenezer Jeyakumar, A., Vijeyakumar, K.N., Removal of High density Impulse noise using Morpological based Adaptive Unsymmetrical Trimmed Mid point Filter. *J. Comput. Sci.*, 1, 7, 1307–1314, 2014.

12. Wang, S.-S. and Wu, C.-H., A new impulse detection and filtering method for removal of wide range impulse noises. *Pattern Recognit.*, 42, 2194–2202, 2009.

13. Lan, X. and Zuo, Z., Random-valued impulse noise removal by the adaptive switching median detectors and detail-preserving regularization. *Optik*, 125, 3, 1101–1105, 2014.

14. Dong, Y., Chan, R.H., Xu, S., A Detection Statistics for Random-Valued Impulse Noise. *IEEE Trans. Image Process.*, 16, 4, 1112–1120, 2007.

15. Zhang, W.G., Liu, F., Jiao, L.C., SAR image despeckling via bilateral filtering. *Electron. Lett.*, 45, 15, 81–783, 2009.

Performance Analysis of Nature-Inspired Algorithms in Breast Cancer Diagnosis

K. Hariprasath[1]*, S. Tamilselvi[2], N. M. Saravana Kumar[3],
N. Kaviyavarshini[1] and S. Balamurugan[4]

[1]*Department of Information Technology, Vivekanandha College of Engineering for Women, Namakkal, India*
[2]*Department of Biotechnology, Bannari Amman Institute of Technology, Erode, India*
[3]*Department of Artificial Intelligence and Data Science, M Kumarasamy College of Engineering, Karur, India*
[4]*Intelligent Research Consultancy Services (iRCS), Coimbatore, India*

Abstract

Nature-inspired computing (NIC) is a fascinating computing paradigm that applies the methodology and approaches of nature that addresses various real-time complex problems ranging from how an organism finds its prey to genetic evolution. One of the unique features is that it has been provisioned with a decentralized control of computational activities naturally. In this chapter, to have a better insight of such NIC-based algorithms, the problem of identifying the breast cancer is used to exhibit their performances. Also, this chapter briefs about the application of stand-alone and hybridized approaches to identify the disease. Finally, it concludes with the experimental results and other statistical measures. The purpose of the chapter is to guide the new researcher in the area to get inspired from the conventional works and to bring out a new advanced approach that can perform further better. The three swarm algorithms are ant colony optimization, firefly, and particle swarm optimization algorithm. These swarm algorithms were used to optimize the support vector machine (SVM) which was trained to classify the malignant and benign images from the Wisconsin breast cancer dataset. With respect to the experimental results, it has been found that naïve algorithm with

---

Corresponding author: khariprasathit@gmail.com

S. Balamurugan, Anupriya Jain, Sachin Sharma, Dinesh Goyal, Sonia Duggal and Seema Sharma (eds.) *Nature-Inspired Algorithms Applications*, (267–294) © 2022 Scrivener Publishing LLC

PSO optimization demonstrates better discriminating property of the underlying conventional classifiers.

Keywords: Nature-inspired computing, PSO optimization, Wisconsin breast cancer, malignant, benign

10.1   Introduction

Breast cancer is turning into a major and inevitable effect of women death across entire earth, in the interim, can be affirmed only at the initial disclosure in the pre-mature stages and an appropriate treatment of this deadly cancer will conform the prolong endurance in such sufferers. Around the world, breast cancer is considered as the second basic sort of disease by following lung carcinoma because 10.4% of disease rate also fifth basic reason for deaths due to cancer [22, 23]. In addition, it is, presently by a wide margin, the most well-known disease among ladies, the occurrence percentage is double than colorectal malignancy also and cervical malignant growth around multiple points than lung carcinoma. Anyway, the mortality rate of breast cancer overall is simply 25% more prominent than that of lung disease among women. Thus, it prompts many researchers who have been funded to model a system that automatically detects the breast cancer in its initial stages so that it can be treatable [19, 20].

The investigator has newly recommended numerous techniques by utilizing intelligence methodologies for infectious analysis; fewer sufferers fulfill the demand of good efficiency. More researches have been done about the analysis of breast cancer diagnosis in the past; this particular work confines in two aspects. First is to select the appropriate optimization technique that suits better and another is to ensure the best-in-class performance to detect the cancer autonomously from supervised to semi-supervised as a test-case analysis. The familiar swarm algorithms FA and PSO were used for analysis breast cancer. The statistical conclusion finds that swarm intelligent techniques are used for the purpose of breast cancer analysis along with high performance. In addition, PSO analyzes breast cancer for better efficiency compared to remaining swarm intelligent algorithms.

10.1.1   NIC Algorithms

Particle swarm optimization (PSO) is one of techniques that enhances a classifier to optimize itself and tends to pick an improved solution from its alternative result set in accordance with known quality proportion and tries to optimize the candidate solution set of the particular iteration with the respective particle velocity and position by searching throughout the entire state space of particles. It is the most successful metaheuristic optimization algorithm used in variety of medical applications and one of the algorithms considered in the chapter to analyze the performance while hybridizing with other conventional classifiers [16–18].

Ant colony algorithm is widely deployed in data mining applications where ant colony clustering method is implemented in the synthesized correlated ant colony. One of the famous applications is that these types of artificial ant colony synthesizing approach has applied in solving traveling salesman problem used for local search in max-min ant systems. Also, to find minimum distance for data routing problem in heavily distributed networks and to exhibit accessing list for heavily decentralized database, systems deal with familiar ant swarm-based approach and scheduling. It has applications in manufacturing industry, market segmentation, feature selection, cloud computing, and resource allocation.

FA was developed for the purpose to tackle with complex issues of peculiar kind those were either does not fit into the true- or false-based conditions; perhaps, it deals with the values that are intermittent too. The basic idea of the algorithm relies on the natural characteristic trait of a firefly that flashes the guiding signals to other fireflies and the same phenomenon is followed by the other fireflies of the same group so as to follow the guiding signals to find prey or mates by minimal effort by the firefly group. The fireflies are closely having similar association in its behavior to that of swarms in terms of message communication, self-organization, and regionalized decision-attaining ability. It seems well suited for solving NP-hard problems, classification in complex datasets problems, multiobjective searches, parallel computational domains, combinatorial computational domains, and incessant search space domains. Because of ability of FA that would efficiently handle continuous data, it is widely used for solving manufacturing drugs, image compression, stock market price forecasting, load dispatch problems, and other biomedical researches studying about cell mutation at DNA sequence level.

The bat algorithm is one of the lately established NIC-based learning algorithms, which exploits the ability of exploring the new routes by using its ability to sense and follow the echo-based location prediction mechanism similar to that of bats and few other nocturnal animals to obtain solutions for a continuous indeterminist search space problems. Because of such ability, it is widely employed in obstacle tracking robots, autonomous cars, game planning, remote wireless multi-hop network management, prioritization problems, feature selection problems, global search problems, and resource scheduling problems. Cuckoo search algorithm depends on generation of cuckoo fowls. Cuckoos are a group of winged creatures with one of a kind conceptive system progressively forceful contrasted with other flying creature's species. Some of cuckoo winged creature's species like Ani and Guira laid eggs on common homes and expel others eggs to build incubating likelihood of their own eggs. Different species use brood parasitism technique for laying their eggs in the homes of different flying creatures or host homes. The parasitic cuckoos are acceptable in donning homes where eggs have quite recently been laid and their planning of laying eggs is precisely. They lay one egg in the host home which will ordinarily incubate faster than different eggs.

Harmony Search Algorithm (HSA) is a fair mix of exploring in the continuous undesirable space search and exploiting the well-known trained cases to classify the cases, i.e., to pick the better candidate solution. Above all, it is very straightforward, robust, and simplicity to implement and ease of use. The HAS is enlivened by the procedure of melodic execution, comprises of three administering criterions: arbitrary inquiry, amicability memory thinking about the criteria of the particular harmony, and appropriate pitch modifying rule. These characteristic features make HSA a very special nature-inspired computing (NIC) algorithm that predominantly employed as a metaheuristic optimizing algorithm.

This particular chapter can be foreseen as a common stage that used to exhibit the individual performances of such algorithms is by detecting the breast cancer malignant figures from Wisconsin breast cancer dataset. This work also quickly clarifies about the use of individual and hybridized ways to deal with the identification of the disease. At long last, it finishes up with the trial results and other factual measures. The purpose of the chapter is to guide the new researcher in the area to get inspired from the conventional works and to bring out a new advanced approach that can perform further better.

10.2   Related Works

Dhahri *et al*. [1] recommended a study based on algorithms of machine learning which has an objective to develop a model to compare the tumours of breast between benign and malignant and to learning algorithm is optimized. The perfect features and parameters of the classifier of machine learning are selected by the technique of genetic algorithm. This approach concentrates on the parameters like accuracy, sensitivity, precision, ROC curves, and specificity. This study demonstrates that programming of genetic has the ability to automatically detect the preeminent approach with the help of algorithm of classifiers and methods of preprocessing. This approach has three important phases. In the first phase, three evolutionary algorithms have same result after the performance of effective configuration. In second phase, it focuses on feature selection method which will progress the performance of accuracy. In the third phase, the supervised classifier of the machine learning is utilized to design pattern that performs automatically.

In programming of genetic algorithm, it is resolved the problem of hyper parameter that performs the challenges of algorithm in machine learning. This proposed algorithm is used to select the suitable algorithm from different types of configurations and this research is done on the library of python. The estimation of ensemble method for the technique of machine learning using comprehensive method and the rate of time consumption is high. This model is best suitable for settings of parameter control of algorithms in machine learning at one side and automatic diagnosis of breast cancer on other side. Determination of model which is best suited for the data and designing the model by automatic and adjustment method of parameter are the two major challenges of this approach.

Kumar [2] proposed that breast cancer has high mortality rate as it is a significant reason between the women but diagnosis of breast cancer manually takes long time. Diagnosis of breast cancer automatically was designed to decrease the time through manually and spread rate of the cancer cells is decreased. This approach is trained as well as tested on dataset Wisconsin using four different types of machine learning algorithm, namely, support vector machine (SVM), naive Bayes, logistic regression, and k-nearest neighbor. This paper concentrates about the comparison of sensitivity, specificity, and accuracy. After comparison analysis is done by the result of accuracy and the finest algorithm is selected. The various types of hyper parameter used are selected manually. The paper presented results that SVM gives the best performance. The performance of machine learning algorithm is done on texture and cell radius with more accuracy than diagnosis done manually.

Idri *et al.* [3] recommended that breast cancer is considered as the primary sources in women death. Various result-based assisting methods were suggested to support cancer treating doctors to analyze meticulously the sufferer. These result-based assisting methods majorly used here is machine learning approach to segregate the analyzation of the mild or benignant cancer. This paper discussed the classification and investigation of the influence of attributes calibration on the accurate three well-defined machine learning approaches. They are SVM, multi-layer perception, and decision trees.

The three attribute calibration methods used in this paper are PSO, grid search, and Weka software. The datasets are gathered from the machine learning repository. The global outcomes recommend that applying PSO and grid search helps to develop the specific classifiers, and thereby, the doctors can do the effective analyses.

Arafi et al. [4] introduced the machine learning approach about the breast cancer data evaluation and categorization, using PSO and SVM. This approach utilizes SVM as design for machine learning approach with the target of reducing standardization inaccuracy error. PSO is a technique for inevitable decision of top first element of two attributes in SVM. Its efficiency in resolving identification issues is analytically proved for realistic benchmark datasets. The final conclusion values are distinguished to the required four techniques using three various methods of efficiency.

This paper proposes the framework and a few exploratory decisions of machine learning techniques toward breast cancer. This technique is in accordance with SVM for categorizing the whole data with the motive of developing the efficiency of the out-coming classifier. Based on this paper, kernel is used also attributes that are systematically kept by applying PSO method.

This technique was executed in Linux PC utilizing LIBSVM library and C++ language. Subsequent programming device had tentatively tried on original benchmark of breast cancer dataset index openly accessible at popular VCI archive of ML. Data collection was partitioned into three distinct manners and into three subsets of various sizes, and substance was individually used for practicing, for approval, and for testing information. Test results had been contrasted with acquired of similar information models by four different strategies utilizing three various measures of efficiency. The observation values show that the proposed technique can additionally upgrade.

Purwaningsih et al. [5] suggested that there are a few investigations in the medical area that order information to analyze and examine choices. To investigate breast cancer, this examination analyzes two techniques: the neural network technique and the SVM technique depend on PSO which recommends deciding most efficiency result in the Coimbra dataset information. To execute the neural network and SVM strategy depending on PSO, Rapid Miner programming is utilized. At that point, the application result values are looked at utilizing Confusion Matrix and ROC curve. In light of the efficiency of the two models, it is realized that PSO-based neural network model has a highest efficiency estimation of 84.55% than the consequences of the PSO-based SVM with an efficiency estimation of 80.08%.

The computation results and the precision of the AUC execution were got by the conclusion of the experiments; the two techniques are PSO-based neural network with AUC estimation of 0.885 and PSO-based SVM with an estimation of 0.819 comprised for the class of classification.

Data collecting systems utilized in this paper using auxiliary data, where the dataset utilized was included from the UCI machine learning repository and planned by leading PSO and SVM-based neural network method to decide most significant level of efficiency in breast cancer coordination.

The phases of researches for the categorization of breast cancer comprised of the following:

1. Preprocessing information is finished by erasing records that are missed elements and copies. Discretization systems are a piece of data transformed that is utilized to change the information types.
2. After the information is transformed, at that point, the information is handled and verified by Rapid Miner utilizing the neural network and SVM model which depends on PSO.
3. Moreover, this work creates an efficiency level, in particular Confusion Matrix, to analyze efficiency esteems in the SVM technique with the neural network technique depends on PSO.

The technique given in this paper is about the SVM technique and PSO-based neural network strategy. In the process of the underlying dataset, it is through verifying and studying the information, the dataset is changed into 0 and range 1, at that point, the dataset is split into 10-fold cross-validation. The dataset was verified utilizing the SVM and PSO-based neural network technique to approve the model efficiency. This technique has a high level of efficiency compared to the PSO-based SVM. In this way, the PSO-based neural network technique can be utilized for categorization in breast cancer investigation.

Mazen et al. [6] proposed model that is partitioned into two phases. From the start organize, firefly algorithm has applied; further, it produces utmost results as beginning populace of genetic algorithm in subsequent stage. At end of second stage, the utmost results created by genetic algorithm have viewed as utmost results at all and values produced by genetic algorithm for mean squared error are likewise studied low estimation of fitness function. This paper explored effectiveness of using genetic algorithm–based firefly algorithm which hybridizes the arrangement development technique of firefly algorithm and genetic algorithm is a meta-heuristic enhancement method of practicing neural systems improving the loads among the layers and also biases of neuron organize in order to limit wellness function. The development pattern surveyed by various assessment criteria and contrasted and models improved utilizing meta-heuristic algorithms like biogeography-based optimization, PSO, and ant colony optimization (ACO). Final decision outcome demonstrates that optimized pattern utilizing the genetic algorithm–based firefly algorithm beats other metaheuristic algorithms in accomplishing increased efficiency and decreased mean squared error.

Fallahzadeh et al. [7] proposed that the pathology as a typical diagnosis evaluation of cancer is an intrusive, tedious, and, in part, idiosyncratic technique. Thus, optical methods, particularly Raman spectroscopy, have engaged in consideration in the diagnosis of cancer analysts. Nonetheless, Raman spectra consists of various pinnacles associated with atomic bounds of the patterns, evaluating that the best attributes identified with dangerous changes can improve the efficiency of analysis. The current research endeavored to enhance the intensity in the cancer which is based on the Raman spectroscopy for the analysis to examine the utmost Raman attributes utilizing ant colony algorithm.

Based on current analysis, 49 spectra had been estimated among the ordinary, generous, and even the carcinogenic tissues of the breast tests, utilizing very low measurable Raman framework. Subsequent to pre-processing for the reduction in non-harmonious foundation luminance and force, about 12 significant Raman groups among the natural sampling were extricated from the attributes in every range.

At that point, the ACO algorithm was used to locate the optimal attributes for analysis. As the outcomes illustrated, by choosing five attributes, the categorization efficiency of the typical, favorable, and harmful class expanded by 14% and arrived at 87.7%. ACO attribute collection can improve the symptomatic efficiency of Raman-based analysis models.

10.3   Dataset: Wisconsin Breast Cancer Dataset (WBCD)

In experimental analysis, the algorithms were tested on the datasets of Wisconsin breast cancer from repository of UCI machine learning. The datasets of Wisconsin breast cancer are composed of 10 different attributes. The samples were records collected from 699 Fine Needle Aspirates (FNA) from tissue of human breast. They were simply categorized into two classes, namely, Benign and Malignant. From acquired dataset of WBC, it is found that about 65.5% of the samples are benign and the rest of the 34.5% have been classified as malignant by the doctors while diagnosing. The attributes of the dataset are cell marginal adhesion, thickness, bare nuclei, normal metric and nucleoli, bland chromatin and shape of cell with homogeneity and size of cell with homogeneity, and single epithelial. It is also found to that the WBC dataset is in complete since 16 records were missing. In our experiments, the images of these 16 records were excluded and the remaining 683 samples were used.

10.4   Ten-Fold Cross-Validation

The procedure includes arbitrarily separating the dataset of Wisconsin breast cancer into 10 gatherings with around equivalent size. For testing, the main fold is kept and the prototype is prepared on 10 folds. The procedure is iterated for n intervals and in each interval diverse fold or an alternate gathering of data arguments is used for justification. Cross-validation is a resampling way implemented to assess machine learning on a restricted data model.

$$Cross - Validation(cv_{(n)}) = \frac{1}{n}\sum_{j=0}^{n} MSE_i \qquad (10.1)$$

Cross-validations are essentially utilized in techniques of machine learning for estimation of the skill of a model in machine learning on hidden dataset. That is, to utilize a restricted example so as to gauge how the model is relied upon to perform all in all when used to make forecasts on data not utilized during the training of the sample.

10.4.1   Training Data

The procedure involves training the model in dataset; it can differ however ordinarily can utilize 60% of the accessible data to train.

10.4.2   Validation Data

The well-performed data is selected and it is made run in the validation data. Usually, 10% to 30% of data belong to subgroup. The model is said to be over fitting when it consists of more errors.

10.4.3 Test Data

Test data is also termed as holdout data. The dataset can hold data that will not be implemented in the data training. Test data advantage is that it has absolute sample estimation. This may range from 5% to 20%.

10.4.4 Pseudocode

Step 1: Train data is divided into 10 portions
Step 2: For i = 0 to 9
Step 3: Network is trained by 9 parts
Step 4: Accuracy is computed by 1 part
Step 5: Average of accuracy computed for 10 runs

10.4.5 Advantages of K-Fold or 10-Fold Cross-Validation

• Time of computation is diminished as it repeats the procedure just for 10 intervals when the estimation for n is 10.
• Minimum bias value.
• Information focuses acquire the chance that is tried precisely after and utilized in preparing 1-n intervals.
• There will be difference in subsequent gauge is diminished and n increments.

10.5 Naive Bayesian Classifier

Naive Bayesian is one of the techniques that belong to classification which was introduced by Thomas Bayes (1702–1761). Naive Bayesian classifier is said to be statistical classifier and it is supervised learning [24–28]. Naive Bayesian is one of inductive learning algorithm which is most effective and efficient learning algorithm for data mining and machine learning. Naive Bayesian classifier is a straightforward probabilistic type of classifier that is reliant on applying theorem of Bayes along with robust of objectivity prospects. The goal of the performance is to predict the test class instance with more accuracy. The Naive Bayesian classifier is based on two simple prospects. They are predictive attributes that are tentatively unconventional in the class and the result of non-categorical attribute is commonly separated inside the class. There are many different ways to treat the discrete and continuous attributes [21].

Naive Bayesian classifier is used explicitly to calculate the probabilities for hypothesis. Naive Bayesian classifier in input data is strong to sound.

In this case, the Naive Bayesian classifier can be realistic to huge dataset [8]. It will result in maximum precision and promptness. In Naive Bayesian classifier, the result of the parameter on the known class will not depend on the result of another parameter and the above statement is known as class-conditional independence. Naive Bayesian classifier has the ability to work better in any difficulty situation and most commonly in computer aided prediction. Naive Bayesian classifier study from train data, the conditional probability of a single variable I_z, and the label of class are given by C. To calculate the probability by applying the classification through Naive Bayesian of particular instance $I_1,....,I_m$ by the method:

$$P(C = c | I_1 = i_1,....,I_m = i_m) \tag{10.2}$$

As the Naive Bayesian classifier is found on assumption, the variables are conditionally not dependent and subsequent of the class is given by the method

$$P(C = c | I_1 = i_1,...., I_m = i_m) = P(C = c) * \prod_{I_z} P(I_z = i_z | C = c) \tag{10.3}$$

The effect of the Naive Bayesian classifier is discussed and it has the maximum subsequent probability

$$max_c \prod_{I_z} P(I_1 = i_1 | C = c) \tag{10.4}$$

Naive Bayesian classifier has four conditions. They are as follows:
1. If class C is a class with his subsequent probability, then the method is

$$max_{c_x \in C} P(c_x | i)$$

2. To identify this class, the subsequent probabilities P(Cx|i) must be calculated. By the use of

$$P(c_x | i) = \frac{P(i | c_x) P(c_x)}{P(i)}$$

This is more sufficient to calculate the probability of the class with given input.

3. The evaluation of probability $P(i|c_x)$ of a parameter to be conditionally not dependent known class

$$P(i|c_x) = \prod_{y=1}^{m} P(a_y|c_x)$$

4. The last step is to evaluate the probabilities for $P(C_x)$ and $P(a_y|c_x)$ by the train set. By giving all the parameters of dataset as continuous, the Gaussian distribution is used to calculate the probability

$$P(a_y|c_x) = \frac{1}{\sqrt{2\pi}\sigma_{yx}} e^{\left(-\frac{(a_y - \mu_{yx})^2}{2\sigma_{yx}^2}\right)}$$

10.5.1 Pseudocode of Naive Bayesian Classifier

Step 1: Read the train set.
Step 2: Estimate the mean and standard deviation of attribute in every class.
Step 3: Repeat
Calculate the probability using density equation.
Until all probability is calculated.
Step 4: Calculate the probability of every class.
Step 5: Get the greatest probability.

10.5.2 Advantages of Naive Bayesian Classifier

- It is mainly based on statistical model.
- It produce efficient training algorithm.
- It is easy to understand.
- It is utilized across many domains.
- The order of instance in this has no effect.
- Predicting new data is easy.

10.6 K-Means Clustering

Given below are the phases that involved in the algorithm of k-means. Figure 10.1 represent the working of K-means clustering.

1. Initialization: K input vectors or data points are chosen for initializing the clusters.
2. Search for nearest neighbors: For every input vector, the cluster center that is the closest is found and that input is assigned to the cluster that is corresponding to it.
3. Updated mean: The centers of cluster in every center are updated by the value of mean or the centroid for the vectors of input that have been assigned to the cluster.
4. Stopping rule: steps 2 and 3 are repeated till such time there is no more change in the means and their values.

There are certain variants of the k-means that differ in the selection of the centroids of initial groups, their choosing of measure of similarity and also the strategies for calculation of cluster means. The usual procedure for the Euclidean data is using the mean as centroid and choosing initial centroids in a random way. This converges to one solution even though it is normally the local minimum [29, 30]. As it is only the vectors that are

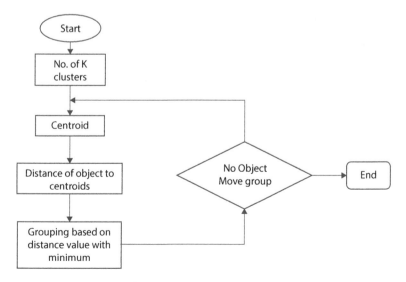

Figure 10.1 K-means centroid computation.

stored the requirement for space is O(m*n), in which the point number is referred as m and the attributes number is referred as n. The requirement for time is O(I*K*m*n), in which I is referred as the iteration number that is needed for convergence. The I is small and is bounded easily as most of the changes take place only in the initial iterations. So, the K-means is an effective and simple method for clusters that are less than m in number.

10.7   Support Vector Machine (SVM)

SVM is introduced by Vapnikthat is created on theory of Vapnik-Chervonenkis (VC) and principle of structural risk minimization (SRM). SVM discovers the adjustment among the reducing of train set and exhausts the possibilities of the boundary. This is done in for the achievement of the finest simplification capacity [14]. This also remembers hardy to over fitting. The sample for grouping is produced by the training set method along with the trained data. Next grouping is implemented on the model of training. The difficulties come across in position of the SVM prototype that is by choosing the function of kernel and its factor values. Settings of unfitting factor clue to reduce in grouping outcomes. This problem includes count of features and not all features is important for particular task. They may include both redundant and irrelevant, when some features are discarded the optimality of the performance is achieved and also result in decreasing the dimensionality space of input to preserve computation effort but might result in lower accuracy in classification. The smallest count of feature is used to make the classification procedure fast and exact. This procedure will be attained by the utilization of feature selection. This is feature selection schemes are inferred to discover the result of inappropriate features on the enactment of classifier systems [9].

The binary classification task is $\{i_x, j_x\}$, $x = 1 \,....n$, $j_x \in \{-1,1\}$, $i_x \in R^d$, in which i_x is point of data and j_x are labels of correspondence. They can be sliced along with the hyper plane denoted by $v^t i + k = 0$ where v is the coefficient of d-dimensional vector in typical vector to the hyper plane, and k is equalizer from origin. The linear type of SVM discovers an ideal splitting boundary by cracking the subsequent ideal activities:

$$\text{Decrease to: } g(v,\xi) = \frac{1}{2}||v||^2 + c\sum_{x=1}^{w} \xi_x$$

$$\text{Subject to: } j_x(v^t i_x + k) \geq 1 - \xi_x \xi_x \geq 0$$

Lagrangian multipliers are introduced $\alpha_m (m = 1,2,\ldots\ldots w)$; the problem of primal can be decreased to a Lagrangian problem with dual property.

Increase to $\sum_x^w \alpha_i - \dfrac{1}{2} \sum_{x=1}^w \sum_{y=1}^m \alpha_x \alpha_y j_x j_y i_x^t i_y$

Subject to: $0 \le \alpha_x \le C, \sum_{x=1}^w \alpha_x j_{x=0}$

Quadratic optimization problem (QP) by means of linear constraints: The Karush-Kuhn-Tucker (KKT) states that

$$\alpha_x (j_x (v^t i_x + k) - 1) = 0 \tag{10.5}$$

If $\alpha_x > 0$, the points of the corresponding data are called support vector. This result receipts the method is $v = \sum_{x=0}^w \alpha_x y_x i_x$, in which w is number of SVs. k can be attained by $j_x (v^t i_x + k) - 1 = 0$, in which i_x is SVs. When v and k are identified, the functions of linear discriminate are assumed by

$$g(i) = sgn\left(\sum_{x=1}^w \alpha_x j_x i_x^t i + k\right) \tag{10.6}$$

The classes of vectors are not separated linearly, and to make the linear model of machine learning to perform better in nonlinear model, a new idea is implemented. The new idea in real space of input is mapped with the function where the dimensional space of feature is maximum for the trained dataset [10]. The decision with this mapped function can be represented as

$$g(i) = sgn\left(\sum_{x=1}^w \alpha_x j_x \varnothing(i_x)^t \varnothing(i) + k\right) \tag{10.7}$$

where $i_x^t i$ input space is represented in procedure of $\varnothing(i_x)^t \varnothing(i)$ in the space features. The practical procedure for planning $\varnothing(i_x)$ needs not be known because it is subliminally well-defined by the use of designated kernel, which is given by $K(i_x, i_y) = \varnothing(i_x)^t \varnothing(i)$. This function of decision can be conveyed as follows:

$$g(i) = sgn\left(\sum_{x=1}^w \alpha_x j_x K(i_x, i_y) + k\right) \tag{10.8}$$

For positive functions for semi-definite which will fulfill the condition of Mercer's and the function of kernel, where function of kernel is included that can be utilized by SVM. The values of parameters can be selected in advance by

- C is a regularized parameter which controls the transaction among the decreasing the error of training as well as the model with complexity.
- The gamma parameter of the function of the kernel that describes the mapping functions of nonlinear space from the input to the dimensional space feature which is maximum.
- SVM utilizes the function of kernel that designs a hyper plane with decision for nonlinear function space of input.

Advantages of Support Vector Machine

- SVM is utilized when there is no idea about the data.
- SVM unstructured and semi structured data like text, Images and trees.
- The real trick of SVM is kernel strength that is with kernel we can solve complex problem.
- The over-fitting risk is minimum in SVM.
- SVM utilizes programming in technique of convex quadratic that delivers merely minima in global way to circumvent the confined in minima in local way.

10.8   Swarm Intelligence Algorithms

In 1989, Gerardo Beni and Jing Wang acquainted Swarm Intelligence (SI) in connection with cell automated frameworks. Piece of a huge number of animals that have chosen their own will for focus on a typical objective is called swarm. How do swarms (winged animals, fish, and so on) figure out how to move so well altogether. How do ants locate the best wellsprings of nourishment in their surrounding? To respond to these inquiries, new incredible streamlining technique, i.e., SI, is planned.

SI is simply the order that manages advanced collection, self-managed, collaborate, flexible, and incredible behavior of class which observes the straightforward principles. The idea of swarm insight depends on artificial intelligence. Individual can be considered as idiotic yet numerous specialists' display self-association conduct and in this manner can act like community-oriented intelligence. SI–based calculation is famous and broadly utilized. A biologic staging arrangement of nature gives the motivation [11]. Case of SI incorporates ant colony, bird congregation, animal or bird grouping, bacterial development, and fish tutoring. Swarm telerobotics is the methodology of SI, alludes to increasingly regular setup of algorithms. "Swarm forecasting" is utilized for determining issues.

10.8.1 Particle Swarm Optimization

PSO is presented by Kennedy and Eberhart in 1995 aspired from the behavior of social creatures in gatherings, for example, flying creature and fish schooling or subterranean ant colonies. This algorithm imitates the communication between individuals to share data. PSO is realistic to different types of fields for development as well as in coordination with other existent calculations.

Swarm optimization (PSO) is a strategy of computational which reduces an issue by regularly and attempting to expand an individual answer based on a specified value of proportion. This understands an issue by the way of having a populace of individual response that is named particles here and particles movement around in the space of searching as per the normal statistical principle from the particle's location and promptness. The development of each particle is attacked by its near most popular location but at the similar period which is guided toward is the most popular situations by the seeking environment that are restored with correct location is sort by particles of different types [12]. Figure 10.2 explains the working of PSO.

PSO will make not maximum or no presumptions about the advanced issue and that can stare over massive spaces of individual solutions. Nonetheless, metaheuristic algorithm like PSO will not ensure an ideal solution at all times. Additionally, PSO will not utilize the changing of the issue that is improved and implies that PSO will not impose that the issue of optimization can be differentiated as it is required by strategies of classical development.

Its applications include combination with a back engendering calculation, to prepare a neural system framework structure, multi-target optimization, classification, image clustering and image clustering, image processing, automated applications, dynamic, pattern recognition, image segmentation, robotic applications, time frequency analysis, decision-making, simulation, and identification [15].

Pseudocode for Particle Swarm Optimization
   Step 1: Initialize particle

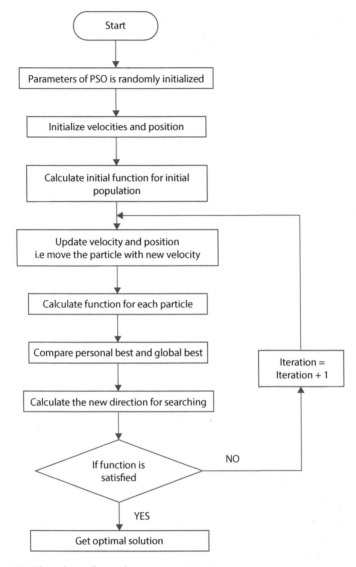

Figure 10.2 Flow chart of particle swarm optimization process.

Step 2: Do till iterations reaches maximum value or error crite-
ria reaches minimum value
Data value for fitness is calculated
Case 1: If value of fitness is better than personalBest then
Set personalBest = currentvalue of fitness
Case 2: If personalBest is superior to globalBest

Set globalBest = personalBest
Step 3: Velocity of particle is calculated and updated

Advantages

- PSO technique is a simple method for execution.
- PSO technique can perform parallel computation.
- PSO has high performance in finding global optima.
- PSO coverage of particle is fast.
- PSO time of computation is short.

10.8.2   Firefly Algorithm

Firefly algorithm is the swarm-based metaheuristic approach which is introduced by Xin. The behavior such as flashing lights of the fireflies is inspired and utilized in the algorithm. The algorithm utilizes the concept that fireflies are always both sex and implies any firefly can be engrossed by some fireflies, and the ability of the desirability of the firefly is directly relational to the ability of its brightness which depends upon the goal work. A firefly will be pulled in to the firefly with more brightness [31, 32].

The working function firefly algorithm has the following steps. Figure 10.3 explains the working of firefly algorithm.

1. Objective function is initialized by absorbing the light intensity.
2. Initial population of the firefly is generated.
3. For every firefly, the light intensity is determined.
4. Attractiveness of the firefly is calculated.
5. The firefly which has brightness level of minimum is moved toward the firefly which as brightness level of maximum.
6. Light intensity of the firefly is updated.
7. Fireflies are ranked based on the intensities and best solution is found.

The advantages of the firefly algorithm are that it has an ability to death with nonlinear more effectively, optimization of multimodal problem can be solved naturally, there is no need of velocity as it is needed in PSO, solution to the global optimization problem can be found as soon as possible, flexible to integrate with other technique of optimization, and initial solution is not required [13]. The disadvantage of firefly algorithm is it consumes more time to reach the optimal solution. Firefly algorithm are used in the field of semantic web composition, classification and clustering problems, neural network, fault detection, digital image compression,

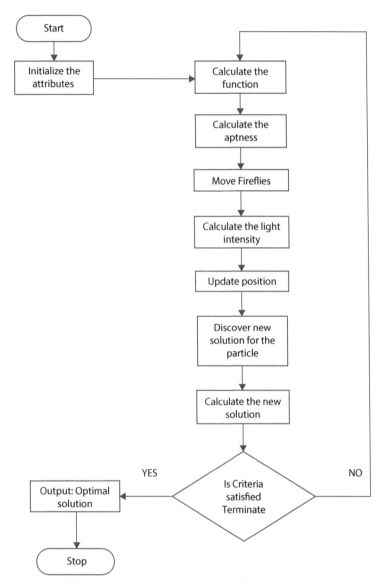

Figure 10.3 Flow chart of firefly algorithm process.

feature selection, digital image processing, scheduling problems, and traveling sales man problem.

Pseudocode for Firefly

Step 1: Randomly generate m fireflies as initial population

Step 2: Calculating appropriateness of each fireflies
   While condition terminates do
   for x = 1: N do (fireflies)
      for y = 1: N do (nflreflies)
         if(aptness(jx) > aptness(jy))
            swap(jy.jx)
       differ attractiveness with distance d between fireflies
   arrange the fireflies and global best in ascending order

10.8.3   Ant Colony Optimization

ACO is a populace-oriented method of metaheuristic which is utilized for discovering inexact results for troublesome enhancement issues. This method is probabilistic in resolving the problems of issues computational that is diminished with the help of discerning new ways through plans. In ACO, a lot of software transmitter referred as artificial ants will probe for respectable answers for optimal for a given issue of appreciation. For the use ACO, the issue of optimization can be transformed into the issue for identifying the best way on a pattern with weight. The artificial ants gradually built by proceeding onward the pattern.

Artificial ants represent multi-agent techniques roused by the behavior of ordinary ants. The pheromone-based correspondence of natural ants is regularly the overwhelming prototype used. Combinations of artificial ants and neighborhood search algorithms have become a technique for decision for various development jobs including a type of graph, e.g., vehicle steering and web directing. The expanding movement right now prompted conferences devoted exclusively to artificial ants and to various business applications by particular organizations, for example, AntOptima [7].

This algorithm is hidden for an individual from the ant algorithms, but in SI techniques, it comprises some approach of metaheuristic developments. It is make known by Marco Dorigo in 1992; the primary algorithm was in the family way to look for an ideal result in an illustration, supported by the ant's behavior of observing for path between the portion as well as the feed root. The major assumption is that it has improved to explain a maximum class of extensive for issues if numeric, and as a result, little issues have been developed and illustration on various types of the ant's behavior. ACO plays out a model-based searching and offers a few reproductions technique with over assessment of circulation algorithms.

Its application includes the problem with generalized assignment and the set covering, classification problems, Ant Net for organize directing, and multiple knapsack problem.

10.9   Evaluation Metrics

Accuracy: The accuracy is referred as the exact total of positive and the negatives and separated through the number of classification attributes by total [True Positive (TP) + True Negative (TN) + False Positive (FP) + False Negative (FN)] in the subsequent formula.

$$Accuracy = \frac{TP + TN}{TP + TN + FP + FN} \tag{10.9}$$

Sensitivity: Sensitivity is referred as the classification of positive fraction and calculated as below:

$$Sensitivity = \frac{TP}{TP + FN} \tag{10.10}$$

Specificity: Specificity is referred as the classification of negative fraction and calculated as below:

$$Specificity = \frac{TN}{TN + FP} \tag{10.11}$$

F-measure: F-measure is referred by the mean value of harmonic by recall as well as precision. It takes the final call in the adjustment among the recall as well as precision.

$$F - Measure = \frac{2 \times (\text{Pr}\,ecision \times \text{Re}\,call)}{\text{Pr}\,ecision \times \text{Re}\,call} \tag{10.12}$$

In which,

$$Precision = \frac{TP}{TP + FP}$$

$$Recall = \frac{TP}{TP + FN}$$

$$Misclassification\ rate = 1 - \left[\frac{TP + TN}{TP + TN + FP + FN} \right]$$

10.10   Results and Discussion

Figure 10.4 show the accuracy of various clustering methods performed in Wisconsin dataset. It is observed that, the accuracy of PSO-SVM possesses higher value of 90.41 than PSO– K-means having accuracy of 88.41, while the accuracy of PSO-Bayesian is 86.84. Figures 10.5 and 10.6 show the

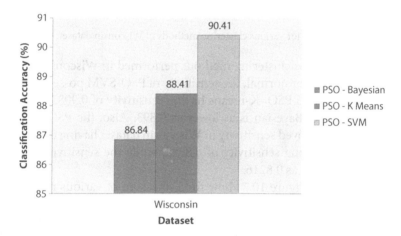

Figure 10.4 Classification accuracy for various clustering methods.

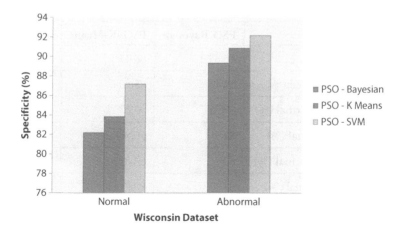

Figure 10.5 Specificity for various clustering methods in Wisconsin dataset.

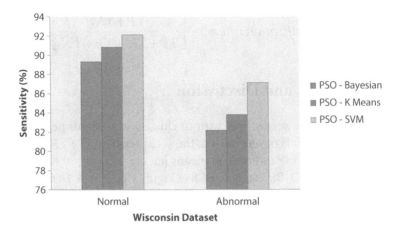

Figure 10.6 Sensitivity for various clustering methods in Wisconsin dataset.

sensitivity of various clustering methods performed in Wisconsin dataset. It is observed that for normal, the sensitivity of PSO-SVM possesses higher value of 0.9214 than PSO–K-means having sensitivity of 0.9083, while the sensitivity of PSO-Bayesian is as lower as 0.893. Also, the PSO-SVM for abnormal has improved sensitivity in Wisconsin dataset having 0.8714 than PSO–K-means having sensitivity of 0.8382, while the sensitivity of PSO-Bayesian is as lower as 0.8216.

Table 10.1 and Figure 10.7 show the F-measure of various methods of clustering performed in dataset of Wisconsin. It is observed that for normal, the F-measure of PSO-SVM possesses a higher value of 0.8625 than 0.833 of PSO–K-means and 0.8115 of PSO-Bayesian. Also, the PSO-SVM

Table 10.1 Performance of various PSO optimized classifiers.

Classifiers	PSO-Bayesian	PSO–K-Means	PSO-SVM
Accuracy (%)	86.84	88.41	90.41
Specificity for Normal (%)	82.16	83.82	87.14
Specificity for Abnormal (%)	89.3	90.83	92.14
Sensitivity for Normal (%)	89.3	90.83	92.14
Sensitivity for Abnormal (%)	82.16	83.82	87.14
F-Measure for Normal (%)	81.15	83.3	86.25
F-Measure for Abnormal (%)	89.89	91.13	92.65

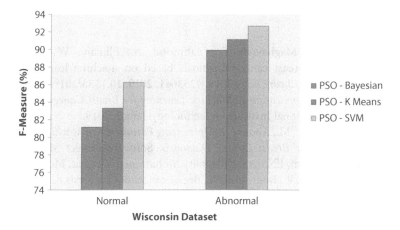

Figure 10.7 F-measure for various clustering methods in Wisconsin dataset.

for abnormal has improved F-measure having 0.9265 than PSO–K-means having F-measure of 0.9113, while the F-measure of PSO-Bayesian is as lower as 0.8989.

10.11   Conclusion

The evaluation metrics plays a key role to assess the quality of a strategy among which the PSO tops in sensitivity, specificity, and precision. For any medical diagnosing model that possess higher sensitivity and precision implies that it enjoys a higher diagnosing power to identify the disease accurately more often. We believed that a very important characteristic of a diagnosing system lies in rejecting the normal images and to identify and pick the cysts. This ideology motivates to carry out the experimental result analysis in all the possible ways considering both to pick the normal as well as abnormal images. In this particular case of breast cancer, if the disease has been diagnosed in the beginning stage, then the percentage of survival of patient will be increased by providing with an appropriate treatment. The obtained result is very promising and claims that PSO-based classifier outperforms the other conventional algorithms.

As a future scope, with respect to the obtained results, it is seen that the accuracy can be further improved to propose an ideal diagnosing model of the disease by employing other NIC algorithms as well. The attempts will be made to implement the most successful proposed model in a physical hospital over a period of time to get trained and the model shall be tested with real-time cases to assess the performance. Also, the metaheuristic approach can be considered to improve further.

References

1. Dhahri, H., Maghayreh, E., Mahmood, A., Elkilani, W., Nagi, M., Automated breast cancer diagnosis based on machine learning algorithms. *J. Healthcare Eng.*, 2019, 4253641, 2019, 10.1155/2019/4253641.

2. Kumar, N., *Application of Machine Learning for Breast Cancer Diagnosis*, Malaviya National Institute of Technology, Jaipur, 2019.

3. Idri, A., Hosni, M., Abnane, I., *Optimizing Parameters of Machine Learning techniques for Breast Cancer Diagnosis*, Software Project Management Research Team, ENSIAS, University Mohammed V Rabat, Morocco.

4. Arafi, A., Fajr, R., Bouroumi, A., Breast cancer data analysis using support vector machines and particle swarm optimization. *2014 Second World Conference on Complex Systems (WCCS)*, Agadir, pp. 1–6, 2014.

5. Purwaningsih, E., Application of the support vector machine and neural network model based on particle swarm optimization for breast cancer prediction. *SinkrOn.*, 4, 66, 2019, 10.33395/sinkron.v4i1.10195.

6. Mazen, F., Abul Seoud, R., Gody, A., Genetic algorithm and firefly algorithm in a hybrid approach for breast cancer diagnosis. *Int. J. Comput. Trends Technol. (IJCTT)*, 32, 62–68, 2016.

7. Fallahzadeh, O., Dehghani-Bidgoli, Z., Assarian, M., Raman spectral feature selection using ant colony optimization for breast cancer diagnosis. *Lasers Med. Sci.*, 33, 1799–1806, 2018, https://doi.org/10.1007/s10103-018-2544-3.

8. Kharya, S., Agrawal, S., Soni, S., Naive Bayes classifiers: A probabilistic detection model for breast cancer. *Int. J. Comput. Appl.*, 92, 10, 0975–8887, April 2014.

9. Furey, T.S., Cristianini, N., Duffy, N., Bednarski, D.W., Schummer, M., Haussler., D., Support vector machine classification and validation of cancer tissue samples using microarray expression data. *Bioinformatics*, Oxford Acad., 16, 10, 906–914, 2000.

10. Chao, C.-F. and Horng, M.-H., The construction of support vector machine classifier using the firefly algorithm. *Comput. Intell. Neurosci.*, Hindawi, 2015, 1–7, 2015.

11. Chen, H.-L., Yang, B., Wang, G., Wang, S.-J., Liu, J., Liu., D.-Y., Support Vector Machine Based Diagnostic System for Breast Cancer Using Swarm Intelligence. *J. Med. Sys.*, 36, 4, 2505–2519, 2011.

12. Lin, S.-W., Ying, K.-C., Chen, S.-C., Lee, Z.-J., Particle swarm optimization for parameter determination and feature selection of support vector machines. *Expert Syst. Appl.*, Elsevier, 35, 4, 1817–1824, 2008.

13. Olatomiwa, L., Mekhilef, S., Shamshirband, S., Mohammadi, K., Petkovic, D., Sudheer, Ch., A support vector machine–firefly algorithm-based model for global solar radiation prediction. *Solar Energy*, Elsevier, 115, 632–644, 2015.

14. Tuba, E., Mrkela, L., Tuba, M., Support vector machine parameter tuning using firefly algorithm, in: *26th Conference Radioelektronika*, IEEE, 2016.

15. Selvaraj, C., Siva Kumar, R., Karnan, M., A survey on application of bio-inspired algorithms. *IJCSIT*, 5, 1, 366–370 2014.

16. Sousa, T., Neves, A., Silva, A., Swarm optimisation as a new tool for data mining. *Proceedings of the International Parallel and Distributed Processing Symposium (IPDPS'03)*, IEEE Computer Society, 2003.

17. Wang, Z., Sun, X., Zhang, D., Classification rule mining based on particle swarm optimization. *ICIC*, Springer-Verlag Berlin Heidelberg, 2006.

18. Wang, Z., Sun, X., Zhang, D., A PSO-based classification rule mining algorithm. *ICIC*, Springer-Verlag Berlin Heidelberg, 2007.

19. Aalaei, S., Shahraki, H., Rowhanimanesh, A., Eslami, S., Feature selection using genetic algorithm for breast cancer diagnosis: Experiment on three different datasets. *Iran. J. Basic Med. Sci.*, 2016.

20. Zamani, H. and Nadimi-Shahraki, M.-H., Swarm intelligence approach for breast cancer diagnosis. *Int. J. Comput. Appl.*, 151, 1, 40–44, October 2016.

21. Dumitru, D., Prediction of recurrent events in breast cancer using the Naive Bayesian classification. Annals of University of Craiova, 36, 2, 92–96, 2009.

22. Aruna, S., Rajagopalan, S.P., Nandakishore, L.V., Knowledge based analysis of various statistical tools in detecting breast cancer at CS&IT – CCSEA, 2, 37–45, 2011.

23. Soria, D., Garibaldi, J.M., Biganzoli, E., Ellis, I.O., A comparison of three different methods for classification of breast cancer data. *Seventh International Conference on Machine Learning and Applications*, Computer Society, IEEE, 2008.

24. Aci, M., Inan, C., Avci, M., A hybrid classification method of k nearest neighbor, Bayesian methods and genetic algorithm. *Expert Syst. Appl., Elsevier*, 37, 7, 5061–5067, 2010.

25. Shah, C. and Jivani, A.G., Comparison of data mining classification algorithms for breast cancer prediction, in: *4th ICCCNT 2013*, IEEE, 31661, 2013.

26. Al-Aidaroos, K.M., Bakar, A.A., Othman, Z., Medical data classification with Naïve Bayes approach. *Inf. Technol. J.*, Asian Network for Scientific Information, 11, 9, 1166–1174, 2012.

27. Singh, S. and Gupta, P., Comparative study ID3, cart and C4.5 decision tree algorithm: A survey. *Int. J. Adv. Inf. Sci. Technol. (IJAIST)*, 27, 27, 97–103, July 2014.

28. Xiaoliang, Z., Jian, W., Hongcan, Y., Shangzhuo, W., Research and application of the improved algorithm C4.5 on decision tree. *2009 International Conference on Test and Measurement*, IEEE, 2009.

29. Ture, M., Tokatli, F., Kurt, I., Using Kaplan–Meier analysis together with decision tree methods (C&RT, CHAID, QUEST, C4.5 and ID3) in

determining recurrence-free survival of breast cancer patients. *Expert Syst. Appl. Sci. Direct*, Elsevier, 5, 1, 366–370, 2009.

30. Surya Prasanthi, L. and Kiran Kumar, R., ID3 and its applications in generation of decision trees across various domains- Survey. *Int. J. Comput. Sci. Inf. Technol.*, 6, 6, 5353–5357, 2015.

31. Fister, I., Fister Jr, I., Yang, X.-S., Brest, J., A comprehensive review of firefly algorithms. *Swarm Evol. Comput.*, 13, 34–46, 2006.

32. Atashpaz-Gargari, E. and Lucas, C., Imperialist competitive algorithm: An algorithm for optimization inspired by imperialistic competition, in: *2007 IEEE Congress on Evolutionary Computation*, pp. 4661–4667, 2007.

11

Applications of Cuckoo Search Algorithm for Optimization Problems

Akanksha Deep and Prasant Kumar Dash*

Department of Computer Science and Engineering, C.V. Raman Global University, Bhubaneswar, Odisha, India

Abstract

In recent years, algorithms inspired by nature have congregated a lot of attention in solving the complex real-world problems. The optimization technique is the way to reach the best performance systems by maximizing the output factors and minimizing input. Similar algorithms inspired by nature used for optimization are Ant Colony Optimization, Genetic Algorithm, Bat Algorithm, Firefly Algorithm, Particle Swarm Optimization (PSO) Algorithm, Cuckoo Search (CS), Bird Flocking, Tabu Search (TS), Artificial Bee Colony Optimization, etc. These algorithms are classified on the basis of two key elements such as diversification and aggregation generally called as exploitation and exploration. The challenges with intense exploration are that it does not provide an optimal solution. On the other hand, if deep exploitation is used, then it traps the algorithm with local optima. A harmony between the local and global optima is eminent fundamental for algorithm inspired by nature. According to the statistical results, Cuckoo Search Algorithm (CSA) has been implemented in different area to optimize the solution. The major domains where CSA implements are image processing, pattern recognition, software testing, data mining, cyber security, cloud computing, IoT etc. This chapter aims to sum up the analysis and utilization of CSA in all categories.

Keywords: CSA, PSO, IoT, cloud computing, pattern recognition, GA, meta-heuristic

Corresponding author: prasant.oitburla@gmail.com

S. Balamurugan, Anupriya Jain, Sachin Sharma, Dinesh Goyal, Sonia Duggal and Seema Sharma (eds.) *Nature-Inspired Algorithms Applications*, (295–316) © 2022 Scrivener Publishing LLC

11.1 Introduction

The applications in the real world require complex and scarce resources. Therefore, a shift in scientific thinking is needed to ensure the optimal use of available resources and efficient solutions. Mathematically, the study of planning effective design solutions by the use of mathematical tools is optimization. The optimization process helps in discovering the best design solution concerning system constraints. Optimization is needed everywhere for reducing the consumption and cost of energy along with increasing the efficiency, performance, output, and profit. Techniques of optimization put forward various restrictions while developing the mathematical and operational research models [1].

In traditional algorithms of optimization, the model solution is dependent on the constraint functions and objective types. The efficacy of conventional algorithms is entirely dependent on the solution size, variable number, and constraints required for problem-solving.

Moreover, these algorithms do not provide general solution strategies that are useful for problem-solving with different variables and constraints. Stochastic optimization algorithm and deterministic algorithms are considered as two classes. For specific set of inputs, deterministic algorithm generates the identical outputs and is mostly used like algorithm for local search. A stochastic algorithm has random components and, for particular data, produces different outputs.

Many metaheuristic algorithms are now readily solving optimization problems. Some examples of most widely used metaheuristic algorithms can be particle swarm optimization (PSO), genetic algorithm (GA), and the famous ant colony optimization. Flexibility, easy implementation, and potential to find local optima are some features of these algorithms. The primary source of inspiration for the metaheuristic algorithm is physical or natural phenomenon such as finding the food sources by animals and their movement. As a result, the algorithm is easy to grasp and can be reproduced for different optimization problems as software programs [5].

The metaheuristic algorithms can find globally optimal solutions from many local solutions. A lot of extensive studies have been conducted on metaheuristic algorithm like Cuckoo Search (CS), Back-tracking Search (BSA), Firefly Algorithm, TLBO, ABC, HS, YYPO, and optimization of Squirrel Search. The swarm optimization for the novel diffusion particle was proposed for the optimization of sink placement. According to NFL, i.e., No-Free Lunch Theorem, no algorithm works well for all the optimization problems. Therefore, for optimizing a series, several metaheuristic algorithms can be suitable [8].

Modern optimization algorithms are typically based on swarm intelligence that are often nature-inspired. In today's world, there are a large number of optimizing techniques such as PSO, Bat Algorithm, Ant Colony Optimization (ACO), Evolutionary Algorithm, Grey Wolf Optimizer, Artificial immune Systems, Gravitational Search Algorithm, Firefly Algorithm, Glow Worm Swarm Optimization, CS, Bird Flocking, Animal Herding, Fish Schooling, Taboo Search, Bacteria Growth, and Simulated Annealing.

There are diverse ways of inspiration, and consequently, there can be many different types of algorithms. However, these algorithms mostly tend to use specific characteristics for making the updated formulae. Example inspiration of GAs was taken from the biological systems of Darwinian Evolution and mutation, crossovers, and choosing the fittest. For GAs, chromosomes or binary/real strings are representation of solution. On the other hand, behavior of birds and fishes inspired the PSO, i.e., Partition Swarm Optimization.

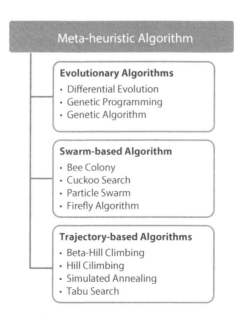

Figure 11.1 Types of meta-heuristic algorithms.

Swarm or group intelligence characteristics may be present in such multi-agent systems [4]. There are several variants and improvements of PSO existing in literature and also many new meta-heuristic algorithms have been developed (Figure 11.1). The central focus of this chapter is on the Cuckoo Search Algorithm (CSA) along with its application. Yang and Deb [2] developed the optimization algorithm CS in the year 2009. Special features and characteristics of breeding and laying the eggs by a cuckoo is the root motivating factor for the CS optimization algorithm. An overview of CS is described in this chapter along with its applications in different sections for optimization of problems. The reviewed categories are engineering, image processing, neural networks, and wireless sensor networks. The aim is to summarize the generalized run-through and provide the analysis of applications of CS in above categories.

11.2   Related Works

Particle Swarm Optimization (PSO) imitates the behavior of birds. Birds search for food in flocks and follow a trail. In this algorithm approach, it treats each bird as a particle. Each particle has certain parameters like velocity, position, etc. There are two solutions called the local particle best solution and the global best solution [3]. The algorithm continuously updates both the local and the global best solutions until it reaches a global optimal solution. These optimization techniques are far-reaching in many domains and have successful applications in areas such as in training neural network system design, time frequency analysis, image segmentation, pattern recognition and image processing, classification, image clustering, and many more.

Another such nature-inspired algorithm is the CSA. This algorithm was developed by Suash Deb and Xin-She. The indication of this algorithm is motivated by the way of life of the Cuckoo bird species. Aggressive reproduction strategy also known as obligate brood parasitism is common in the Cuckoo bird. These species lay their eggs (only one egg in one nest) in the nest of other birds. The algorithm is motivated on simple rules like the egg laying behavior, egg's quality, and availability of hosts [6]. It also considers the probability that host bird catch the Cuckoo's eggs. Using these rules, we determine the chances of survival of chick. Fitness value for each solution is varied and the output, the nest having best eggs (best fitness value), is the best solution. The process is repeated again and again, to attain the global optimum result.

In 2009, Deb and Yang presented a unique diagnosis system using CS to work out mechanical engineering design optimization complications comprising of the springs' design and structure of welded beam for reducing the spring's weight, therefore minimization of combined cost fabrication. Author also presented comparisons with different techniques similar to the CSA, i.e., PSO and GA for being more efficient than previously used algorithms [2]. Then, the author also compares with differential evolution methods and shown that CSA is a better substitute to balance the synaptic weights of the neuron. The proposed software functioned efficiently in the standard assessment proving proof that the solution is suitable for implementation in advanced tasks of solving problems.

In the year 2012, Natrajan proposed the enhanced CS has for optimizing spam filtering [7]. In a similar manner, CSA has been planned for optimizing the manufacturing system. The algorithm does it by reducing the cost and increasing the system active time. Particle approach based on the CSA has been industrialized which successfully attained a wireless sensor network with energy efficient system. The simulation results exhibit that the Cuckoo-based Particle Approach in clustering provides output comparable with standard LEACH protocol. CSA has been implemented to top quality optimal parameters in the milling operation. It was successful in optimizing embedded system and semantic web service, for solving non-linear problems.

11.3 Cuckoo Search Algorithm

In 2009, Yang and Deb developed an optimization algorithm known as Cuckoo Search Algorithm, also abbreviated as CSA [2]. The inspiration for the development of this algorithm is derived from a bird species, called cuckoo. This bird with a beautiful voice has a unique method of reproduction. The uniqueness lies in the fact that these birds do not build their own nest. Instead, they lay their eggs in the nests of other birds. Such mechanism of reproducing is known as obligate brood parasitism.

11.3.1 Biological Description

Kingdom: Animalia

Phylum: Chordata

Class: Aves

Order: Cuculiformes

Families: Musophagidae, Cuculidae, and Opisthocomidae

Aggressive reproduction of some species of cuckoo is discussed in the following paragraph. Typically, 16–22 eggs are laid by a female cuckoo. The eggs may vary in color and shape or similar to the host bird's eggs. The various species of cuckoo lays variety of eggs. The cuckoos do not target a particular type of birds to be the host. Instead, there is an also a variety in the host birds targeted by the various species of cuckoo.

The eggs of cuckoo mostly have red, yellow, green, gray, monochrome, or white surface color with spots. Their radius is mostly about 21.9 to 16.3 mm.

Brood parasitism for hatching is used by almost half of these birds. The female cuckoo hides near the nest of suitable host, waiting for a chance to lay the egg. Some cuckoo female also imitates the colors of the host eggs, thereby reducing the probability of the eggs being discovered and thus increasing the reproductively. Because the host birds on discovering, foreign eggs either throw the eggs or leave the nest to build a new one. Cuckoos very often pick a nest in which the bird has already laid its eggs.

Generally, cuckoo birds' eggs hatch slightly before the other birds. Once the primary brooded cuckoo chick comes out of the shell, it propels the host eggs out of the nest to eliminate them. As a result, it ensures to get more share of food which the host provided. Studies also show that to get more food, these chicks can also imitate the call of the host birds' chicks.

11.3.2 Algorithm

Yang and Deb identified three rules that idealize the behavior of cuckoo so that it can be implemented as a computer algorithm.

- One cuckoo produces single egg at one time and dumps it in a nest that has been chosen randomly.

- The nest with eggs of high quality will be carried over to the subsequent generation.
- Host nest count is fixed and the host can detect foreign egg with the probability between [0, 1]. In case of detection, host can either obviate the cuckoo egg or leave the nest and build a new one.

The following is the implementation of CS based on the above rules:

Candidate solution is represented by each egg in nest. Therefore, one cuckoo can put a single egg in a nest. However, each nest may have more than one egg. This group of eggs may mostly represent multiple solutions.

It is now the responsibility of the CS to get a new solution with more potential so that it can replace the solutions currently in the nest. A target function is used to evaluate the standard of solutions. It is generally a maximization function.

However, for some problems in the real world, we need the minimum values of the target function. Such problems are mathematically related to min-max equation and problems.

$$Min(f(x)) = Max(-f(x))$$

A fitness function is derived which is a transformed function of the objective function. The probability parameter in the last rule is now called as the switching probability. This probability helps in determining when n unflavored host nests get substituted by an arbitrarily generated one.

Exploration and exploitation are two components of the CS, which were identified by Crepinsek. Both of these components get balanced by the above-mentioned parameter.

Every single egg is equivalent to a solution and every cuckoo egg is a replacement solution. The objective is to use newer and potentially better solution for exchanging inadequate solutions within the nest. For simplicity, only one egg is present in one nest.

This algorithm is also suitable for more complex cases when each nest has more than one egg, representing a cluster and each cluster is a solution.

In nature, animals look for foodstuff using a quasi-random or random approach.

Mostly, the scourge of animal path is a stochastic process as the subsequent step is predicted based on both present direction and state/location. This may even be mathematically modeled.

A Levy flight is a stochastic process in which heavy-tailed probability distribution makes the distribution of step-length consistent.

Step 1:

1. Initialize size of host nests (n), probability ($p_a \in [0,1]$), and max no of iterations Max_{itr}.
2. Initialize counter to t = 0
3. For(i = 1; i ≤ n) start
   a. Produce primary population of host of size n
   b. Check fitness function $f(xi^{(t)})$
4. Stop for
5. Repeat
   a. Create new solution $x_i^{(t+1)}$
      i. Verify fitness function of a solution $f\left(x_i^{(t+1)}\right)$
   b. Randomly select a nest from n solutions, x_j
   c. If $f\left(x_i^{(t+1)}\right) > f\left(x_i^{(t)}\right)$ then
      i. Substitute solution x_j with $x_i^{(t+1)}$
   d. End if
   e. Discard fraction p_a of worst nests
   f. Make fraction $p_{a(of\ worst\ nests)}$ number of new nests at different place
   g. Keep nests with best-quality solutions
   h. Compare the solutions and find the current best
   i. Make t = t + 1
6. Until (t ≥ Max_{itr}) - Terminate
7. Generate best solution

Step 2:

Cuckoo's egg

Host bird's eggs
Nest k

Lay egg(rk,sk') within nest k
Nest k is selected at random

Cuckoos' egg is almost like a host egg.
Where
rk' = rk + Randomwalk(Levy flight)rk
sk' = sk + randomwalk(Levy flight)sk

Step 3:

Nest k

Compare health of host and cuckoo egg
Find Root Mean Square Error (RMSE)

Step 4:
If the fitness of cuckoo's egg is best than the host egg, then replace the egg within the nest k by cuckoo's egg.

If cuckoo egg is of better quality than host egg, then switch egg of nest k with cuckoo's egg.

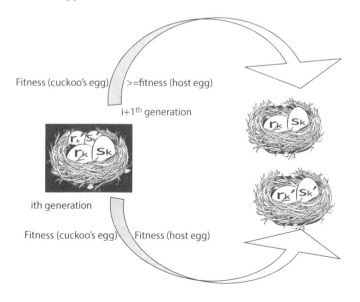

Step 5:

If discovered by host, then nest is abandoned and another nest is built (p < 0.25) to avoid local optimization.

Nest k   New Nest

Repeat steps 2 to 5 until termination.

11.4 Applications of Cuckoo Search

CSA has various applications in both optimization and real-world problems. A number of publications have compared the performance of other optimization algorithm with CSA. In this section, CSA's application in field such as image processing, clustering, data mining, power, energy, and engineering designs has been discussed (Figures 11.2 and 11.3).

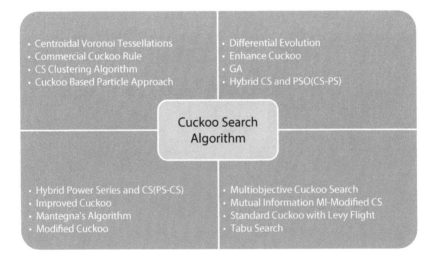

Figure 11.2 Types of Cuckoo search algorithm.

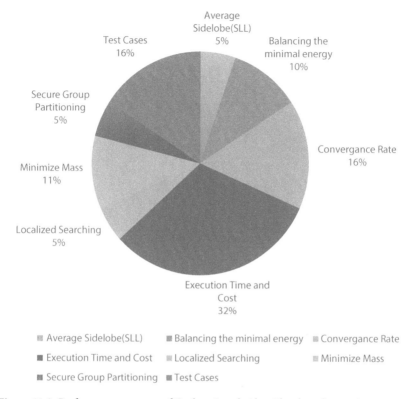

Figure 11.3 Performance measure of Cuckoo Search Algorithm based on various parameters.

11.4.1   In Engineering

In engineering, the rapid advancement in computing technology needed more optimized engineering solution. As a result, many engineering problems are solved using CSA algorithm.

11.4.1.1   *Applications in Mechanical Engineering*

11.4.1.1.1   Laser Cutting

It is widely used contour cutting process for cutting wide choice materials including non-conventional materials. In order to make accurate prediction of roughness of laser cut material surface, MilošMadic *et al.* effectively

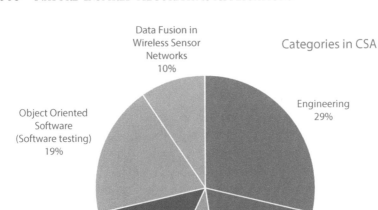

Categories in CSA

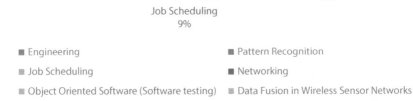

Figure 11.4 Major categories of application of CS.

used neural network and CSA. An experiment integrating CSA and mural network using CO2 laser and Chrome Steel (AISI304) was conducted. In this chapter, it was observed that CSA obtain 90.44% accuracy and was highly efficient in giving optimal parameters for laser cutting.

To reduce the cost and increase productivity, cutting is optimized both non-linearly and with constraints. Esfandiari optimized the cutting conditions by applying CS, GA, and SA. The output showed that CSA achieved better global optimum solution with higher accuracy and faster convergence (Figure 11.4).

11.4.1.1.2   Four-Bar Mechanism

Optimization of synthesis of path generating four bar mechanism has a lot of problems. It is therefore very hard task and has mostly being solved using DE (Differential Evaluation) algorithm and its variance. But Wen-Yi Lin and Kuo-Mo Hsiao used CSA to solve these problems using a single user parameter CSA (Figure 11.5). The results proved CSA to be better than both DE

Implementation	Reference & Author
❖ Antenna arrays	Khodier (2013)
❖ Engineering optimisation	Yang and Deb (2010)
❖ Allocation and sizing of DG	Tan *et al.* (2012)
❖ Antenna arrays synthesis	Ahmed and Abdelhafid (2013)
❖ Capacitor placement	Arcanjo *et al.* (2012)
❖ Constrained engineering tasks	Kanagaraj *et al.* (2013b)
❖ Design optimisation of truss structures	Gandomi *et al.* (2012)
❖ Design space exploration	Kumar and Chakarverty (2011a, 2011b)
❖ Electrostatic deflection	Goghrehabadi *et al.* (2011)
❖ Integrated power systems	Piechocki *et al.* (2013)
❖ Linear antenna array	Rani and Malek (2011), Rani *et al.* (2012b)
❖ Non-linear state estimation	Walia and Kapoor (2013)
❖ Optimal capacitor placement	Reddy and Manohar (2013)
❖ Optimisation of sequence	Lim *et al.* (2012)
❖ Phase equilibrium calculations	Bhargava *et al.* (2013)
❖ Photovoltaic models	Ma *et al.* (2013)
❖ Planar EBG structures	Pani *et al.* (2013)
❖ Reliability problems	Valian *et al.* (2013), Valian and Valian (2012)
❖ Stability analysis	Rangasamy and Manickam (2013)
❖ Steel frames	Kaveh and Bakhshpoori (2013)
❖ Steel structures	Kaveh *et al.* (2012)
❖ Structural design optimisation	Durgun and Yildiz (2012)
❖ Structural optimisation problems	Gandomi *et al.* (2013)
❖ Synthesis of six-bar	Bulatovič *et al.* (2013)
❖ Wind turbine blades	Ernst *et al.* (2012)

Figure 11.5 Some specific applications of CS [9].

and TLBO (teaching learning bases optimization). The unique combination of search modes, flight with only relevant individual and model, makes CSA's efficiency comparable to that of CMDe (cloud model–based DE) algorithm.

11.4.1.1.3   Trajectory Planning of Quadrotar

Based on the way CSA is used in planning of trajectory Hanjie Hu, Yu Wu, Jinfa Xu, and Qingyun Sunbuilt a CSA-based method for planning trajectory of quadrotar in urban environment. CSA based method proved advantageous over swarm-based algorithm for planning trajectory. It is better in terms of number of computation and quality of solution. The CSA convergence rate does not depend on parameters.

11.4.2   In Structural Optimization

Nowadays, structural optimization plays a significant role in the engineering field. It helps an engineer by means of constructing the structure economic, lightweight, etc. It is also applied within the world of aircraft and aerospace structures for minimum weight, electrical network, control, etc.

Structural optimization is done basically for shape, size and topology. The target of this optimization is basically reduction of mass.

Optimization of topology in this connectivity with nodes and elements is altered to get the optimum design of a layout. Challenge appears in changing truss topology structure to a mechanism.

Optimization of Size: For this, the continuous or discrete properties of the cross-section of an element are changed to get the optimum property values.

Optimization of Shape: In this, the nodes are moved while keeping the node-element connectivity same, thus results in optimizing shape without altering topology. CSA has been extended to optimize the shaping of truss structures.

11.4.2.1   Test Problems

Jayanthi V., Manigandan M., Velrajkumar G., Saravanan M. did a comparative study of CSA with GA and PSO based on performance measures; in this, it was inferred that CSA is highly efficient for all test problems. This is due to the less number of parameters in CSA as compared to GA and PSO. Keeping first effective solution (productive nests) ensures that the leading effective solution gets transferred to subsequent iteration, minimizing the risk of most effective solution getting discarded in later iterations.

11.4.3   Application CSA in Electrical Engineering, Power, and Energy

11.4.3.1   Embedded System

CSA is used to create a reliable secure embedded system. Such systems are highly complex and need lengthy processing. Therefore, CSA is used to design solutions with optimum performance, availability, cost, and reliability. The results deduce that such solution were better in quality and insensitive to variation of parameters.

11.4.3.2 PCB

PCB takes a lot of time it drilling path. Combining CSA with PCB has reduced production time, cost, and increased productivity.

Bhargava used this modified version to resolve equilibrium, its phases, and stability in both reactive and non-reactive systems. In this case, comparing CSA performance with DE matrix adoption and FA proved that CSA showed more efficiency in solving thermodynamic calculation.

11.4.3.3 Power and Energy

Renewable resources are becoming widely used due to less pollutions and abundance. Windmill is used to provide clean electricity. Supplying electricity generated from wind to remote location is not cheap. CSA proposed to resolve this by designing an optimized system. In this, CSA uses different parameter wattage component for designing appropriate system. It provides almost optimum if not optimum solutions.

Hydroelectricity is another important source of clean energy. CSA is used in Abrasive Water Jet (AWJ) to find surface roughness and was found to give better result than SBM and neural network.

In the field of power and energy numerous problems like capacitor allocation power transmission network, wind-based generators, etc., are solved by CSA. In order reduce power loss in distribution network and improve voltage CSA was applied, small scale technologies were employed using distributed generation approach to supply power to end-users. The criteria for improvement of power quality were determined by minimum and maximum voltage deviations. Results show that CSA can be accommodated for any problem without prior knowledge because of its convergence rate. CSA was exceedingly used to cut back power loss by Buaklee. The effectiveness of CSA was demonstrated through a redial nine bus distributed system by Provincial Electricity Authority of Thailand (PEA) and DIgSILENT. Sudabattula used CSA with the aim to locate optimum renewable–based DG. On testing CSA on IEEE 69 bus test system, it proved to have better performance than GA and PSO.

PV system has been used to supply power to homes for several years now. Ahmed and Salam proposed a new approach for location MPP within PV system. For this, three samples of voltages were generated over the span

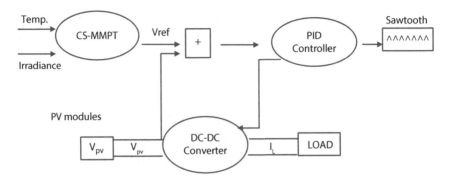

Figure 11.6 PV system using MPPT with CSA.

of PV system. CSA was observed to be most effective solution. To replace the single diode for commercial PV generator a CSA-based parameter was proposed. CSA was found to be able to optimize PI controller gain for PV microgrid. It achieved less peak values and balance.

In PV system, CSA was also applied for outlet tracking (MPPT) (Figure 11.6). In this system, the change in temperature, gradual irradiance, and quick change in both temperature and irradiance is evaluated, thereby accommodating shading conditions (partial).

11.4.4   Applications of CS in Field of Machine Learning and Computation

Machine learning algorithms such as support vector machines (SVM), K-nearest neighbors (KNN), extreme learning models (ELM), decision trees (DT), Naive Bayes (NB), and Bayesian networks (BN) were used to estimate a location in a building. As compared to others, KNN and SVM outperform. Besides, SVM is based on the structural risk minimization principle with good generalizability and can solve problems with few samples, nonlinear data, avoid local minima, and so on. SVMs depend on parameter optimization for high classification accuracy or position estimation. Nature-inspired optimization algorithms such as particle swarm, bee, bad reference distribution, and cuckoo search can therefore be applied.

Cuckoo is one of the most recent algorithms that are inspired by the breeding behaviours of the cuckoo bird and applied to solve nonlinear optimization problems. Alternative optimization algorithms do not always reach the local best solution. It is possible that they will not be able to solve the nonlinear optimization or multidimensional optimization problems. By using Levy's flight process, combining local and search capability increases the probability of obtaining a global optimal solution in cuckoo search.

11.4.5   Applications of CS in Image Processing

Image processing extricates useful information from the image to reinforce its view by transforming it into a digital form and performing some operations. It forms a core research area for engineering and engineering science domains, and due to its critical application in various aspects, it has shown a gradual growth in the field of business.

Face recognition is a process that helps to identify anonymous individuals who might be dangerous. However, this process faced some challenge, for example, noisy and redundant data, which leads to decrease in accuracy in face recognition process. When CSA is applied to an array of feature vector drown out by a 2D discrete cosine transform of a picture and the first matched image from the database using Euclidean distance. Study says that CSA provides much better solution compared to PSO and ACO optimization algorithm.

For a satellite image, high and expensive computation is required to draw out meaningful pattern as it has extended to multilevel thresholding. To resolve the problems, Bhandari proved another approach which combined both CSA using Kapur's entropy.

DWT is used for analysing the image while CSA is used to optimize each sub-band selecting the singular value. In the final step, DWT is used to enhance the image, and the result is use to verify the efficiency and effectiveness of the proposed combined algorithm. This algorithm is used for deducting surface features of varied visible area and in remote sensing applications.

In this algorithm, by taking random initial threshold, value of the most effective solution is achieved. In other studies, the combination of DWT and CSA is taken into consideration, a low-constraint straight-like image.

While studying the RGB's optimal segmentation using the entropy value of Kapur's method of image multi-thresholding based on CSA, the algorithm was targeted to find an efficient threshold value, used for segmentation of image. The design of the fitness function supports entropy values of the identical images. The observed results were then compared with PSO and firefly algorithms through universal models. It was noticed that the performance of the CSA was improved through fast convergence along with less computational time.

11.4.6   Application of CSA in Data Processing

Basically, clustering process is an unsupervised classification which divides patterns into multiple groups. The clustering is aimed to separate a mixed dataset into multiple clusters supporting the association between weather inside the similar cluster. Data clustering application has been identified various fields, like pattern recognition, computer vision, mechanics, statistical physics, and computer vision.

Besides having the importance, some inaccuracies are there while using the standard mechanism. For example, segmentation of the medical image has configuration errors of first few centroids and also the accurate number of the clusters with fuzzy e-means is foremost effective in forming clusters. In this regard, CS and PSO techniques enforce a hybrid method which is accustomed in increasing the duvet for e-means imperfections. The mixed algorithm attained better results as compared to the standard means by reduced time of computation and making convergence during some iteration irrespective of what was the number of clusters initially.

Web computer program's clustering has significant amount of importance in scientific and academic communities which are related to the domain of information retrieval. Engines for web clustering attempt in providing solutions for users. They increase the focus of presented documents and the time spent in reviewing is also reduced. However, several clustering have already performed this work.

Distributed systems use the task input from the users to the server and servers process the request and return the results to the tasked user. There can be many servers and locating the foremost and most effective server will be difficult. Here, the concept of mobile agent can be an example. But the basic job of a mobile agent is to work as an intermediary system in interaction process of users and servers. A mobile agent carries the task of a user, so they travel in the server's network to find best suitable location of server to perform the allocated task. While migrating from one server to another, the job is paused, and they might resume the tactic upon the new sever. It is a difficult job for a mobile agent to find the path. The solution of migration of mobile agent was attempted by Akajit Salim who applied the modified CSA. The problem for migration of mobile agent can be compared to the problem of finding paths in graph theory. So, the data of the graph theory can be used rather than the real data of the network. They compare MCS method with FOR (the real CS and ACS algorithm) method which was proposed earlier. Accuracy and path length of the graph data were used to measure the performance. Improved accuracy and shorter targeted path length proved the efficiency of the experiment.

11.4.7   Applications of CSA in Computation and Neural Network

In the area of optimization and computational intelligence, CS has been applied and presented the efficient results. Examples in favor of Cuckoo

Search are the engineering design where the CS algorithm has performed better than the other algorithms for selecting the problems of continuous optimization. The other problems in engineering include design of welded beam and spring. Additionally, the modified CS demonstrated by the Walton *et al.* has been very efficient for solving the nonlinear problems such as mesh generation. The famous model, spiking neural network, gets trained by CS algorithm. This was demonstrated by the Vazquez, while the known semantic web service was optimized by Chifu using the CS. Continuing the further work on CS algorithm, Chakarverty and Kumar attained promising design for embedded systems. Bakshpoori and Kaveh applied CS to design frames of steel. Yildiz implemented the CS for selecting the best suitable machine parameters for milling operation. The results are very motivational. Zhou and Zheng provided a modified CSA, based on the Gaussian process. Their results show encouraging behavior of CSA.

Tein and Ramli proposed discrete CSA for scheduling problems. It can generate independent paths for generating test data and software testing. A CSA variant and quantum-based approach is used to solve knapsack problems very effectively. A comparison study based on optimization problems by Gandomi showed CSA to be robust and extensively efficient. Use of CSA to for training neural network has shown drastic performance enhancement. This result was obtained by Valian.

Back propagation neural network trains neural network very slowly, gives locally optimal solution, and needs initial weight and bias. An integrated algorithm of CSA and back propagation is used to overcome these issues. On comparison with regression neural network and back propagation, this integrated approach produces better output.

Hybrid Accelerated Cuckoo PSO (HACPSO) is another integration of CSA and Accelerated PSO (APSO) has been used for training Artificial Neural Networks (ANN). It provided search solutions. Experimental results of this hybrid algorithm used benchmarked datasets. The performance comparison on basis of accuracy and convergence with ABC (artificial bee colony optimization) and other variant algorithms showed better results by the hybrid algorithm.

11.4.8 Application in Wireless Sensor Network

Among the algorithm to estimate positions of unknown network of sensor, CSA has proved to be better than most algorithm techniques. Efficiency of CSA can enhanced using the feature that it is not controlled the ability of global searching. For achieving more accuracy, we can also propose a hybrid stochastic algorithm. The CSA effectiveness can be verified by using experimental setup of sensor network.

On applying soft computing web algorithm, the outcome time of results exceeded the expected time. Hybridization within CSA, K-means, and Bayesian information solved the above problem. CSA has a combination of both global and local searching strategy which offers diversity by preventing next population convergence.

Document retrieval based on clustering is one of the major retrieval challenges. Finding relevant information comes under the domain of document information retrieval. For helping users, navigations, summarizations, and organization of information were based on Levy's flight. Use of CSA in clustering of web document helps in locating optimal centroids, and finding global solution for the above clustering algorithm on benchmark dataset, the work performs very good in document clustering.

Modifying CSA with K-means clustering provides another new method of partitioning clusters. The proposal of this work was to find methods for practical and efficient analysis of cluster in an extensive database. So, it has no need for entering values of cluster point for obtaining best clustering using validity in clustering.

11.5 Conclusion and Future Work

The algorithm of CSA is present in various domains that include image processing, flood forecasting, wireless sensor network, clustering, job scheduling, shortest path, in engineering design, and more. PSO and CSA are swarm intelligence–based algorithm that are very good in solving large range of non-linear optimization problems. This is the reason that they show diversity in application in science and engineering. Algorithm such as CSA can have excellent global convergence. There persist sum challenging issues that are required to be resolved in feature investigation. An important point is that there is a gap between theory and practical.

Metaheuristic algorithm not only having less application in practice but the mathematics too lacks far behind. Apart from limited results related to convergence and stability of particular algorithm such as genetic, particle swarm, and cuckoo do not have theoretical analysis.

The metaheuristic algorithm has dependent parameters. Therefore, supplying values to these parameters greatly affect algorithm performance. Thus, tuning of parameter also becomes an optimization requirement. As a result, parameter-tuning requires more research attention. Such issues must inspire more research and undoubtedly more application of CSA.

CSA is predicted to be applied in various fields in near future. Variant implementations of CSA will not only improve performance but also ensure application and reliability in complicated tasks.

References

1. Yang, X.S. and Koziel, S., Computational Optimization: An Overview. In: Koziel, S., Yang, X.S. (eds) *Computational Optimization, Methods and Algorithms. Studies in Computational Intelligence*, vol 356. Springer, Berlin, Heidelberg, 2011. https://doi.org/10.1007/978-3-642-20859-1_1

2. Yang, X.S. and Deb, S., Cuckoo search via Lévy flights, in: *Nature & Biologically Inspired Computing, 2009. NaBIC 2009. World Congress on*, December, IEEE, pp. 210–214, 2009.

3. Omran, G.M., Engelbrecht, A.P., Salman, A., "Particle Swarm Optimization Method for Image Clustering. *Int. J. Pattern Recognit. Artif. Intell.*, 19, 03, 297–321, 2005.

4. Kennedy, J. and Eberhart, R., Particle swarm optimization. *IEEE international conference on neural networks*, 1942–1948, 1995.

5. Agarwal, P. and Mehta, S., Nature-Inspired Algorithms: State-of-Art, Problems and Prospects. *Int. J. Comput. Appl.*, 100, 14–21, 2014.

6. Yang, X.S. and Deb, S. Cuckoo search: recent advances and applications. *Neural Comput & Applic*, 24, 169–174, 2014. https://doi.org/10.1007/s00521-013-1367-1.

7. Natarajan, A. and Subramanian, P.K., An enhanced cuckoo search for optimization of bloom filter in spam filtering. *Global J. Comput. Sci. Technol.*, 12, 1, 67–73, 2012.

8. Mohamad, A., Zain, A. & Bazin, N.E.N., Cuckoo Search Algorithm for Optimization Problems—A Literature Review and its Applications, *Applied Artificial Intelligence*, 28, 5, 419–448, 2014.

9. Fister jr, I., Fister, D., & Fister, I., A comprehensive review of Cuckoo search: Variants and hybrids. *Int. J. Math. Model. Numer. Optim.*, 4, 387, 2013.

12

Mapping of Real-World Problems to Nature-Inspired Algorithm Using Goal-Based Classification and TRIZ

Palak Sukharamwala[1,2*] **and Manojkumar Parmar**[1,3†]

[1]Robert Bosch Engineering and Business Solutions Private Limited, Bangalore, India
[2]Institute of Technology, Nirma University, Ahmedabad, India
[3]HEC Paris, Jouy-en-Josas Cedex, France

Abstract

The technologies and algorithms are growing at an exponential rate. The technologies are capable enough to solve challenging and complex problems, which seemed an impossible task. However, the trending methods and approaches face challenges on various fronts of data, algorithms, software, computational complexities, and energy efficiencies. Nature also faces similar challenges. Nature has solved those challenges, and formulation of those is available as Nature-Inspired Algorithms (NIAs), which are derived based on the study of nature. A novel method based on TRIZ to map real-world problems to nature problems is explained here. TRIZ is a theory of inventive problem-solving. Using the proposed framework, the set of best NIA can be identified to solve real-world problems. For proposed framework to work, a novel classification of NIA based on the end goal that nature is trying to achieve is devised. The application of this framework, along with examples, is also discussed.

Keywords: Classification, TRIZ, AI, ML, algorithm, software complexity, energy efficient computing, taxonomy

*Corresponding author: manojkumar.parmar@bosch.com
†Both authors have contributed equally.

S. Balamurugan, Anupriya Jain, Sachin Sharma, Dinesh Goyal, Sonia Duggal and Seema Sharma (eds.)
Nature-Inspired Algorithms Applications, (317–340) © 2022 Scrivener Publishing LLC

12.1   Introduction and Background

Nature does things in an incredible way. Behind the visible phenomena, sometimes, there are innumerable invisible causes. Scientists have been observing nature for hundreds of years and trying to understand, explain, adapt, and reproduce artificial systems based on it. There are countless living and non-living agents, act in parallel and sometimes against each other, to define nature and regulate harmony. This is considered the dialectic of nature that resides in the concept of evolution of the natural world. The evolution of complexity in nature follows a distinctive order. There is also a distributed, self-organized, and optimal processing of information in nature without any central control. The whole series of forms, mechanical, physical, chemical, biological, and social, are distributed and aligned according to the complexity of the lowest to the highest.

Table 12.1   Acronyms used in this chapter.

Acronym	Full name
NIA	Nature-Inspired Algorithm
TRIZ	Russian: Teoriya Resheniya Izobretatelskikh Zadatch English: Theory of inventive problem solving
AI	Artificial Intelligence
ML	Machine Learning
DL	Deep Learning
FOA	Fruit Fly Optimization
FOA-MHW	Fruit Fly Optimization Algorithm–Multiplicative Holt-Winters
BA	Bat Algorithm
LSSVM	Least Square Support Vector Regression Model
MARS	Multivariate Adaptive Regression Splines
DP	Dynamic Programming
GA	Genetic Algorithm
TSP	Traveling Salesman Problem
ACO	Ant Colony Optimization

This sequence expresses its mutual dependence and its relation in terms of structure and history. Associated activities also change due to changing circumstances. All of these phenomena known or partially known so far emerged as new areas of study in science and technology. Computer science helps to study nature-based problem-solving techniques, underlying principles, mechanisms of natural, physical, chemical, and biological organisms which perform complex tasks appropriately with limited resources and capabilities [1].

Science is a bridge between scientists and nature which has evolved over the centuries by enriching itself with new concepts, methods, and tools and has developed into well-defined disciplines of scientific activity. Since then, humanity has been trying to understand nature by developing new tools and techniques. The field of Nature-Inspired Computer science (NIC) is interdisciplinary, combining computer science with knowledge from different branches of science, mathematics, and engineering, which allows the development of new computational tools such as algorithms, hardware, or software to solve the problem. This chapter provides limitations of current technology, an overview of existing classification on Nature-Inspired Algorithm (NIA), a new approach called end goal–based classification, framework examples to understand its use.

Readers are suggested to refer to Table 12.1 to get an understanding of acronyms used throughout the chapter.

12.2 Motivations Behind NIA Exploration

In the first two decades of the 21st century, access to large amounts of data (known as "big data"), faster computers, and advanced machine learning techniques was successfully applied to many problems for commercial benefits. The AI/ML algorithms and their applications are pervasive today, and they are solving many specific problems and making life easier. However, data scientist's favorite algorithms and many other technologies from various engineering branches have their limitations. We will discuss limitations in detail in the following subsections.

12.2.1 Prevailing Issues With Technology

12.2.1.1 Data Dependencies

Data is the essence of the AI/ML algorithm to achieve reasonable accuracy. Today's algorithms are highly data-dependent. However, issues like the cost of data acquisition, processing it, maintaining it, and storing it in a compliant way, makes it challenging to have a sufficient amount of data many times. The cost of data is one the most significant investment for any organization who want to leverage AI/ML. In the absence of data, the AI/ML algorithm's accuracy suffers and renders them unfit for use [2]. The critical question is can we develop algorithms and alternatives which are not highly dependent on data, which can leverage a "less data approach"?

We need to be aware of AI's limitations and where humans still need to take the lead. Data and algorithms cannot solve all types of problems. For a specific set of problems, the available set of algorithms fails to perform adequately despite the massive amount of available data [3].

For a long time, Facebook believed that problems like the spread of misinformation and hate speech could be algorithmically identified and stopped. However, under recent pressure from legislators, the company quickly pledged to replace its algorithms with an army of over 10,000 human reviewers. The medical profession has also recognized that AI cannot be considered a solution for all problems. The IBM Watson for Oncology program was a piece of AI that was meant to help doctors treat cancer. Even though it was developed to deliver the best recommendations, human experts found it difficult to trust the machine. As a result, the AI program was abandoned in most hospitals, where it was trialed.

These examples demonstrate that there is no AI solution for everything. Not every problem is best addressed by applying machine intelligence and machine learning to it despite the availability of large amount of data and state-of-the-art algorithms [4].

12.2.1.2   Demand for Higher Software Complexity

The increasing software demands, also lead to an increase in complexity. The complexity is increasing at a rapid rate as the demand for intuitive and complex solutions is growing. The traditional methods of software programming and solutions are already proven inadequate to manage complexity [5]. The question is can we develop software with reduced complexity yet rich in features?

12.2.1.3   NP-Hard Problems

There are sets of intractable problems (NP-hard) that are not solvable due to computational complexity arising from a known set of algorithms, such as the Traveling Salesman Problem (TSP). TSP is discussed in detail in the following sections. The question is can we adequately solve NP-Hard problems with available computational power today [6, 7]?

12.2.1.4 Energy Consumption

Deep Learning (DL) algorithms are claimed to mimic human brains, they still lack accuracy of human intelligence and energy efficiency of biological system. There is a long way to go to mimic human brains perfectly.

Despite the availability of data, algorithms, and computational power, it is impossible to solve a set of problems due to the sheer amount of energy usage. The cost-benefit analysis produces unfavorable results due to the impact of energy usage in general and impact of it on the environment [8]. The critical question is can we solve the problem in an energy-efficient way to match human brains' energy efficiency frontier?

The discussed problems are considered small today; however, they are growing drastically. These problems indicate that ML/DL-based algorithms and applications' growth is not sustainable from a technical, business, and environmental perspective. Therefore, to tackle the stated problem, there is a need to explore alternative solutions. Scientists believe NIA is the best suitable alternative as nature has perfected them over time in iterative way.

12.2.2 Nature-Inspired Algorithm at a Rescue

Nature faces varied problems, and it has found the best way to solve them using constrained optimization over time. The species on earth are doing various forms of optimization for the rest of their life in their respective environment. The survival of many species is proof that the evolved optimizations are one of the best possible solutions. Nature has its way of transferring minimum intelligence from one generation to another using genes. Later on, life forms acquire a higher intelligence level based on their experiences interacting with the environment. In the entire process of acquiring intelligence, the usage of data is very minimum. At the same time, the decisions derived from intelligence are good enough at the least. The life forms are capable of managing the real-world complexity, and their decisions are the most efficient way as their survival depends on it.

Today's digitally powered world is facing significant complex problems due to temporal and spatial complexity, variability, and constrained environments. The similarity between problems faced by nature and the digital world is striking. Hence, the proposition is to take over solutions of nature and implement them to the digital problems. The solution formalized by studying nature is referred to as NIA [9]. NIA is a set of metaheuristic algorithms, which provide approximate answers. They are designed to optimize numerical benchmark functions and multi-objective functions and solve NP-hard problems for many variables and dimensions.

The growth of current technologies is bound to diminish and pave the way for new technologies to emerge. We believe that NIA will be the next disruptive technology to address the problems faced by current technologies and provide answers to crucial questions asked above.

12.3 Novel TRIZ + NIA Approach

12.3.1 Traditional Classification

There exists a classification for NIAs, which is solution-based. It focuses on the techniques used by algorithms. According to traditional classification, algorithms are classified into the following classes [1, 10–12]. Figure 12.1 classifies NIA into the below-mentioned classes.

- Swarm intelligence
- Evolutionary algorithms
- Bio-inspired algorithms
- Physics-based algorithm
- Other NIAs

12.3.1.1 Swarm Intelligence

Swarm intelligence (SI) is something in which agents work in parallel to achieve a specific task. SI is simply the aggregate conduct of decentralized, self-organized entities. A similar idea is utilized for artificial intelligence (AI) in the early days. Firstly, Gerardo Beni and Jing Wang presented it in 1989 regarding cellular robotic systems [13].

SI systems typically consist of a population of simple agents or bots interacting locally with one another and with their environment. The inspiration often comes from nature, especially biological systems. The agents follow simple rules, and although there is no centralized control structure dictating individual agents' behavior. Their random interaction leads to the emergence of "intelligent" global behavior, unknown to the individual agents. Examples of SI in natural systems include ant colonies, bird flocking, hawks hunting, animal herding, bacterial growth, fish schooling, and microbial intelligence.

The application of swarm principles to robots is called swarm robotics, while "swarm intelligence" refers to the more general algorithms. "Swarm prediction" has been used to solve forecasting problems. Similar approaches to those proposed for swarm robotics are considered for genetically modified organisms in synthetic collective intelligence [14]. Animal Migration

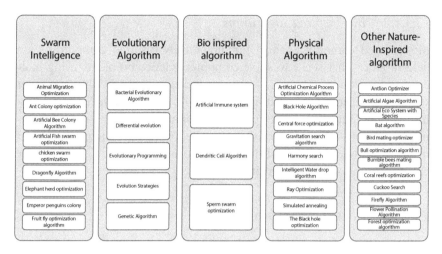

Figure 12.1 Categories of traditional classification of NIAs.

Algorithm, Ant Colony Optimization, Artificial Fish Swarm Optimization, and Fruit fly Optimization Algorithm are examples of SI.

12.3.1.2 Evolutionary Algorithm

In AI, an evolutionary algorithm (EA) is a subset of evolutionary computation [15], which represents a generic population-based metaheuristic optimization algorithm. An EA uses biological evolution mechanisms, such as reproduction, mutation, recombination, and selection. For optimization problems, the candidate solution plays the role of the individual in the population, and the fitness function determines the quality of the solutions (see also loss function). The evolution of the population then takes place after the repeated application of the fitness function over generations.

EAs often perform well by approximating solutions to all types of problems as they ideally do not make any assumption about the underlying fitness landscape. Techniques from EAs applied to biological evolution modeling are generally limited to explorations of microevolutionary processes and planning models based upon cellular processes. In most real applications of EAs, computational complexity is a prohibiting factor [16]. In fact, this computational complexity is due to fitness function evaluation. Fitness approximation is one of the solutions to overcome this difficulty. However, seemingly simple EA can often solve complex problems [16] like the knapsack problem, which is explained below. Therefore, there might not be any direct link between algorithm complexity and problem complexity. Bacterial EA and Genetic Algorithm (GA) are famous EAs.

12.3.1.3   Bio-Inspired Algorithms

Bio-inspired computing, short for biologically inspired computing, is a field of study that seeks to solve computer science problems using biology models. It relates to social behavior and emergence. Within computer science, bio-inspired computing relates to AI and machine learning. Bio-inspired computing is a significant subset of natural computation. In simpler words, bio-inspired algorithms imitate a particular biological system of an animal body. Artificial Immune System and Dendrite Cell System are examples of bio-inspired algorithms.

12.3.1.4   Physics-Based Algorithm

Physics-inspired algorithms employ basic physics principles, for example, Newton's laws of gravitation, laws of motion, and Coulomb's force law of electrical charge. They are all based on deterministic physical principles. Black Hole Algorithm, Artificial Chemical Process Optimization Algorithm, Central force Optimization Algorithm, and Gravitational Search Algorithm fall under the physics-based algorithm category.

12.3.1.5   Other Nature-Inspired Algorithms

The set of algorithms that do not fit directly to the above classification is put into this category. Artificial algae algorithm, Bat Algorithm, Coral Reef Optimization, Cuckoo Search, Firefly Algorithm, and Flower Pollination Algorithm are famous examples of other NIAs.

12.3.2   Limitation of Traditional Classification

The drawback of the traditional classification is that it does not help map real-life problems to conceptual problems. For an application, the selection of an algorithm is achieved using brute force. This classification does not make it easy to select an algorithm. Hence, the solution-based approach is not ideal for mapping problems.

The drawbacks of traditional classifications are following:

- It is a solution-based approach. The classification focuses on how nature is solving an issue, not on what nature wants to achieve.
- It does not help map real-life problems to conceptual problems as it does not factor in nature's problem.

12.3.3   Combined Approach NIA + TRIZ

From our analysis, it has been clear that traditional classification and approaches lack a systematic method and framework to map real-world problems to NIA. They are mainly brute force in nature. Hence, a novel approach to systematically map real-world problems to NIA using TRIZ methodology is proposed [17]. TRIZ principles are used along with a new classification approach.

12.3.3.1   TRIZ

TRIZ is the Russian acronym for the "Theory of Inventive Problem Solving [18]". TRIZ presents a systematic approach for understanding and defining challenging problems, and it is the most useful in roles such as product development, design engineering, and process management. TRIZ includes a practical methodology, tool sets, a knowledge base, and model-based technology for generating innovative solutions for problem-solving.

The TRIZ helps in problem formulation, system analysis, failure analysis, and patterns of system evolution. The TRIZ was developed on three primary findings:

1. Problems and solutions are repeated across industries and sciences.
2. Patterns of technical evolution are also repeated across industries and sciences.
3. The innovations generally use the solution and scientific findings from outside the focused field.

The prism of TRIZ, as depicted in Figure 12.2, represents the four-step approach for problem-solving. The real-world problem is mapped to a conceptual problem using abstraction. The conceptual problem and corresponding solutions (40 TRIZ Principles) database are then used to find the conceptual problem's analogous solution. The conceptual solution is then converted to a real-world solution. In simple words, prism TRIZ suggests taking help from the solved problem to solve newer problems. Here, NIAs are used as solved solutions to nature's problems.

12.3.3.2   NIA + TRIZ

We envisioned that the TRIZ prism is the most suitable methodology to map real-world problems to nature problems and then provide corresponding

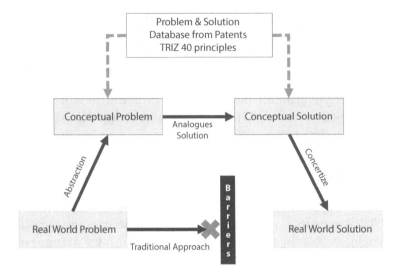

Figure 12.2 TRIZ problem-solution approach [19].

NIA solutions. A novel methodology, as depicted in Figure 12.3, combines TRIZ with end goal–based classification. According to the TRIZ foundation, if problems and solutions are repeated across industries and sciences, then existing pairs of problems and solutions can be used. For us, that pair of problems and solutions are inspired by nature. However, for this approach to work, we need a new classification that is based on problems. For this reason, we introduce novel classification. Here, modified four-step TRIZ process is explained.

1. The real-world problem is mapped to the conceptual problem using abstraction.
2. The conceptual problem is then mapped to the end goal of NIA.
3. From an available database of NIA problems and solutions, analogous NIA is derived into a conceptual solution.
4. The conceptual solution is then converted to a real-world solution.

12.3.4   End Goal–Based Classification

End goal–based classification mainly focuses on problems nature has solved. It also considers the goal nature wants to achieve by solving the problem. The classification is four levels deep and varies based on goals

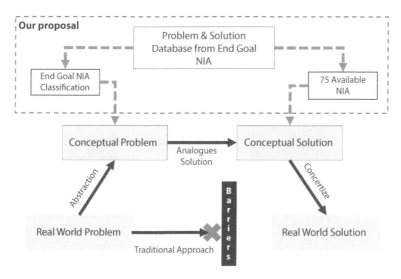

Figure 12.3 NIA + TRIZ approach [19].

and sub-goals, as depicted in Figure 12.4. In total, 75 NIAs are classified using this approach and are present at one of the leaf nodes. Figure 12.4 represents the classification diagram, and Tables 12.2 and 12.3 explain the respective levels of classification.

- Level 1: Biology and non-biology based to distinguish living from non-living
- Level 2: Based on the primary goal
- Level 3: Based on the sub-goal
- Level 4: Based on the behavior

The detailed mapping of leaf nodes for NIA is available in Table 12.2 for biology-based and Table 12.3 for nonbiology-based. For non-biology-based, the classification is available based on primary goals only as sub-goals, and behavior has no real implications.

12.4   Examples to Support the TRIZ + NIA Approach

12.4.1   Fruit Optimization Algorithm to Predict Monthly Electricity Consumption

Jiang *et al.* [20] demonstrated the fruit fly optimization algorithm's use to improve the prediction of monthly electricity consumption with the

Table 12.2 Biology-based algorithms.

Level 2: primary goal	Level 3: sub-goal	Level 4: behavior	NIA
Resource Seeking	Food Seeking	Hunting	Antlion optimizer
			Bat algorithm
			Grey wolf optimizer
			Lion optimization algorithm
			Salp swarm algorithm
			Whale optimization algorithm
		Migration	Animal migration optimization
			Artificial algae algorithm (AAA)
		Herd Behavior	Ant colony optimization
			Artificial bee colony algorithm
			Artificial fish swarm optimization
			Chicken swarm optimization
			Dragonfly algorithm
			Fruit fly optimization algorithm
			Grass hoper optimization
			Krill herd algorithm

(Continued)

Table 12.2 Biology-based algorithms. (*Continued*)

Level 2: primary goal	Level 3: sub-goal	Level 4: behavior	NIA
			Locust search algorithm
			Particle swarm optimization algorithm
			Strawberry algorithm
	Habitat Seeking	Herd Behavior	Monarch butterfly optimization
			Moth flame optimization algorithm
			Sperm swarm optimization
Survival	Self		Artificial immune system
			Dendritic cell algorithm
			Grass hoper optimization
	Offspring		Cuckoo search
			Emperor penguins colony
	Dependent		Tree physiology optimization

(*Continued*)

limited amount of training data. The proposed solution uses a hybrid forecasting model named FOA-MHW (Fruit Fly Optimization Algorithm–Multiplicative Holt-Winters). The Holt-Winters algorithm is an exponential smoothing algorithm for forecasting time series data. The parameters of exponential smoothing are generated using FOA.

Table 12.2 Biology-based algorithms. (*Continued*)

Level 2: primary goal	Level 3: sub-goal	Level 4: behavior	NIA
Reproduction	Mate Searching		Elephant herd optimization
			Firefly algorithm
			Honey bee mating optimization
			Social spider optimization
	Evolution		Artificial eco-system with species
			Bacterial evolutionary algorithm
			Bird mating optimizer
			Bull optimization algorithm
			Bumblebees mating algorithm
			Coral reefs optimization
			Differential evolution
			Evolutionary programming
			Evolution strategies
			Genetic algorithm
			Memetic algorithm
	Pollination		Flower pollination algorithm
			Forest optimization algorithm

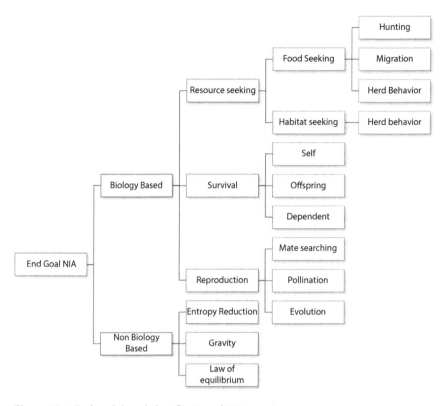

Figure 12.4 End goal–based classification of NIA.

Table 12.3 Non-biology–based algorithms.

Level 2: primary goal	NIA
Gravity	Black hole algorithm
	Central force optimization
	Gravitation search algorithm
Entropy Reduction	Artificial chemical process optimization algorithm
	Intelligent water drop algorithm
Law of Equilibrium	Harmony search
	Water wave optimization
	Wind-driven optimization

The real-world problem of MHW is to find optimal parameters for smoothing with the minimum amount of data. The parameter finding is converted into a conceptual problem of the food-seeking problem under resource seeking (resource seeking -> food-seeking problem -> herd behavior) as referred to in Figure 12.4. For food-seeking in a herd, the fruit fly is one of the superior species as it uses acute smell sensing in a swarm with intelligent communication. Hence, the corresponding solution, as shown in Figure 12.5, of fruit fly optimization is suitable for the identified problem. Therefore, for the stated problem, FOA is found most suitable and outperformed traditional algorithms.

12.4.2   Bat Algorithm to Model River Dissolved Oxygen Concentration

Yaseen *et al.* [21] use Bat Algorithm (BA) in modeling river dissolved oxygen concentration. Here, NIA is integrated with Least Square Support Vector Regression Model (LSSVM). The LSSVM-BA model's accuracy compared with those M5 trees and MARS models are found to increase by 20% and 42%, respectively, in terms of root-mean-square error.

Studies have reported that LSSVM models' efficiency significantly depends on the values of the kernel and regularization parameters. The hyper-parameters of LSSVM can be considered decision variables and should be determined accurately by optimization algorithms for better performance of LSSVM models. In this study, the hyper-parameters of LSSVM were optimized using the BA. In BA, as shown in Figure 12.6, bats' hunting behavior is mimicked where multiple bats are trying to echolocate

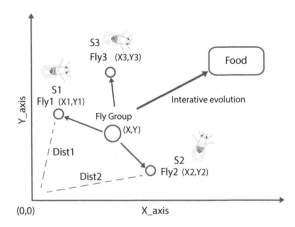

Figure 12.5 Diagram for fruit fly optimization algorithm FOA.

prey and differentiate it from obstacles. Bat hunting comes under resource seeking followed by the food-seeking category (resource seeking -> food-seeking problem -> hunting) as referred to in Figure 12.4. It can be concluded that the parameter optimization problem can be mapped with the food-seeking problem.

12.4.3   Genetic Algorithm to Tune the Structure and Parameters of a Neural Network

Frank *et al.* [22] discuss tuning of neural network parameters using Genetic Algorithms (GA). This is the first paper from 2003, where it was proposed to use NIA to train and search optimal neural networks.

The neural network is proved to be a universal approximator. A three-layer feed-forward neural network can approximate any nonlinear continuous function to arbitrary accuracy. However, a fixed structure may not provide optimal performance within a given training period. A small network may not provide good performance owing to its limited information-processing power. A large network, on the other hand, may have some of its connections redundant.

Moreover, the implementation cost for a large network is high. It could be best if the algorithm suggests the best structure for a neural network.

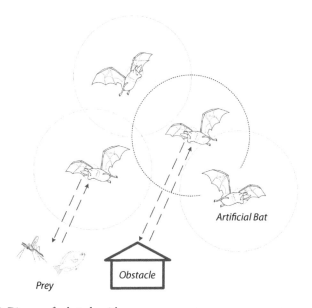

Figure 12.6 Diagram for bat algorithm.

It can lead to a low cost of implementing the neural network in terms of hardware and processing time.

Here, parameters like number of neurons, number of levels, dense layer activation function, and network optimizer are presented in one array. An array is also used to present an output solution. Choosing the correct representation of an output solution is very important in NIAs. In initialization, any random value for these parameters is taken. Priory can also be used instead of random values. Networks are trained using these parameters. The difference between the predicted and actual value is the fitness function. The change values of the parameter are according to the improved GA. Figure 12.7 depicts a pseudo algorithm along with the procedure.

If we talk about abstraction from real-world problems to nature issues, then we can say the best structure is the result of survival among the rest. Self-survival can be mapped with the survival of the best structure. That is

```
Procedure of the improved GA
begin
        τ←0        // τ: number of iteration
        initialize P(τ)                      //P(τ): population for iteration τ
        evaluate f(P(τ))       // f(P(τ)):fitness function
while (not termination condition) do
        begin
        τ←τ+1
        select 2 parents p₁ and p₂ from P(τ−1)
        perform crossover operation according to equations (7) to (13)
        perform mutation operation according to equation (14) to generate three
        offspring nos₁, nos₂ and nos₃
        // reproduce a new P(τ)
                if random number < pₐ  // pₐ: probability of acceptance
                        The one among nos₁, nos₂ and nos₃ with the largest fitness value
                        replaces the chromosome with the smallest fitness value in the
                        population
                else begin
                        if f(nos₁) > smallest fitness value in the P(τ−1)
                                nos₁ replaces the chromosome with the smallest fitness value
                        end
                        if f(nos₂) > smallest fitness value in the updated P(τ−1)
                                nos₂ replaces the chromosome with the smallest fitness value
                        end
                        if f(nos₃) > smallest fitness value in the updated P(τ−1)
                                nos₃ replaces the chromosome with the smallest fitness value
                        end
                end
        end
        evaluate f(P(τ))
        end
end
```

Figure 12.7 Procedure of improved genetic algorithm.

why the GA algorithm from biology-based -> survival -> self-category as referred to in Figure 12.4 is chosen.

12.5   A Solution of NP-H Using NIA

12.5.1   The 0-1 Knapsack Problem

The knapsack problem is part of the combinatorial optimization problems' family. Here, the 0-1 knapsack problem is one of the variants of the knapsack problem. Knapsack problems appear in real-world decision-making processes in a wide variety of fields. Few traditional applications are finding the least wasteful way to cut raw materials in the construction; scoring of tests in which the test-takers choose as to which questions they answer, and others [23]. The knapsack problem has been studied for more than a century. Computer scientists always have a fascination for knapsack problems because the decision problem form of the knapsack problem is NP-complete; thus, there is no known algorithm both correct and fast (polynomial-time) in all cases.

The knapsack problem is defined as a set of items (x_i) is given, each with a weight (w_i) and a value (v_i). Determine the number of each item included in a collection so that the total weight is less than or equal to a given capacity (W) and the total value is as large as possible. In 0-1 knapsack, the condition is that each chosen item must be whole; a fraction of an item cannot be selected in solution [23].

Dynamic programming solution for the 0-1 knapsack problem also runs in pseudo-polynomial time. Solution runs in $O(nW)$ time and $O(nW)$ space. Another algorithm for 0-1 knapsack, discovered in 1974 and sometimes called "meet-in-the-middle" due to parallels to a similarly named algorithm in cryptography, is exponential in the number of different items but may be preferable to the DP algorithm when capacity (W) is large compared to a number of total items (n). The algorithm takes $O(2^{n/2})$ space and $O(n2^{n/2})$ time. George Dantzig proposed a greedy approximation algorithm to solve the knapsack problem. However, for the bounded problem, where each item's supply is limited, the algorithm is incapable of giving an optimal solution [23]. These results conclude that dynamic programming is the best approach among the traditional algorithms to treat the knapsack problem.

Generally, a knapsack is a packing kind of problem. As we all know, some operations get better over time. Experience makes those tasks perform better and make better decisions. Experience comes with the generations, and generations are part of evolution. Here, we can take the help of biology-based algorithms -> reproduction -> evolutionary algorithms for the knapsack problem. In which GA is one of the best choices. Figure 12.8 shows a flow diagram to use a GA to solve the 0-1 knapsack problem.

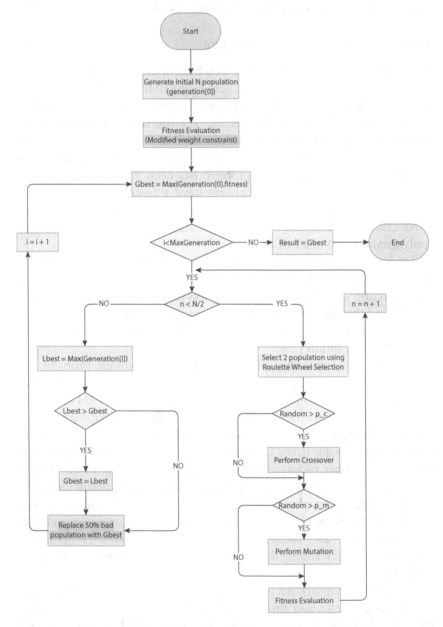

Figure 12.8 Flow chart of genetic algorithm to solve 0-1 knapsack problem.

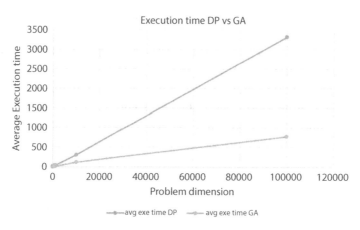

Figure 12.9 Execution time comparison between dynamic programming and genetic algorithm class.

When this flow diagram is implemented, it shows better results than dynamic programming. Figure 12.9 shows the execution time compression. Here, problem size is the total number of items, so it is observable that the slope of execution time for GA is lesser than the slope of execution time for DP. In terms of execution time, GA performs much better than DP.

12.5.2   Traveling Salesman Problem

Traveling Salesman is also an NP-hard problem in combinatorial optimization, significant in operations research and theoretical computer science. In the computational complexity theory, the TSP decision version (given a length L, the task is to decide whether the graph has a tour of at most L) belongs to the NP-complete problems. Thus, the worst-case running time for any TSP algorithm increases super-polynomially (but no more than exponentially) with the number of cities. The TSP has several applications even in its purest formulation, such as planning and logistics.

TSP is defined as a list of cities, and the distances between each pair of cities are given, and the question is to find the shortest possible route that visits each city and returns to the origin city.

The most straightforward solution would be to try the brute force approach. Testing all permutations (ordered combinations) takes a running time of a polynomial factor of $O(n!)$, the factorial of the number of cities, so this solution becomes impractical even for only 20 cities. Another approach is branch-and-bound algorithms, which can be used to process TSPs containing 40–60 cities.

AI researcher Marco Dorigo described in 1993 a heuristically generating "good solutions" to the TSP. As we all know, NIAs are the best metaheuristic algorithms. Route finding task is a matter of teamwork, and simultaneous searching helps to achieve the best solution. Herd behavior can be helpful for this type of problem. Scientists' concerned problem is already solved by nature. Ants are the best solver of a route optimization problem. Hence, (biology-based algorithms -> resource seeking -> herd behavior -> ant colony optimization) leads to the end of our algorithm search.

Ant Colony Optimization Algorithm sends out many virtual ant agents to explore many possible routes on the map. Each ant probabilistically chooses the next city to visit based on a heuristic combining the distance to the city and the amount of virtual pheromone deposited on edge to the city. The ants explore, depositing pheromone on each edge they cross until they have all completed a tour. At this point, the ant which completed the shortest tour deposits virtual pheromone along its complete tour route (global trail updating). The amount of pheromone deposited is inversely proportional to the tour length: the shorter the tour, the more it deposits.

12.6   Conclusion

The main purpose of introducing "The End Goal–based Classification" is to convey the missing pattern to link problem and solution. The identification of the problems and classification of them helps to narrow down the range of suitable NIAs. A task like parameter tuning, structure selection, and parameter optimization, which follows the brute force approach, can be solved with NIA classification and mapping with conceptual problems. The novel approach is expected to benefit researchers and engineers working on computationally intensive and data-starved problems to identify solutions in the most efficient way.

References

1.   Siddique, N. and Adeli, H., Nature-inspired computing: An overview and some future directions. *Cognit. Comput.*, 7, 6, 706–714, Dec 2015.

2.   T. C. Redman. If your data is bad, your machine learning tools are useless. *Harv. Bus. Rev.*, Apr 2018, https://hbr.org/2018/04/if-your-data-is-bad-your-machine-learning-tools-are-useless..

3. Lando, G., *Top 5 limitations of machine learning in an enterprise setting*, FileCloud blog, Jun 2018. https://www.getfilecloud.com/blog/2018/06/top-5-limitations-of-machine-learning-in-an-enterprise-setting/.

4. Polonski, V., Here's why ai can't solve everything, 27 May 2018. https://thenextweb.com/news/why-ai-cant-solve-everything.

5. Braude, E.J. and Bernstein, M.E., *Software engineering: modern approaches*, Waveland Press, Illinois, USA, 2016.

6. Žerovnik, J., Heuristics for np-hard optimization problems-simpler is better!? *Logist. Sustain. Transp.*, 6, 1, 1–10, 2015.

7. Woeginger, G.J., Exact algorithms for np-hard problems: A survey, in: *Combinatorial optimization—eureka, you shrink!*, pp. 185–207, Springer, Berlin, Heidelberg, 2003.

8. Hao, K., Training a single ai model can emit as much carbon as five cars in their lifetimes. *MIT Technol. Rev.*, Jul 2019, https://www.technologyreview.com/2019/06/06/239031/training-a-single-ai-model-can-emit-as-much-carbon-as-five-cars-in-their-lifetimes/.

9. Yang, X.-S., *Nature-inspired metaheuristic algorithms*, Luniver press, Frome, United Kingdom, 2010.

10. Nanda, S.J. and Panda, G., A survey on nature-inspired metaheuristic algorithms for partitional clustering. *Swarm Evol. Comput.*, 16, 1–18, 2014.

11. Binitha, S., Siva Sathya, S. *et al.*, A survey of bio inspired optimization algorithms. *Int. J. Soft Comput. Eng.*, 2, 2, 137–151, 2012.

12. Fister Jr., I., Yang, X.-S., Fister, I., Brest, J., Fister, D., A brief review of nature-inspired algorithms for optimization. *arXiv preprint arXiv: 1307.4186*, 2013. https://arxiv.org/abs/1307.4186.

13. Beni, G. and Wang, J., Swarm intelligence in cellular robotic systems, in: *Robots and biological systems: towards a new bionics?*, pp. 703–712, Springer, Berlin, Heidelberg, 1993.

14. Solé, R., Amor, D.R., Duran-Nebreda, S., Conde-Pueyo, N., Carbonell-Ballestero, M., Montañez, R., Synthetic collective intelligence. *Biosystems*, 148, 47–61, 2016.

15. Vikhar, P.A., Evolutionary algorithms: A critical review and its future prospects, in: *2016 International Conference on Global Trends in Signal Processing, Information Computing and Communication (ICGTSPICC)*, IEEE, pp. 261–265, 2016.

16. Cohoon, J., Kairo, J., Lienig, J., Evolutionary algorithms for the physical design of vlsi circuits, in: *Advances in evolutionary computing*, pp. 683–711, Springer, Berlin, Heidelberg, 2003.

17. Parmar, M. and Sukharamwala, P., Mapping of real world problems to nature-inspired algorithm using goal based classification and triz. *Proc. Comput. Sci.*, 171, pp. 729–736, 2020. https://www.sciencedirect.com/science/article/pii/S1877050920310474.

18. Altshuller, G.S., *The innovation algorithm: TRIZ, systematic innovation and technical creativity*, Technical innovation center, Inc., Worcester, MA, USA, 1999.

19. Nakagawa, T., A new paradigm for creative problem solving: Six-box scheme in usit without depending on analogical thinking, in: *27th Annual Conference of the Japan Creativity Society*, October, pp. 29–30, 2005.

20. Jiang, W., Wu, X., Gong, Y., Yu, W., Zhong, X., Monthly electricity consumption forecasting by the fruit fly optimization algorithm enhanced holt-winters smoothing method. *arXiv preprint arXiv:1908.06836*, 2019. https://arxiv.org/abs/1908.06836.

21. Yaseen, Z., Ehteram, M., Sharafati, A., Shahid, S., Al-Ansari, N., El-Shafie, A., The integration of nature-inspired algorithms with least square support vector regression models: application to modeling river dissolved oxygen concentration. *Water*, 10, 9, 1124, 2018.

22. Leung, F.H.-F., Lam, H.-K., Ling, S.-H., Tam, P.K.-S., Tuning of the structure and parameters of a neural network using an improved genetic algorithm. *IEEE Trans. Neural Networks*, 14, 1, 79–88, 2003.

23. Knapsack problem.

Index

Also of Interest

Check out these published and forthcoming related titles from Scrivener Publishing

Smart Systems for Industrial Applications
Edited by C. Venkatesh, N. Rengarajan, P. Ponmurugan and S. Balamurugan
Forthcoming 2022. ISBN 978-1-119-76200-3

Impact of Artificial Intelligence on Organizational Transformation
Edited by S. Balamurugan, Sonal Pathak, Anupriya Jain, Sachin Gupta, and Sachin Sharma and Sonia Duggal
Forthcoming 2022. ISBN 978-1-119-71017-2

Nature-Inspired Algorithms Applications
Edited by S. Balamurugan, Anupriya Jain, Sachin Sharma, Dinesh Goyal, Sonia Duggal and Seema Sharma
Forthcoming 2022. ISBN 978-1-119-68174-8

Artificial Intelligence for Renewable Energy Systems
Edited by Ajay Kumar Vyas, S. Balamurugan, Kamal Kant Hiran Harsh S. Dhiman
Forthcoming 2022. ISBN 978-1-119-76169-3

Artificial Intelligence Techniques for Wireless Communication and Networking
Edited by Kanthavel R., K. AnathaJothi, S. Balamurugan and R. Karthik Ganesh
Forthcoming 2022. ISBN 978-1-119-82127 4

Advanced Healthcare Systems
Empowering Physicians with IoT-Enabled Technologies
Edited by Rohit Tanwar, S. Balamurugan, R. K. Saini, Vishal Bharti and Premkumar Chithaluru
Forthcoming 2022. ISBN 978-1-119-76886-9

The manufacturer's authorised representative in the EU for product safety is Oxford
University Press España S.A. of El Parque Empresarial San Fernando de Henares,
Avenida de Castilla, 2 – 28830 Madrid (www.oup.es/en or product.safety@oup.com).
OUP España S.A. also acts as importer into Spain of products made by the manufacturer.

Printed in the USA/Agawam, MA
January 13, 2025

880951.002